Frederick Edward Warren

The Antiphonary Of Bangor

Part II: An Early Irish Manuscript In The Ambrosian Library At Milan

Frederick Edward Warren

The Antiphonary Of Bangor
Part II: An Early Irish Manuscript In The Ambrosian Library At Milan

ISBN/EAN: 9783744740432

Printed in Europe, USA, Canada, Australia, Japan

Cover: Foto ©Thomas Meinert / pixelio.de

More available books at **www.hansebooks.com**

HENRY BRADSHAW SOCIETY

Founded in the Year of Our Lord 1890

for the editing of Rare Liturgical Texts.

VOL. X.

ISSUED TO MEMBERS FOR THE YEAR 1895,

AND

PRINTED FOR THE SOCIETY

BY

HARRISON AND SONS, ST. MARTIN'S LANE,

PRINTERS IN ORDINARY TO HER MAJESTY.

THE

ANTIPHONARY OF BANGOR

AN EARLY IRISH MANUSCRIPT
IN THE AMBROSIAN LIBRARY AT MILAN

EDITED BY

F. E. WARREN, B.D., F.S.A.

PART II.

London:
HARRISON AND SONS, ST. MARTIN'S LANE,
Printers in Ordinary to Her Majesty.

1895.

LONDON :
HARRISON AND SONS, PRINTERS IN ORDINARY TO HER MAJESTY,
ST. MARTIN'S LANE.

TABLE OF CONTENTS OF PART II.

vi CONTENTS.

LIST OF ABBREVIATIONS.

B. = The Antiphonary of Bangor.

Dan. = Daniel (H. A.) Thesaurus Hymnologicus. Halis et Lipsiae, 1841–1855.

H. & S. = Haddan and Stubbs, Councils and Ecclesiastical Documents. Oxford, 1869.

Hamm. = Hammond (C. E.) Liturgies Eastern and Western. Oxford, 1878.

Holst. = Holstenius (W.) Codex Regularum, etc. Parisiis, 1643.

L.H. = Liber Hymnorum, or the MS. Book of Hymns in the Library of Trinity College, Dublin. Paginal references are to the uncompleted edition of this MS. by Dr. J. H. Todd, for the Irish Archæological and Celtic Society, in two parts, Dublin, 1855, and 1869. Dr. Todd assigned the MS. to a date not later than the ninth or tenth century (p. 1.) Mr. Whitley Stokes has more recently assigned it to the eleventh or early twelfth century (W.S. p. ci.) It may be inferred from this variety of opinion that it is extremely difficult to date the MS. with precision. It may be provisionally assigned to the eleventh century, and most probably to the later part of it.

L.H.* Another copy of the Liber Hymnorum, now in the Franciscan Convent, Merchants' Quay, Dublin. It is about fifty years later than L.H. A complete catalogue of its contents is given in W.S. pp. cii–cix.

M. = Muratori, Anecdota Bibliothecae Ambrosianae, Tom. iv. Patavii, mdccxiii.

Mart. = Martene, de Antiquis Ecclesiae Ritibus, Bassani, mdcclxxxviii. Tom. iv. of this work contains ' De Antiquis Monachorum Ritibus Libri quinque,' with an Appendix.

P.L. = Migne, Patrologiae Latinae Cursus Completus.

S. = Southampton Psalter. This is an eleventh century Irish MS. Psalter, now in the Library of St. John's College, Cambridge. It contains the Psalms divided into three divisions of fifty Psalms each, and the following Canticles :

After the first division of Psalms :

Title.		First words.
f. 35v. [Benedictio trium puerorum]	...	Benedicite omnia opera.
f. 36v. Canticum issaiae	...	Confitebor tibi domine.
f. 37r. Canticum ezechiae	...	Ego dixi in dimidio.

After the second division of Psalms :

f. 69v. Canticum annae matris samuelis	... ...	Exultauit cor meum.
f. 70r. Canticum mariae sororis moysi	... ...	Cantemus domino gloriose.
f. 70v. Canticum ambacuc profetae ...	... ...	Domine audiui.

After the third division of Psalms :

f. 99v. [Canticum moysi]	... ...	Audite caeli.

V. = Biblia Sacra Vulgatae Editionis, Augustae Taurinorum, mdccclxxv.

W. = Warren (F. E.) Liturgy and Ritual of the Celtic Church. Oxford, 1881.

W.S. = Whitley Stokes, Edition of the Tripartite Life of St. Patrick. Rolls Series, London, 1887.

W.T. = The Winchester Troper, edited for the Henry Bradshaw Society, by W. H. Frere, London, 1894.

EXPLANATION OF CERTAIN TERMS OR SYMBOLS.

Anthem = Latin 'Antiphona.'

Chora = a group of three Psalms.

Missa = a Lection, from Holy Scripture or from some other source.

Mattins. This word is always used in its ancient meaning of Lauds, and not in its modern sense as equivalent to the Night Hours. In the Celtic Divine Office, 'Matutina' is the name of the last and longest of the Night Hours ending with the three Psalms 148–150. For various meanings of 'officium matutinum' see Mabillon, *Disquisitio de Cursu Gallicano*, § v. n. 53 in P.L. t. lxxii. col. 405.

Quinquagesima = Easter-tide.

† following a word signifies that the manuscript has been exactly followed.

The Vulgate numeration of the Psalms has been employed throughout.

LIST OF EDITIONS OF CERTAIN SERVICE BOOKS TO WHICH REFERENCE IS SOMETIMES MADE.

Breviarium Ambrosianum	Mediolani, mdcccxxx.
Breviarium Monasticum...	pro omnibus sub regula SS. P. Benedicti militantibus. Venetiis, mdciv.
Breviarium Mozarabicum ...	P.L. Tom. lxxxvi.
Breviarium Romanum ...	Tornaci Nerviorum. mdccclxxix.
Breviarium Sarisburiense	Ed. F. Procter et Chr. Wordsworth. Cantabrigiae, mdccclxxix.
Euchologion	Venice, 1863.
Horologion	Venice, 1876.
Missale Ambrosianum	MS. saeculi xᵐⁱ editum ab Ant. Ceriani [no place or date.]
Missale Mozarabicum	P.L. Tom. lxxxv.
Missale Romanum	Mechliniae, mdccclxx.

Missale Gallicanum Vetus ... .⎫
Missale Gothicum ... ... ⎬ Ancient Liturgies of the Gallican Church, Burntisland,
Missale Richenovense ... ... ⎪ 1855, Part i. edited by J. M. Neale and G. H.
Missale Vesontionense ... ... ⎪ Forbes. Part ii. 1858, and Part iii. 1867, edited by
Sacramentarium Gallicanum (Missale Vesontion-⎪ G. H. Forbes.
ense.) ⎭

Sacramentarium Gelasianum ... ...⎫
Sacramentarium Gregorianum ... ... ⎬ Muratori, Liturgia Romana Vetus, Venetiis, mdccxlii.
Sacramentarium Leonianum ... ...⎭

INTRODUCTION.

§ 1. Nature and Object of the Bangor Book.   § 2. The Divine Office in the Celtic Church.   Distribution of the Psalter.   § 3. Distribution of Collects.   § 4. Traces of Eastern influence.   § 5. Traces of Hispano-Gallican influence.   § 6. Commemoration of Martyrs.   § 7. Version of Holy Scripture.

§ 1. *Nature and Object of the Bangor Book.*—In the Introduction of Part I. the history and palæography of the MS. of the Antiphonary of Bangor have been narrated and described. In the present Introduction the nature and object of that MS. regarded as a Service Book will be discussed.

The Antiphonary evidently falls into three divisions.

Division i. extends from f. 1r. to f. 17v. *i.e.* to the end of the first half of the second gathering. We may regard the Collect written on the lower part of f. 17v. as merely due to a desire to utilize vacant space. This division contains Canticles and Hymns.

Division ii. extends from f. 18r. to f. 29v., *i.e.* from the commencement of the second half of the second gathering to the end of the first half of the third gathering. This division consists almost exclusively of Collects, having in some cases Anthems prefixed.

Division iii. extends from f. 30r. to f. 36v. *i.e.* from the commencement of the second half of the third gathering to the end of the MS. This division consists mainly of 'Antiphonae' or Anthems. It also contains a quantity of miscellaneous matter, the Anthems being mainly comprised between ff. 31v. and 33v. inclusive. It opens and closes with a Hymn. Nearly two pages after the opening Hymn on f. 30r. are filled up by an Exorcism, and an additional Collect 'De Martyribus.' The twelve Anthems appended to 'Gloria in Excelsis' have the full text of that Hymn preceding them, though in itself that 'Gloria' might have been thought to belong more properly to Division i. The contents on and after f. 34r. are of too miscellaneous a character to be reduced under any classification.

It has been suggested there may be found five main divisions of the Antiphonary,[1] but we think that the above triple division is simpler, and palæographically and sectionally more complete. See Diagram facing page xviii. in Part I.

What then is the proper description, and what is the *raison d'être* of this book, which is partly a Hymnarium, partly a Collectarium, partly an Antiphonarium, with the occasional introduction of Eucharistic and other elements?

It has been suggested that its fragmentary character may be explained in this manner: "that an Antiphonary of a particular monastery did not contain all the Divine Office, but only some portions of it which were peculiar to that monastery, just as the Irish supplement of the Breviary contains only those prayers or offices supplementary to the Roman Breviary, and intended for the use of the Irish Clergy."[2]

But this explanation will not hold. Such Hymns as 'Te Deum laudamus' and 'Gloria in excelsis' were not peculiar to a particular monastery, and the same remark is true of

---

[1] *Church Quarterly Review*, vol. xxxvii. p. 347.
[2] J. O'Laverty, *An Historical Account of the Diocese of Down and Connor*, Dublin, 1882, vol. ii. Preface (not paged.)

nine-tenths of the contents of the Bangor Antiphonary. The idea of its being a local supplement is borrowed from the practice of to-day, and then thrown back more than a thousand years. The present uniformity of Roman Missal and Breviary, which causes local supplements to be made, had no existence in the seventh century.

It has been suggested that the Bangor MS. is only the end of a Psalter, being the concluding portion of a much larger MS. volume, of which the greater part has been lost. Canticles with miscellaneous formulae of devotion are frequently appended at the end of Psalters, which from the ninth century onward generally include long litanies to the Saints, and later on Collections of Hymns, ' Vigiliae Mortuorum,' etc.

But there is nothing to prove and little to support such a suggestion in the case of the Bangor MS. On the contrary, the completeness of the gatherings of which it is composed ; the large capital A on f. 1ʳ. and the motto on its top margin ; the fact that Irish Psalters were almost always divided into three divisions of fifty Psalms each, and that Canticles and Collects, if added at all, were inserted at the beginning or end of these divisions, instead of being written together at the end of the volume ;[1] the general and, to a certain extent, systematic character and arrangement of the contents of the Bangor MS. put such a suggestion out of court.

It has been suggested that the Bangor MS. is an abbreviated Breviary, a portable service-book for the use of travellers: ' pro sacerdotibus aut monachis itinerantibus.' Some singularly thin MS. Missals such as the Stowe Missal, and MS. A. 566 in the public Library at Rouen, have been accounted for in this way. Speaking of the latter MS. Mons. L. Delisle says : " Il a cependant dû exister, à toutes les époques du moyen âge, de petits livres ou même de simples cahiers dans lesquels les prêtres pouvaient trouver les prières des messes les plus usuelles. On s'en servait dans les voyages et probablement aussi dans les églises trop pauvres pour se procurer des recueils plus complets."[2]

But the contents of the Bangor MS. do not at all bear out the travelling theory, and one cannot think of poverty in connection with the celebrated and much-frequented monastery of Bangor.

Setting then on one side these possible explanations as inapplicable in the present case, which theory remains to be offered as to the origin, character and use of the Bangor MS. ?

We believe that it is a companion volume to the Psalterium and Lectionarium for use in the Divine Office,

> either (1) on Easter Even and Easter Day.
>
> or (2) on Saturdays and Sundays in Easter-tide.
>
> or (3) on Saturdays and Sundays throughout the year, and also on Feasts of Martyrs.

[1] This is the case with the Southampton Psalter (S.) and the two Irish Psalters in the British Museum (Cott. MS. Vitell. F. xi. ninth or tenth century, and Cott. MS. Galba A. v. eleventh or twelfth century.) The Psalter of Ricemarch, a twelfth century MS. Trin. Coll. Dublin (A. 4. 20) is divided into the three fifties, but contains neither Canticle nor Collect. The Psalters of St. Columba, a sixth century MS. in the Royal Irish Academy, Dublin, and of St. Columbanus, a ninth century manuscript in the Ambrosian Library at Milan, are not arranged in three fifties, and yield neither Canticle nor Collect, but in its present mutilated and decayed condition the former only extends from Ps. xxx. 20—Ps. cv. 13. [2] *Mémoire sur d'anciens sacramentaires*, Paris, 1886, p. 292.

In favour of (1) there are the Hymn [9] and Collect [127] for the 'Benedictio Cerei, and frequent allusions to Baptism and the Resurrection. But as has been pointed out in notes to [9] and [127] the 'Benedictio Cerei' now solemnly performed and exclusively associated with Easter Even is probably, like other of the services and ceremonies of Holy Week, only the solitary survival of a ceremonial act much more frequently performed in earlier times. The administration of Baptism in the early Irish Church was not confined to Easter, but was also performed at the Feasts of Pentecost and of the Epiphany. An early Irish Canon directed 'Octavo die chatechumeni sunt ; postea solemnitatibus Domini baptizantur, id est, Pascha, et Pentecoste, et Epiphania.'[1]

Apart from this, references to Baptism would not be inappropriate, at any season of the Christian year, in connection with the Canticle 'Cantemus Domino.'

So likewise with regard to the Resurrection, every Sunday in the Christian year is a reflection of Easter Day, and commemoration of the Resurrection might be made on every Sunday, or even on every day in the early Irish Church. In the Sarum Breviary there is a daily commemoration of it throughout Easter-tide in the shape of a special Versus ante Laudes.[2] In the Greek Church there is a daily commemoration of it throughout the year in the Troparion at the end of Lauds.[3] This is in addition to the special Troparion in Easter-tide.[4] There are also eleven gospels on the Resurrection read successively at Nocturns on Sundays, except on a few Festivals when a special Gospel is appointed.[5]

The four complete or incomplete sets of Collects for the Day and Night Hours, and the seven sets of Collects for use after Canticles, Hymns, etc.,[6] point at least to the wider period of the 'Quinquagesima Paschalis' or Easter-tide.

We think that they point to a wider period still, and have come to the conclusion that the Bangor MS. contains Collects, Anthems, etc., for use on Saturdays and Sundays, and Feasts of Martyrs, either in Easter-tide or throughout the whole year, and that the preponderance of evidence is in favour of the wider alternative.

THE DIVINE OFFICE IN THE CELTIC CHURCH.

§ 2. *Distribution of the Psalter.* No Psalm is written down *in extenso* in the Bangor MS. The only references to particular Psalms are in the following titles :

(1) 'Collectio post tres Psalmos' [64] 'Post laudate Dominum de coelis,' [73], [78], [83], [90], [93.]

(2) 'Incipit antiphona in Natale Domini super Domine refugium ad Secundam.' [98.]

(3) 'Super Domine refugium in Dominico die' [105.]

(4) 'Alia cotidiana' [108.]

(1) An inspection of the wording of [64] and of other Collects under the more frequently used title 'Post laudate Dominum,' proves that the three Psalms referred to are Pss. 148,

---

[1] Canons attributed to St. Patrick (but though early Irish, not his) No. xix. in H. and S. vol. ii. pt. 11. p. 336.
[2] p. dcccxxvi.   [3] Άκολουθία τοῦ Ὄρθρου. *Horologion*, p. 73.   [4] *Ibid.* p. 379-396.
[6] *Euchology.* Edit. G. V. Shann. Kidderminster, 1891, p. 488.   [5] See § 3.

149, 150, which no doubt were daily recited at Bangor at Mattins, as they are still recited at Mattins, or in the office corresponding to Mattins, in all Breviaries Eastern and Western.

(2), (3), (4). From these titles we learn that the 89th Psalm ' Domine refugium ' was used on Christmas Day, Sundays, and Ferial days, and therefore probably daily throughout the year at Prime. It is used daily at Prime in the Eastern church, whereas it is not part of Prime in Roman, Benedictine and other Western Breviaries.

These references are too few and scanty to throw light on the distribution of the Psalter in the Divine Office at Bangor. There can, however, be no reasonable doubt that such distribution was identical with that which is described and laid down in the Rule of St. Columbanus, himself, in his younger days, a monk at Bangor under its founder and first abbot St. Comgall, and which is also referred to in certain other Celtic or semi-Celtic monastic Rules.

This arrangement is so peculiar, and so dissimilar from the arrangements of any extant Western Breviaries, both secular and monastic, that it deserves to be described at length. The subject will not, it is hoped, be considered an irrelevant digression in an introduction to the only known extant MS. Service-book, apart from Psalters, connected with the Divine Office of the Celtic Church.

The following is the direction for the use of the Psalter as laid down in the *Regula S. Columbani Abbatis* Cap. vii. De Cursu [Psalmorum.]

" De Synaxi, ergo, id est, de cursu Psalmorum et orationum modo canonico quaedam sunt distinguenda, quia varie a diversis memoriae de eo traditum est. Ideo juxta vitae qualitatem ac temporum successionem varie a me quoque litteris idem insinuetur. Non enim uniformis esse debet pro reciproca temporum alternatione ; longior enim per longas noctes, breviorque per breves esse convenit. Inde et cum senioribus nostris ab 8 Calendas Julii cum noctis augmento sensim incipit crescere cursus a duodecim choris brevissimi modi in nocte Sabbati sive Dominicae, usque ad initium hyemis, id est, Calendas Novembris ; in[1] quibus viginti quinque canunt Antiphonas Psalmorum ejusdem numeri duplicis, qui semper tertio loco [duobus] succedunt Psaltis,[1] ita ut totum Psalterium inter duas supradictas noctes numero cantent duodecim choris, caeteras temperantes tota hyeme noctes. Qua finita, per ver sensim per singulas hebdomadas terni semper decedunt Psalmi, ut duodecim in singulis noctibus tantum Antiphonae remaneant, id est, quotidiani hyemalis triginta sex Psalmi cursus, viginti quatuor autem per totum ver et aestatem, et usque ad autumnale aequinoctium, id est, 8 Calendas Octobris in quo similitudo Synaxeos est : sicuti in vernali aequinoctio, id est, in 8 Calendas Aprilis, dum per reciprocas vices paulatim crescit et decrescit.

Igitur juxta vires consideranda vigilia est, maxime cum ab authore salutis nostrae jubemur

---

[1]—[1] 'in quibus . . . Psaltis.' Dom G. Morin has recently suggested the following interpretation of this difficult sentence : ' *L'antiphona psalmorum* désigne ce mode de psalmodie qui consiste à intercaler un refrain entre chaque verset ou chaque groupe de versets d'un psaume ; la *psalta* un autre mode de psalmodie, sans doute plus simple et plus primitif, tel que celui qui était en usage chez les Pères des déserts . . . On arrive ainsi au commencement de Novembre, et alors il faut s'arranger de manière à distribuer le psautier tout entier entre ces deux nuits du samedi et du dimanche. Pour cela, Colomban prescrit vingt-cinq *antiphonae psalmorum* ou psaumes antiphonés avec le nombre double de *psaltae.* De la sorte on obtiendra le nombre voulu de soixante-quinze psaumes, et chacun des psaumes antiphonés viendra toujours en troisième lieu après deux de ces psaltae.' *Revue Bénédictine*, Mai, 1895, Maredsous, p. 201.

vigilare et orare omni tempore,[1] et Paulus praecipit *sine intermissione orare.*[2] Sed quia orationum canonicarum noscendus est modus, in quo omnes simul orantes horis conveniant statutis, quibusque absolutis unusquisque in cubiculo suo orare debet. Per diurnas terni Psalmi horas pro operum interpositione statuti sunt a Senioribus nostris, cum versiculorum augmento intervenientium, pro peccatis primum nostris, deinde pro omni populo Christiano, deinde pro Sacerdotibus et reliquis Deo consecratis sacrae plebis gradibus, postremo pro eleemosynas facientibus, postea pro pace regum, novissime pro inimicis, ne illis Deus statuat in peccatum quod persequuntur et detrahunt nobis, quia nesciunt quid faciunt.

Ad initium vero noctis duodecim Psalmi, ad mediumque noctis duodecim similiter psalluntur : ad Matutinum vero bis deni bisque bini per tempora brevium, ut dictum est, noctium sunt dispositi, pluribus, jam ut dixi, nocti Dominicae ac Sabbati vigiliae deputatis. In quibus sub uno cursu septuaginta quinque [Psalmi] sigillatim cantantur. Haec juxta communem dicta sunt synaxim."

[Here follows a passage allowing dispensations for various causes ; then the Rule proceeds] . . .

. . . "Sunt autem quidam Catholici, quibus idem est canonicus duodenarius Psalmorum numerum,[3] sive per breves sive per longas noctes : sed per quaternas in nocte vices hunc canonem reddunt, ad initium noctis, ad mediumque ejus, pullorum quoque cantus, ac Matutinum. Qui cursus sicut in hyeme parvus aliis videtur, ita in aestate satis onerosus et gravis invenitur, dum crebris in noctis brevitate expeditionibus non tam lassitudinem facit, quam fatigationem. Noctibus vero reverentissimis, Dominicae scillicet† vel Sabbati, ad Matutinum ter idem volvitur numerus, id est, ter denis et sex Psalmis.

Quorum pluralitas ac sancta conversatio hunc numerum canonicum multis dulci indixit suavitate, tanquam et reliquam disciplinam, sub qua nimirum regula nullus invenitur lassus ; et cum tanta pluralitas eorum sit, ita ut mille Abbates sub uno Archimandrita esse referantur, nulla ibi a conditione coenobii inter duos Monachos rixa fuisse fertur visa ; quod sine Dei ibi habitatione dicentis ' *Ego in eis habitabo, et inter illos ambulabo, et ero illorum Deus, et ipsi erunt mihi populus* '[4] esse non posse manifestum est. Merito itaque creverunt, et quotidie, Deo gratias, crescunt, in quorum medio Deus habitat : quorum meritis mereamur salvari a Salvatore nostro. Amen."[5]

Fleming calls this chapter 'prolixum pariter et obscurum,' and later writers have echoed his complaint. He also calls attention to the fact that it is only found in one MS. but he does not on that account suggest that it is spurious. He gives up the attempt to explain it, or rather postpones the attempt to a second edition which never made its appearance. After first expounding the meaning of 'Synaxis' he proceeds :

"Reliqua quae sequuntur hujus capitis, in quibus de solemnitate laudis perpetuae per duodecim choros (*sic*) distributa, tam sunt obscura et intricata, ut sine magna veterum rituum et caeremoniarum Congregationis Luxoviensis notitia, ad plenum explicari non possint.

Quare cum ad praesens circa haec non simus sufficienter instructi, in aliud tempus hujus capitis ulteriorem expositionem dimittimus, in secunda forsan editione adjungendam."[6]

---

[1] Luc. xviii. 1.   [2] 1 Thess. v. 18.   [3] for numerus.   [4] Levit. xxvi. 12.

[5] P. Flemingius, *Collectanea Sacra*, Lovanii, 1667, pp. 5, 6. There are many various readings in the text as printed by Holst. pt. ii. p. 93, and in P. L. Tom. lxxx. col. 212.   [6] *Ibid.* p. 15.

Martene complains that the chapter is so obscure as to be barely intelligible, but proceeds to explain it thus : " S. Columbani cursus expressus habetur in ejus Regulae capite 7. sed ita obscure, ut vix intelligi possit. Quapropter ejus non verba sed sensum hic referemus. Itaque noctes prolixiores a brevioribus distinguens, hyemis tempore, hoc est, ab aequinoctio autumnali, hoc est, ab 8 Calendas Octobris usque ad Calendas Februarias, triginta sex psalmos cum duodecim antiphonis ad singulas noctes dici praescribit, ita ut singulis tribus psalmis una interseratur antiphona, a Calendis vero Februariis usque aequinoctium autumnale, hoc est toto vere, aestate, et autumni parte anteriori, viginti quatuor psalmos cum octo dumtaxat antiphonis eodem prorsus modo, hoc est, ut singulis tribus psalmis una interseratur antiphona ; aliter vero Dominicis et Sabbati vigiliis, ut dicemus, cum de die Dominica agemus. Hunc cursum S. Columbanus a senioribus acceperat, hoc est, a monasterio Benchor, in quo vitam monasticam professus fuerat."[1]

Other passages connected with the name of St. Columbanus bearing on the Divine Office are these :

' Qui humiliationem in Synaxi, id est, in Cursu oblitus fuerit (haec est humiliatio in ecclesia post finem cujusque Psalmi) similiter poeniteat.'[2]

' In ecclesia dum duodecim Psalmos ad Duodecimam canunt.'[3]

" Qui ergo in nocte Dominica et tempore Quinquagesimae penitentes genua flectunt in commune cum omnibus fratribus omnibus diebus ac noctibus tempore orationum in fine omnium Psalmorum genua in oratione, si non infirmitas corporis hoc fecerit, flectere aequo animo debent sub silentio dicentes ; ' Deus, in adjutorium meum intende ' ' Domine ad adjuvandum me festina.' Quem versiculum postquam ter tacite in oratione decantaverint, aequaliter a flexione orationis surgant, exceptis diebus Dominicis, et a primo die Sancto Paschae usque ad quinquagesimum diem, in quibus moderate se in tempore Psalmodiae humiliantes, genua non flectentes, sed sedulo Dominum orent."[4]

In the Rule of St. Donatus, which was Celtic in its distribution of the Psalter, and in the severity of its monastic punishments, the ' Cursus Psalmorum ' is thus laid down.

" Cap. lxxv. De Ordine quo psallere debeant.

De Synaxi, id est, de Cursu Psalmorum et orationum modo Canonico, juxta normam Regulae nostrae quaedam in breve sunt distinguenda. Ab octavo Kalend. Octobris crescit cursus usque ad summum ejus viginti quinque choris ; quas tota hieme, quae a Kalendis Novembris incipit, et finit in Kalendis Februarii cantandas in nocturnis vigiliis per noctem Sabbati et Dominicae patres nostri sanxerunt.

Duodecim vero chorae in hyeme omni nocte cantandae sunt usque ad octavo Kalendas Aprilis, et post hyemem quindecim chorae in sacris Martyrum vigiliis.

[1] Mart. Tom. iv. Lib. i. cap. ii. § ix. p. 5.

[2] Regula S. Columbani Coenobialis, cap. ii. (P. Fleming, *Collectanea Sacra*, Lovanii, 1667, p. 19.)

[3] *Ibid.* cap. iii. Fleming *ut supra*, p. 22. The title ' Duodecima' does not occur as a title of one of the Hours in the Bangor MS. but we know that it was sometimes another name for ' Hora Vespertina ' or ' Vespers ' e.g. : ' Sed prima sic debet dici quomodo Duodecima quae dicitur Vespera.' *Regula Magistri* (probably Gallican) cap. 34. Holst. Pt. ii. p. 232. For further authorities see Du Cange *Glossarium*, etc. *sub voce*. Mabillon, *Disquisitio de Cursu Gallicano* § 1, n. 18, printed at the end of his book *De Liturgia Gallicana*, Paris, 1685.

[4] *Ibid* cap. iii. Fleming *ut supra* p. 22, and note on p. 32. We have, in this extract, incorporated some of Fleming's marginal readings from the Codex Augustanus.

Et sicut crescit, ita etiam decrescit quinque choris; quae in primo Sabbato quinque chorae augendae sunt, ut sint viginti, per alium autem Sabbatum una chora augenda est usque ad Kalendas Novembris, usque totus cursus compleatur, id est, viginti quinque[1] chorae psalmorum; qui per tres menses hyemis numerus complendus est in duabus supradictis noctibus, et post hoc decrescit per Sabbatum.

Primo Sabbato quinque chorae, et singula per alterna Sabbata, quia longius spatium est ad finem hyemis, usque ad aequinoctium veris, in cursu decrescendo quam crescendo, ideo per alterna Sabbata singulae decidant chorae usque octavo Kalendas Aprilis.

Duodecim namque chorae tempore aestatis in sanctarum noctium cursu, id est, Sabbati et Dominicae, cantandae sunt.

Octo vero [semper] reliquis noctibus de aequinoctio veris in aequinoctium cantandae sunt, id est, per sex menses. De aequinoctio veris in aequinoctium autumni, viginti quatuor psalmi canendi sunt."[2]

St. Donatus, from whose rule the above is an extract, was a monk under St. Columbanus in the monastery of Luxeuil. In 624 he was consecrated Bishop of Besançon. There he founded the monastery of St. Paul (Palatius) for Canons Regular, and placed it under a mixed Rule of St. Columbanus and St. Benedict, and also, through his mother Flavia, a monastery for women, called St. Joussan, which was said to be placed under the Rule of St. Caesarius of Arles. It is obvious that so far as the recitation of the Psalter was concerned, the Rule of St. Donatus was modelled upon the Columbanian type.

It will be seen that the Celtic Rule draws a distinction between Saturday and Sunday nights and the other five nights of the week. On each of those two nights from Nov. 1 to March 25, seventy-five Psalms are said, 'ad matutinam' under twenty-five Anthems, each Anthem being said after three Psalms, so that the whole Psalter was recited every week during those two nights. From the 25th of March to the 24th of June, the amount of Psalms is diminished weekly by one Anthem and three Psalms, so that on Midsummer Day there remain but twelve Anthems and thirty-six Psalms. Then, as the nights grow longer, every week brings an additional Anthem, with three additional Psalms, so that by the 1st of November the total is reached again of twenty-five Anthems and seventy-five Psalms. This is the rule for Saturdays and Sundays. The rule for the other five nights seems to be as follows. It is laid down that twenty-four or thirty-six Psalms are to be said 'ad matutinam.' Thirty-six is the full number, but in the shorter summer nights only twenty-four Psalms are to be recited. It is possible that there was a gradual *diminuendo* and *crescendo* in their use corresponding to the regulation of a similar kind in force for the Saturday and Sunday, but there is no order expressed to that effect, and it is expressly ordered otherwise in the Rule of St. Donatus (see last sentence quoted above.)

This arrangement of the 'Cursus Psalmorum' in the Celtic Church is unique and interesting. The twelve Psalms 'ad initium noctis,' and again 'in nocturno' together with the prolonged office 'in matutino' point to an Eastern origin, while the difference between the long and short nights in summer and winter shows how such an office was adapted to the altered conditions of the extreme Western country in which it was drawn up for use.[3]

---

[1] 'quoque' text as printed.   [2] Holst. Pars tertia, p. 69.
[3] B. Zimmerman, *The Divine Office in the Greek Church* (reprinted from *the Month*, Jan.–March, 1893) p. 20. A

Three Psalms are assigned to each of the Day Hours which are followed by a number of devotions, or 'Preces' in the form of Versicles introducing Collects. (1) for our sins; (2) for all Christian people; (3) for priests, and for other persons consecrated to God in the various grades of the ministry; (4) for those who give alms; (5) for the peace of kings; (6) for our enemies.

From the position of these intercessions [40]-[56] in the Bangor Book, where they are enlarged in number and slightly varied in the wording of their titles, it would appear that they were used at the end of Mattins, but the wording of the Rule of St. Columbanus, previously quoted, implies their attachment to all the Day Hours.

It may be a convenience to exhibit the arrangement of the 'Cursus Psalmorum' in the Celtic Divine Office in a tabular form :

	Name of Office.	Hour.	No. of Psalms.
1. Ad Secundam ...	Prime	6 a.m.	3
2. Ad Tertiam	Terce	9a.m.	3
3. Ad Sextam	Sext	Noon.	3
4. Ad Nonam	None	3 p.m.	3 } daily.
5. Ad Vespertinam[1] ...	Vespers	6 p.m.	12
6. Ad initium Noctis ...	1st Nocturn	9 p.m.	12
7. Ad medium Noctis ...	2nd Nocturn	Midnight.	12
8. Ad Matutinam ...	{ 3rd Nocturn with Lauds or Mattins. }	3 a.m.[2]	{ 24-36 Monday to Friday. 36-75 Saturday, Sunday. }

The complicated mode of varying the number of Psalms 'Ad Matutinam' has been already described. We would only add that the obscure wording of the Rule may point to the further fact that the four equal divisions of the year were not exactly adhered to, so that the rate of increase or decrease might have to be accelerated or retarded in the autumn or spring. For example the decrease in the number of the Psalms seems to have begun after Midsummer Day and not on Aug. 1st, and if so it would have to be spread over a longer period of time than exactly three months or thirteen weeks.

We now approach a question, not of much importance, but of some difficulty. Does the service 'Ad vespertinam' belong to the series of Day Hours or of Night Hours? The normal hour to which it was attached was, as its name 'Duodecima' indicates, 6 p.m. If Prime said at 6 a.m. was the first of the Day Hours, then, if we divide day and night equally, Vespers said at 6 p.m. ought to be regarded as the first of the Night Hours.[3]

somewhat similar arrangement for the increase and decrease of Psalms 'ad matutinam' is laid down in canon 18 of the second Council of Tours (A.D. 567). See J. Mabillon, *De Cursu Gallicano*, § 5, n. 52. P. L. Tom. lxxii. col. 405.

[1] or 'Ad Duodecimam' see quotation in page xiv. note 3. This hour was also called 'Lucernarium,' 'Eucharistia,' 'Hora Incensi.' (Mart. Tom. iv. p. 32.) Lucernarium has a double meaning. It is sometimes used for Vespers, sometimes for the short service attending the lighting of lamps, which took place immediately before Vespers. So in the 'Regula S. Aureliani' in the 'ordo Psallendi' appended to the Canons (Holst. Pt. ii. p. 67.)

[2] This column represents the normal hours, in theory. They must have been sometimes departed from in practice.

[3] Sed Prima sic debet dici, quomodo Duodecima, quae dicitur Vespera." (Regula Magistri, cap. xxxiv. Holst. Pt. ii. p. 232.) Yet according to this same Gallican Rule, three Psalms were to be said at Prime (cap. xxxv.) but at Vespers six in winter and five in summer. (cap. xxxvi.) Dr. O. Seebass includes Vespers among the five Day Hours at Bangor. (*Columba von Luxeuils Klosterregel* &c. Dresden, 1883, p. 24.)

The twelve Psalms assigned to Vespers in the Rule of St. Columbanus[1] seem to assimilate it to the nocturnal services. But too much stress must not be laid upon this fact. In the Gallican Rule of St. Aurelian we find that twelve was the number of Psalms assigned to Prime, Terce, Sext, and None, as well as to Vespers and Nocturns in Easter-tide, whereas in ordinary seasons the number of Psalms was twelve at Prime, Terce, Sext, and None, but eighteen at Vespers and Nocturns.[2] Twelve Psalms at Vespers are also mentioned in the 18th canon of the second Council of Tours, A.D. 567, which runs :

'Statuta Patrum praeceperunt ut ad Sextam sex Psalmi dicantur cum 'Alleluia,' et ad 'Duodecimam' duodecim denique cum Alleluia.'[3]

In Egypt, as throughout the East, the number of Psalms at Terce, Sext, and None, was three. Cassian tells us : 'Itaque in Palaestinae vel Mesopotamiae monasteriis ac totius Orientis supradictarum horarum solemnitates trinis Psalmis quotidie finiuntur.'[4]

On the other hand there were twelve Psalms at Vespers and twelve at Nocturns, and this number was believed to have been laid down by angelic authority.[5] 'Per universam Aegyptum et Thebaidem duodenarius Psalmorum numerus tam in Vespertinis quam in nocturnis solemnitatibus custoditur.'[6]

We are not surprised, therefore, to find Cassian coupling Vespers and Nocturns together as he does in the following sentence :

"Quamobrem exceptis vespertinis nocturnisque congregationibus, nulla apud eos [i.e. Egyptios] per diem publica solemnitas, absque die Sabbati vel Dominica, celebratur, in quibus hora tertia sacrae communionis obtentu conveniunt."[7]

A modern writer of authority, referring to the twelfth century, says :

"Et l'on distinguait deux sortes de stations, les stations diurnes qui ne comportaient que la messe stationale, et les stations nocturnes ou grandes stations, qui comportaient les premières vêpres la veille au soir, l'office nocturne au milieu de la nuit, la messe solennelle au matin."[8] And still more especially with reference to primitive times : "Ce que nous appelons vêpres fut ainsi, à l'origine, le commencement de la vigile nocturne. Il est vrai que cette pensée d'unité originelle se perdit de bonne heure. Methodius (ob. 311) s'en souvenait pourtant quand il compare sa vie des vierges à une vigile, qui, comme toute vigile, aurait trois moments : la *vespertina vigilia*, la *secunda vigilia*, et la *tertia vigilia*, figures de la jeunesse, de l'âge mûr, et de la vieillesse. Jean Cassien, au commencement du v* siècle, était dans la même tradition, quand il comprend l'office de vêpres et l'office du chant du coq sous le même titre d'office nocturne."[9]

Although the normal hour for Vespers was 6 p.m. yet for purposes of convenience and

[1] quoted on page xiv.
[2] 'De ordine Psallendi' after Canon LV. Holst. Pt. ii. pp. 66, 67.
[3] Mansi, *Concilia*, Tom. ix. col. 797.
[4] Joan. Cassianus, *De Instit. Coenobiorum*, Lib. iii. cap. 4.
[5] *Ibid.* Lib. ii. capp. v. et vi. The chapters are too long to quote. See also Mart. Tom. iii. pp. 4, 5.
[6] Joan. Cassianus, *De Instit. Coenobiorum*, Lib. ii. cap. 4.
[7] *Ibid.* Lib. iii. cap. 2.
[8] P. Batiffol, *Histoire du Bréviaire Romain*, Paris, 1893, p. 144.
[9] *Ibid.* p. 4, referring to Cassian, *Institut.* Lib. iii. cap. 8, and S. Method. *Sympos.* Lib. v cap. 2. See Migne, *Pat. Graec.* Tom. xviii. col. 100. See S. Bäumer, *Geschichte des Breviers*, Freiburg, 1895, pp. 34, 161.

d

economy it varied with daylight. The rule of St. Donatus (Cap. 76), almost verbally copying on this point the Rule of St. Benedict (Cap. 41) ordered :

'Ipsa autem vespera sic agatur, ut lumine lucernae non indigeant reficientes, sed luce adhuc diei omnia consummentur.'[1]

The number of Night Hours has varied, but we have not found anywhere a larger number than three, unless it be in the practice of the 'quidam Catholici' referred to in the Rule of St. Columbanus where four Night Hours seem to be spoken of (p. xiii.) In the Apostolic Constitutions one Hour is specified between Vespers and Mattins, namely, Cockcrow.[2]

In the Benedictine Rule the hour of rising for the 'Officium Divinum Nocturnum,' or 'Nocturna Laus,' or 'Vigiliae Nocturnae' was the 'octava hora noctis' i.e. 2 a.m., so as to enable Mattins to be begun at daybreak.[3]

In the Spanish Rule of St. Fructuosus, the monks are ordered to observe 'Prima, Tertia, Sexta, Nona, Vespera, Media nox' and 'Gallicinium,' and it is added 'Has horas canonicas ab Oriente usque in Occidentem, Catholica, id est, universalis indesinenter celebrat Ecclesia.'[4]

The arrangement of the Night Hours which existed at Bangor seems to have included, after Vespers, three Services, viz. 1. Ad Initium noctis ; 2. Ad Nocturnum ; 3. Ad Matutinam.

It must have been a difficult arrangement to carry out under any circumstances and in any place. If practicable in the warm nights in Southern Gaul and Spain it must have been intolerable in the chilly nights in Ireland. Perhaps, however, it was modified in practice both there and elsewhere.

It will have been noticed that there is no mention in any Celtic Rule, nor in the Bangor MS. of Compline. That Service had probably not yet been introduced into Ireland, although it had long previously obtained a recognised place in the Rule of St. Benedict.[5]

It is only fair to add that Dom Suitbert Baeumer, whose recent death is a great loss to Liturgiology, stoutly maintains that the service 'ad initium noctis' was Compline. He even traces the Confession of Compline in the Anthem 'Injuste egimus' by a flight of fancy in which few will follow him.[6] It seems to us a natural and almost a necessary inference from the paragraph in the Rule of St. Columbanus beginning 'ad initium vero noctis' etc. (p. xiii.) that this service was one of the 'nocturnae vigiliae,' among which it is there plainly enumerated.

The whole scheme of the Celtic Divine Office is an illustration of the great variety originally existing in the structure and arrangement of the Church's services, of which Cassian speaks at length, and deprecatingly, in the second chapter of the second book of his *De Coenobiorum Institutis*,[7] and also of the extraordinary devotion, and capacity for devotion in the Irish nation, to which Walafrid Strabo thus bore evidence in the ninth century : " Quamvis autem geniculationis morem tota servet ecclesia, tamen praecipue huic operi Scotorum insistit natio ; quorum multi pluribus, multi paucioribus, sed tamen certis vicibus, et dinumeratis per

[1] Holst. Pt. iii. p. 70.

[2] Εὐχὰν ἐπιτελεῖτε ὄρθρου, καὶ τρίτῃ ὥρᾳ, καὶ ἕκτῃ, καὶ ἐννάτῃ, καὶ ἐσπέρᾳ, καὶ ἀλεκτοροφωνίᾳ. Lib. viii. cap. 34, Ueltzen's Edit. 1853, p. 227.

[3] *Regula S. Benedicti*, cap. viii.   [4] Cap. x. Holst. Pt. ii. p. 156.

[4] Cap. xviii. Holst. Pt. ii. p. 21.

[6] *Geschichte des Breviers*, Freiburg, 1895, p. 168.

[7] Holst. Pt. i. p. 12.

diem vel noctem genuflectentes, non solum pro peccatis deplorandis, sed etiam pro quotidianae devotionis expletione, studium istud frequentare videntur."[1]

We have not attempted to reproduce the order of Mattins, or of any other part of the Divine Office, out of the collection of Collects, Hymns, Canticles, &c., in the Bangor MS.

In the almost entire absence of rubrics, and in the great diversity of early Gallican Offices, after which it must have been more or less modelled, such a reconstruction must be extremely problematical, and in many of its details incapable of proof or disproof.[2]

§ 3. *Distribution of Collects.—a.* We group together in this section and present in tabular form the Collects which occur in the Bangor MS. Cassian tells us that throughout the East a Collect was used at the conclusion of each Psalm, instead of the 'Gloria Patri' which he found to be the established usage in Gaul on his arrival in that country.[3] Each Psalm was followed by a Collect in the Divine Office at Jerusalem in the fourth century.[4] The early Latin Psalter printed by Thomasius[5] has a Collect at the conclusion of each Psalm. There is not sufficient evidence to prove the usage of Bangor, but it is evident from the second Table of Collects, that Collects were appended to certain Canticles, Hymns, and Psalms, &c., and therefore, perhaps, to all Psalms, either singly or in groups.

b. Two sets and portions of a third and fourth set of Collects for the Day and Night Hours.

First Set (fol. 17v.)	*Second Set* (fol. 18v.)	*Third Set* (fol. 22r.)	*Fourth Set* (foll. 34v. 35r.)
a. [16, 17] ad secundam	[27] ad secundam 'hac hora prima diei'	*deest*	[122] Ad secundam.
b. [18] ad tertiam	[28] ad tertiam	*deest*	*deest.*
c. [19] „ sextam	[29] „ sextam	*deest*	*deest.*
d. [20] „ nonam	[30] „ nonam	*deest*	[121] Ad horam nonam.
e. [21] „ vespertinam ' vespertino sub tempore '	[31] „ vespertinam ' vespertina oratio '	*deest*	*deest.*
f. [22] ad initium noctis	[32-3] ad initium noctis 'evoluta nunc dei temporibus noctiumque spatiis super- venientibus '	*deest*	*deest.*
g. [23] „ nocturnam ' nocte orantes media '	[37] ad nocturnam ' horam mediae noctis '	[57] ad nocturnam ' media nocte '	*deest.*
h. [24-5-6] ad matutinam ' gallorum cantibus ' ' pulsis tenebris ' ' diei lucem tribuis '	[38-9] ad matutinam 'Tu es, domine, illuminator caliginum '	[58-9-60] ad matutinam ' de luce ' ' excita de gravi somno '	[120] Ad matutinam.
	[40-56] orationes communes fratrum		[117-119] A second and shorter set of ' ora- tiones communes fra- trum.'

Note.—Phrases indicating the time of day or night have been appended in smaller type.

[1] *De Rebus Eccles.* cap. xxix. 25. apud Hittorpium, *De Divin. Officiis,* Romae, 1691, p. 350, 1st col.

[2] A more venturesome writer has attempted a partial reconstruction in the *Church Quarterly Review,* vol. xxxvii. Jan. 1894, p. 351, &c. So has B. Zimmerman in the *Irish Eccles. Record* for June, 1895, vol. xvi. No. 7. p. 635 &c.

[3] *De Institt. Coenobiorum,* Romae, 1588, Lib. ii. cap. 8.

[4] *Peregrinatio Sylviae,* § 11 in L. Duchesne, *Origines du Culte Chrétien,* Paris, 1889, p. 473. See also P. Batiffol, *Histoire du Bréviaire Romain,* Paris, 1893, p. 22.

[5] *Opera Omnia,* Romae, 1747, Tom. ii. Nearly the same series of 150 Collects 'ad singulos Psalmos' has been printed by Geo. Cassander, *Opera Omnia,* Paris, 1616, pp. 423-46.

c. Seven sets of Collects after the Canticles, three Psalms (148-150), Gospel, Hymn, and 'of the Martyrs.'

[55] [61] De martyribus apparently misplaced. They should perhaps come after [75] or [80.]

	I.	*II.*	*III.*	*IV.*	*V.*	*VI.*	*VII.*
	fol. 22v. p. 24	fol. 24r. p. 25.	fol. 24v. p. 25.	fol. 25r. p. 26.	fol. 25v. p. 26.	fol. 26v. p. 27.	fol. 26v. p. 27.
	✠	✠	✠	✠	✠	✠	✠
Post Canticum	[62] Post Canticum.	[68] Post Canticum.	[71] Post Canticum.	[76] Post Canticum.	[81] Post Canticum.	[88] Post Canticum.	[91] Post Canticum.
Post Benedicite	[63] Post Benedicite.	[69] Post Benedicite.	[72] Post Benedicite.	[77] Post Benedicite.	[82] Post Benedicite.	[89] Post Benedicite.	[92] Post Benedicite.
Post iii. Psalmos	[64] Post iii. Psalmos.	[70] Post iii. Psalmos.	[73] Post iii. Psalmos.	[78] Post iii. Psalmos.	[83] Post iii. Psalmos.	[90] Post iii. Psalmos.	[93] Post iii. Psalmos.
Post Evangelium	[65] Post Evangelium.	*deest.*	[74] Post Evangelium.	[79] Post Evangelium.	[84-5] Post Evangelium (2).	*deest.*	*deest.*
Post Hymnum	[66] Post Hymnum.	*deest.*	[75] Post Hymnum.	[80] Post Hymnum.	[86] Post Hymnum.	*deest.*	*deest.*
De Martyribus	[67] De Martyribus.	*deest.*	*deest.*	*deest.*	[87] De Martyribus.	*deest.*	*deest.*

fol. 28v. p. 28.
✠
[94] Post Canticum.

This seems to be the commencement of another set; but the scribe of this part of the MS. had come nearly to the end of the space allotted to him, and had to complete [94] on a narrow slip of vellum, specially inserted for that purpose, and now numbered as fol. 29. It is evident that fol. 30 was written upon before fol. 29, otherwise it would not have been necessary to provide a strip to hold the remainder of [94.]

A cross is prefixed to all these sets.

Two more isolated Orationes de martyribus occur later on, viz : [97] on fol. 31r. and [114] on fol. 35r.

The absence of any Collects after 'Te deum laudamus' in the above series suggests the possibility that originally that Hymn did not form part of mattins. Four such Collects are however provided, as by an after-thought, later on, viz : [123] [125] [126][128] under the title of 'Post laudate,' &c.

d. Collectiones post Canticum. There are eight Collects so entitled [62], [68], [71], [76], [81], [88], [91], [94]. They are all for use ' Post Canticum Moysi ' i.e. 'Cantemus Domino gloriose,' &c. [5]. Six out of the eight are addressed to Christ ; one [94] is addressed to God the Father ; of one [88] the address is uncertain.

The phrase ' devictis tenebris nostris ' in [68] point to 3 a.m. or daybreak as the hour at which they were in use. There is no special reference to our Lord's resurrection. The general purport of these Collects is to ask our Lord as the 'Salvator mundi' [62], [68], [71], [91], to protect His people from the 'vetus inimicus' [91], and from all danger, as once He defended His chosen people in the Red Sea from Pharaoh and his pursuing hosts. They contain these four references to Baptism :

> (1) Deus, qui cotidie populum tuum jugo Aegyptiae servitutis absolvis, et per fluenta spiritalis lavacri in terram repromissionis devicto hoste transducis, &c. [68.]
> (2) nos quoque per baptismi gratiam et crucis triumphum &c. [76.]
> (3) nos ergo per gratiam baptismi libera, &c. [88.]
> (4) Israelem verum quae unda salvat [94.]

These allusions might seem to point to the baptismal associations of Easter Even and Easter-tide, but it is obvious that they would be suggested by the triumph song of Moses, at whatever period of the year that Canticle was used.

e. Collectiones post Benedicite. There are seven Collects provided for use after the Canticle ' Benedicite omnia opera' viz. [63], [69], [72], [77], [82], [89], [92]. Their language affords no indication of the time of day, or of the character of the day or season, or of the nature of the service in which they are intended to be used.

They are probably all addressed to Christ. In the case of the first three and the last this is self-evident. In [63], [69] and [92] Christ is addressed as 'Salvator mundi.' In [72] He is named. In the remaining three Collects [77], [82], [82] we infer the fact that He is addressed from the employment of the concluding formula ' Qui regnas.' The mere fact that a Collect commences with the word ' Deus ' by no means proves that it is addressed to God the Father. See [71], [72], [73], all of which commence with ' Deus,' yet evidently are addressed to Christ, and all of which end with ' Qui regnas.'

f. Collectiones post tres Psalmos. There are seven Collects which fall under this head [64], [70], [73], [78], [83], [90], [93]. But the title ' Post tres Psalmos' is only prefixed to the first of them, the remaining six being entitled ' Post laudate Dominum de coelis,' which are the first four words of the first of the three Psalms referred to, viz. Pss. 148, 149, 150. These are universally associated with Mattins, and such is no doubt their association here. The words 'quousque tenebrae iniquitatis nostrae convertantur in lumine' in [73] suggest an early morning hour. For the phrase ' in hac vigilia sollemnitatis ' in the same Collect see note to [73.]

All these Collects seem to be addressed to Christ. In the case of the first three and the last there is no doubt. The phrase ' Salvator mundi ' occurs in [64], [73], [93]. In the case of [78], [83], [90] we infer the fact from the concluding formula ' Qui regnas.'

g. Collectionrs post Evangelium. There are five Collects under this title, viz. [65], [74], [79], [84], [85]. This 'Evangelium' has evidently no connection with the liturgical Gospel, nor does it correspond to the Gospel which is read after the twelfth Lesson in the third Nocturn in the Benedictine Breviary, which is followed by an Oratio, which immediately precedes Lauds. See note to [65]. The language of these ·'Collectiones' implies an early morning hour 'pro reddita hujus diei luce' 'a vigilia matutina' [65]. The following phrases are suggestive of Easter-tide, if not of Easter Day itself, 'diem dominicae resurrectionis nobis sollempniter celebrantibus' [65] 'dominicum nostrae resurrectionis initium venerantes' [74] 'resurgentem in hoc diluculo Dominum' [79] 'diluculo lucis auctore resurgente', [85] yet the suggestion is not necessarily true, for in the Greek Church there are eleven Gospels of the Resurrection, one of which is used every Sunday at Lauds ("Ορθρος) when no special Sunday Gospel is appointed.

The connection of the Bangor Evangelium and its Collect with Mattins or Lauds is testified to by the repeated introduction of the word laus, e.g. laudes, gratiasque referamus [65], debitas laudes et grates unito referamus affectu [74], oblata laudis hostia spiritali [84.]

All these Collects are fashioned rather in the form of ·'biddings' to the people than of prayers addressed to a divine person, but Christ rather than God the Father is addressed or referred to in the last three Collects.

h. Collectionas post Hymnum. There are four ·Collects under ·this title, viz. [66], [75], [83], [86]. The Hymn referred to ·is probably the metrical Hymn of Mattins; Collects so placed are rare. Examples may be seen after the Hymn 'Veni Creator' as said by the priest while vesting for mass, in the Sarum Missal, and after the Hymn 'Aeterne rerum conditor' in the Mozarabic Breviary (Col. 51.)

The wording of these·Collects is not of a sufficiently marked character to enable us to attach them with certainty to specified ·Hymns; but see note to [66]. They would be appropriate to such Hymns as the '.Hymnus S. Hilarii de ·Christo' [2] or the 'Hymnus Apostolorum' [3] or any other Hymn commemorating the life or work of Christ, and especially His resurrection. Some phrases seem to connect this ' Hymnus ' with the ' Canticum Zachariae.' e.g.: '*illuminatio* et salus . . . *illumina* cor nostrum' [66.] 'qui infirmitates *visitasti*' [75] lux *orta* est [86].

The first three Collects are addressed to Christ ; the fourth is addressed to God the Father, but speaks throughout of·Christ.

i. Collectiones de Martyribus. There are six·Collects under this title ·or ' Ad Martyres,' viz. [55], [61], [67], [87], [97], [124]. These commemorative Collects were probably used at Mattins, though the language of them does not·contain allusion to any time of day. The first five Collects are addressed to Christ, who is besought through the prayers [67] or merits [55] [87] of the Martyrs. The sixth is a direct address to the martyrs themselves to remember their suppliants in the sight of the Lord: ·'mementote ·nostri in ·conspectu Domini.' For comment on these commemorations of·martyrs, see § 6.

§ 4. *Traces of an Eastern origin and connection.* In the following details the Bangor book shows traces of Eastern·rather than of'Western usage.

(*a*) The repetition of the refrain in 'Benedicite omnia opera' [6] after each verse in that canticle, 'hymnum dicite, et superexaltate eum in saecula.'

This arrangement is peculiar to the Eastern Church, where, in the Greek Office, the Song of the Three Children forms the eighth of the nine Odes appointed for Mattins (Ὀρθρος), whereas in Western Breviaries, both secular and monastic, the refrain is repeated only four times.

(*b*) The assignment of Collects to the close of each Canticle, and if we may infer from the title to [64] to the close of each Psalm, or set of Psalms, is a primitive Eastern feature, of which we find traces in the *Peregrinatio Sylviae*,[1] the writings of St. Basil,[2] and the Institutes of Cassian,[3] and in some of the Office Books now in use in the Eastern Church, as e.g. the Armenian.

(*c*) The presence in the Divine Office of the ceremony of the kiss of peace. See note to [34.]

(*d*) The use of Psalm lxxxix. daily at Prime. See note to [98.]

(*e*) The long Collects provided for use 'post Cantica,' especially [91]–[94] are very unlike Petrine Collects, which are usually short and terse. They bear far more resemblance to some Oriental prayers.

(*f*) The festal observance of Saturday as well as Sunday. On this point we must go a little more into detail.

In Eastern Christendom both the Saturday and the Sunday, both the Sabbath and the Lord's Day, were marked for festal observation.

In the Apostolic Constitutions, Christians are exhorted to meet together in church daily for worship, " but especially upon the Sabbath Day and on the Lord's Day, which is the Day of the Lord's resurrection, to praise God, Who made all things by Jesus, and Who sent Him to us, and delivered Him to suffer, and raised Him from the dead " (i.e. on the first day of the week.)[4]

They are enjoined to :

" Keep the Sabbath and the Lord's Day as feasts, because one is a memorial of the creation, and the other of the resurrection."[5]

It is ordered :

" Let servants work on five days, but let them rest on the Sabbath and on the Lord's Day, in the Church, with a view to the teaching of piety."[6]

In the Apostolic Canons it is laid down :

" If any cleric be found fasting on the Lord's Day, or on the Sabbath Day, except on one Sabbath Day only, (i.e. Easter Even) let him be deposed ; if a laic, let him be excommunicated."[7]

[1] L. Duchesne, *Origines du Culte Chrétien*, Paris, 1889, p. 471.
[2] Epist. ccvii. Migne, *Patrol. Graeca*. Tom. xxxii. col. 764.
[3] Lib. ii. cap. xi. P.L. Tom. xlix. col. 100.
[4] Lib. ii. cap. 59, § 2. Ültzen's Edit. Suerini et Rostochii, 1853, p. 70.
[5] Lib. vii. cap. 23, § 2. *Ibid.* p. 169.
[6] Lib. viii. cap. 33, § 1. *Ibid.* p. 226.　　　　　　　　[7] Canon 66. *Ibid.* p. 249.

The Council of Laodicea A.D. 364, marked out the Sabbath and the Lord's Day as days to be observed festally even in Lent.[1]

According to the Rule of St. Anthony food was never to be tasted before the ninth hour, except on Saturday and Sunday.[2] Further and corroborative evidence of Eastern practice is given in Smith and Cheetham's *Dictionary of Christian Antiquities*, vol. ii. p. 1824. A plain statement of Eastern practice on this point is made by John Cassian.[3]

In Western Europe, while the Eastern practice of keeping Saturday as a Feast prevailed at Milan,[4] in Gaul,[5] and, as we gather from the Bangor Antiphonary,[6] in Ireland, in the Roman Church Saturday was observed as a Fast.

Evidence on this point might be multiplied. It will be sufficient to quote the explicit testimony of St. Augustine, who says: 'Hence arose the variety [of custom with regard to Saturday.] Some, as especially the people of the East, in order to symbolize His [the Saviour's] rest, prefer to relax the fast; others like the Roman Church and some other Churches of the West, on account of the humiliation of the death of our Lord, prefer to fast.'[7] Further and corroborative evidence of Western practice in this matter is given in Smith and Cheetham's *Dictionary of Christian Antiquities*, vol. ii. pp. 1824-6.

Now the ranking of Saturday (Sabbatum) with the Feasts of Martyrs in the Bangor Antiphonary [11.] is an indication that Saturday at Bangor was kept as a Festival, and not as a Fast, and that Irish practice on this point in the seventh century coincided with that of the East and not with that of Rome.

We must guard ourselves against being supposed to suggest that the Church of Ireland was directly founded by the Eastern Church, as the Church of Southern Gaul has been believed to have been directly founded by the Church of Asia Minor. The connecting link between Ireland and the East was Gaul. Whatever Oriental features may be found in the early Irish Divine Office must have passed into it through a Gallican channel.

In spite of errors of detail, and in spite of a corrupt text, we believe that there is a solid foundation of fact in the following statement made about the origin of the *Cursus Scottorum* i.e. the Irish Divine Office, not the Liturgy, though what is true of one is probably true of the other. The author of the statement is an eighth century continental Scotic monk.

In linking the Irish services through Gaul with St. Mark, he makes a statement uncorroborated in any other quarter, both as regards the *genesis* of the 'Irish Cursus,' and as regards the connection of Eastern monastic rule (which would include regulations as to divine service) with St. Mark.[8]

---

[1] Canons 49 and 51. The latter canon ordered 'Quod non oportet in Quadragesima martyrum natales peragere, sed sanctorum martyrum facere commemorationes in Sabbatis et Dominicis.' Mansi, *Conciliorum Amplis. Coll.* Florentiae, 1759, Tom. ii. col. 572.

[2] Canon ii. Holst. Pt. i. p. 4.　　　　[3] *De Institutis Coenobiorum*, Lib. iii. cap. ix.

[4] See note 7.　　　　[5] *Rule of St. Caesarius of Arles*, Can. xxv. Holst. Pt. ii. p. 56.

[6] Rubric on Fol. 12v. [11.]

[7] *Epist. ad Casulamum*, cap. xiii. § 31. P.L. Tom. xxxii. col. 150. The next Chapter records the sensible advice of St. Ambrose to St. Augustine : 'Quando hic sum [i.e. Mediolani] non jejuno sabbato ; quando Romae sum jejuno sabbato ; et ad quamcumque Ecclesiam veneritis, ejus morem servate, si pati scandalum non vultis aut facere.' *Ibid.* col. 151. See F. Cabrol, *Les Eglises de Jérusalem*, Paris, 1895, p. 139.

[8] But see the passage quoted from Cassian in note below.

"*Cursus Scottorum.* Unde et alium cursum, qui dicitur praesenti tempore Scottorum, quae sit opinione jactatur. Sed beatus Marcus Evangelista,[1] sicut refert Josephus[2] et Eusebius[3] in quarto libro, totum Aegyptum vel Italiam taliter praedicaverunt sicut unam Ecclesiam ut omnis Sanctus, vel Gloria in Excelsis Deo, vel Oratione Dominica, et Amen, universi tam viri, quam foeminae decantarent. Tanta fuit sua praedicatio unita. Et postea in Italia Evangelium ex ore Petri Apostoli edidit.

Beatus Hieronimus affirmat,[4] ipsum cursum, qui dicitur praesenti tempore Scotorum, beatus Marcus decantavit, et post ipsum Gregorius Nazianzenus, quem Hieronimus suum magistrum esse affirmat. Et beatus Basilius, frater ipsius sancti Gregorii, Antonius,[5] Paulus. Macarius, vel Iohannes, et Malchus,[5] secundum ordinem Patrum decantaverunt.

Inde postea beatissimus[6] Cassianus, qui Linerensi (*sic*) monasterio beatum Honorium habuit comparem. Et post ipsum beatus Honoratus primus abba, et S. Caesarius Episcopus qui fuit in Arelata, et beatus Porcarius[7] abbas, qui in ipso monasterio fuit, ipsum cursum decantaverunt, qui beatum Lopum [et] beatum Germanum monachos in eorum monasterio habuerunt. Et ipsi sub normam reguli ipsum cursum ibidem decantaverunt, et postea in episcopatus cathedra summi honoris perseverandi sanctitatis eorum sunt adepti. Et postea in Britanniis vel Scotiis praedicaverunt, quae Vita Germani Episcopi Autisiodorensis, et Vita beati Lupi adfirmant. Qui beatum Patricium[8] spiritaliter litteras sacras docuerunt atque innutrierunt, et ipsum Episcopum pro eorum praedicatione Archiepiscopum in Scotiis et Britanniis posuerunt ; qui vixit annos cliii, et ipsum cursum ibidem decantavit.

Et post ipsum beatus Wandilochus[9] senex, et beatus Gomogillus,[10] qui habuerunt in eorum monasterio monachos circiter tria millia. Inde beatus Wandilochus in praedicationis ministerium a beato Gomogillo missus est, et beatus Columbanus partibus Galliarum ; destinati sunt Luxogilum[11] monasterium, et ibidem ipsum cursum decantaverunt. Et inde postea

---

[1] Cassian tells us about St. Mark : 'Nam cum in primordiis fidei pauci quidem sed probatissimi monachorum nomine censerentur, qui sicut a beatae memoriae Evangelista Marco, qui primus Alexandrinae urbi pontifex praefuit, normam suscepere vivendi, &c.' (*De Institutis Coenobiorum*, Lib. ii. cap. 5.)

[2] Not identified. Is this Josephus the Egyptian anchoret (4th cent.) some of whose sayings are preserved by Cassian in his sixteenth and seventeenth Collations ?

[3] Eusebius tells us that St. Mark preached the Gospel in Egypt and founded the Church of Alexandria. (*Hist. Eccles.* Lib. ii. cap. 16.) He does not mention Italy.

[4] It has not been found possible to verify this quotation from St. Jerome.

[5-5] All Egyptian or Syrian anchorites. See Smith and Wace's *Dict. of Christian Biog.* for dates and details.

[6] The epithet 'beatissimus' indicates a special regard for Cassian, who is here described as the link between Eastern monasticism, and the earliest monastic systems of Gaul, and, through Gaul, of Great Britain and Ireland.

[7] This passage seems to favour the chronology which places the martyrdom of St. Porcarius, abbot of Lerins, and his companions in the fifth century at the hands of Genseric and the Vandals.

[8] The Archbishopric of St. Patrick, the extension of his life to 153 years, and his mission from SS. Germanus and Lupus are unhistorical.

[9] Wandilochus is stated in the next sentence to have been one of the [twelve] companions of St. Columbanus when he left Bangor for the Continent. He is identical with the Waldolenus, frequently mentioned by Mabillon, *Annal. Bened.* Paris, 1703. Tom. i. p. 295, A.C. 611, Lib. x. cap. 53. See also pp. 294, 296, 313. Margaret Stokes, *Six Months in the Apennines*, London, 1892, pp. 112-3.

[10] Gomogillus, i.e. St. Comgall.

[11] This is Luxeuil in Franche-Comté.

percrebuit forma sanctitatis eorum per universum orbem terrarum, et multa coenobia ex eorum doctrina tam virorum quam puellarum sunt congregata.

Et postea inde sumpsit exordium sub beato Columbano, quod ante beatus Marcus Evangelista decantavit. Et si nos non creditis, inquirite in Vita beati Columbani et beati Eustacii[1] abbatis ; plenius invenietis ; et dicta beati Athleti[2] abbatis Edbovensis."[3]

In an Irish gloss in the *Book of Hymns* the following curious statement is made about St. Columba : " Ten canonical Hours he used to celebrate as it is reported, and it is from John Cassian's history that he took this."[4]

We need not lay stress upon the ten Hours, but the statement is interesting as preserving the Irish tradition about the influence of Cassian upon the ecclesiastical arrangements of the early Irish Church. Cassian, who had been a monk at Constantinople, came to Marseilles in 410, where he founded two monasteries, and died c. 448.

§ 5. *Traces of Ephesine or Hispano-Gallican influence.*

In addition to the above features of Oriental origin and influence, we note the following traces of Hispano-Gallican influence, using the term Hispano-Gallican instead of the older term Ephesine, as more convenient wherewith to designate the Old-Gallican and Mozarabic Service books, and including under it points which connect the Bangor book with the ancient services of Gaul and Spain, but which cannot be traced further, directly, to Greek or other Eastern sources.[5]

(a) The expression ' Salvator mundi' occurs frequently in Bangor Collects, i.e. ten times in [62], [63], [64], [68], [69], [71], [73], [91], [92], [93]. This phrase is rarely found in Roman formulae of devotion, and where it does occur it may be taken as a token of a Gallican importation, e.g. it occurs in the Collect ' Dirigere et sanctificare," &c., in the Roman Office of Prime, and also in the longer form of the same Collect at Prime in the Ambrosian Breviary (Pars Vernalis, p. 20).[6] The phrase also occurs twice among the ' Antiphonae ad processionem in Laetania majore' in the *Liber Antiphonarius* S. Gregorii Magni, a part full of

---

[1] Succeeded St. Columbanus as Abbot of Luxeuil in 610.

[2] This is Attala, one of the companions of St. Columbanus from Ireland and his successor as Abbot of Bobio [Edbovensis]. He died in 627.

[3] H. and S. vol. i. p. 138. W. p. 178. It exists in MS. in Cotton MS. Cleop. E. 1. foll. 5r.-7r. where the following note is appended ' Ex antiquo manuscripto litteris Lumbardicis scripto cir[c]a annum 720.'

[4] W. Stokes, *Goidelica*, London, 1872, p. 70.

[5] The term Hispano-Gallican was invented by the Rev. C. E. Hammond in 1878 (*Liturgies Eastern and Western*, Oxford, 1878, p. xvi.) The term ' Ephesine ' is much older. It is found in a letter attributed to Pope John VII. and addressed to Edald, Archbishop of Vienne, c. A.D. 707, in which these words occur ' De officiis missarum, de quibus in litteris vestris requisistis, sciat charitas vestra quia varie apud varias ecclesias fiant. Aliter enim Alexandrina ecclesia, aliter Hierosolymitana, aliter Ephesina, aliter Romana facit, &c.' (Mansi, *Concilia*, Tom. ix. col. 760.) This is not the place to defend that epithet, nor to discuss the rival theories of the Milanese origin of the Old-Gallican Liturgy, held by Duchesne (*Origines du Culte Chrétien*, Paris, 1889, p. 83) or of its Roman origin, as held by Father H. Lucas (*Dublin Review*, July, 1893, p. 564.)

[6] In the process of transplantation into the Sarum Breviary and through it into the Anglican Liturgy. this phrase has been dropped, the person to whom the Collect is addressed being changed. The change seems to have taken place at an early date. The history of the Collect is obscure. For a similar dropping out of the words ' Salvator mundi' in a Collect see the history of the Collect ' Deus, tibi gratias agimus ' &c., on p. xxix.

importations from Gallican sources.[1] But the title 'Salvator mundi' is of frequent occurrence in the devotions of the Old-Gallican Church, e.g. it occurs thrice in as many different Collects in the Christmas Day Mass in the *Missale Gothicum*, pp. 34, 35. It is found in an Oratio ad Pacem in the Mass in Dominica i. in xl. in the Mozarabic Missal (col. 302). It survives in some Tropes in W. T. which are of Gallican origin (pp. 130, 131); and in an anthem in the office 'De Extrema Unctione' in the Sarum Manual, whence it has passed into the 'Service for the Visitation of the Sick' in the Anglican Book of Common Prayer, 'O Saviour of the world, &c.'[2]

(*b*) The form of Creed presented in [35], though not found verbatim elsewhere, bears marked traces of affinity to the Creed in the *Sacramentarium Gallicanum.* For details see note to [35.]

(*c*) The use of the word 'Collectio' for 'Collecta,' as the equivalent of 'Oratio' in [54], [62], and frequently, 'Collectio,' is the term in almost exclusive use in the Old-Gallican Liturgies, but it does not occur in any of the Roman Sacramentaries. Strange to say, it is frequently found, as well as 'Collecta,' in the 'Rituale Ecclesiae Dunelmensis,'[3] but Gallican influence may have been at work there.

(*d*) The Eucharistic anthems [109]-[115] show more than strong Hispano-Gallican influence and affinities. In fact they are Hispano-Gallican anthems. See notes.

(*e*) The frequent use of the specially Gallican epithet 'carus.' See note to [14] stanza ix. line 8.

(*f*) The form 'Gloria et honor Patri &c.' given in [116] anthem (12), is Mozarabic and Ambrosian. See note.

(*g*) The majority of Collects are addressed to the second Person instead of the first Person in the Blessed Trinity. This addressing of Prayers to Christ is a marked Mozarabic feature, and is also found to a great extent in the Old-Gallican Missals. Such Collects in the Mozarabic rite witness to the Church's long struggle with and final victory over the tenacious Arianism of Spain.[4] There was little, if any, Arianism in the Celtic Church of Ireland. The numerous Collects addressed to Christ in the Bangor MS. can only be accounted for by their having been borrowed from some Hispano-Gallican source.

(*h*) The commencement of a considerable number of Collects, &c., with the personal pronouns 'Tu' and 'Te.'

This is mainly a Gallican or Mozarabic feature. Let us first take the case of Collects commencing with 'Tu.' Of ten Collects known to us thus commencing, exclusive of three in the Bangor book,

One occurs in the Sacramentarium Leonianum.   Col. 368.
One   „   „   „   Gregorianum.   Col. 183.

---

[1] P.L. tom. lxxviii. col. 684.

[2] *Missale Gothicum*, &c. passim.

[3] Surtees Society Publications, vol. x. p. 46, &c.

[4] H. P. Liddon, *Bampton Lectures*, London, 1869, 4th Edit. p. 389, where this subject is fully illustrated in a note.

One occurs in the Missale Mozarabicum.   Col. 698.

Five occur ,,   Sacramentarium Gelasianum.   Coll. 526 (*bis*), 702,
720, 748.

Two ,,   ,,   ,,   Gallicanum, pp. 210, 358.

It must be remembered that the Gelasian Sacramentary is a Gallican recension of a Roman Sacramentary, and that it abounds in Gallicanisms.

With regard to Collects commencing with the word 'Te,' of twenty-two collects known to us thus commencing, exclusive of those in the present volume, (See Index.)

Eleven occur in the Missale Mozarabicum, Coll. 114, 138, 179, 187, 194, 240 (frequently repeated) 467, 554, 624, 778, 840.

Six   ,,   ,,   Sacramentarium Gelasianum, Coll. 593, 631, 642, 744, 747, 749.

Three ,,   ,,   ,,   Gallicanum,   pp. 288, 357, 361.

Two   ,,   ,,   Missale Gallicanum,   pp. 160, 168.

On the other hand there is not a single specimen to be found in the Leonian or Gregorian Sacramentaries. This fact may point with others to a Gallican origin of the Hymn 'Te Deum laudamus.'

(*i*) There are traces of the Hispano-Gallican 'Praefatio' or 'Bidding of the people' in the shape assumed by some of the Collects, e.g. [70], [121.]

(*k*) It will have been noticed that in the Bangor MS. the ablative case is sometimes used instead of the accusative, as in the title of [23] 'ad nocturno' &c.

There is a note to the following effect by Dr. Neale quoted with apparent approval by Daniel:

'Notandum hic et saepius in Officii Mozarabici Hymnis eam linguae Latinae corruptelam inveniri, ex qua casus ablativus pro accusativo vel nominativo paullatim in usum venit ; donec in hodierna Hispanorum et Lusitanorum lingua fixum teneret locum, ut 'calle' 'arvore' 'commodo' pro 'callis' 'arbor' 'commodus.'[1]

But this use of the ablative case is not specially Spanish, and cannot be quoted as a mark of Mozarabic influence. It is found in the Utrecht Psalter (ff. 86*v*., 88*r*.), believed to have been written in the north of Gaul ; in the Vatican MS. of the Gelasian Sacramentary, likewise written in Gaul (MS. Reginae Suec. 316 cited as V, and edited by H. A. Wilson, Oxford, 1894, where see p. xxxi.) ; in the Verona MS. of the Sacramentarium Leonianum, written in Italy ; and it is probably a feature common to all European Latin MSS. of the seventh century and onwards. How much earlier it began to make its appearance this is not the place to enquire. There are no Western liturgical MSS. written earlier than the seventh century.

(*l*) We would call attention to the formula 'Qui regnas,' which occurs so frequently at the close of Collects in the Bangor Antiphonary, e.g. in [17], [18], &c.

---

[1] Dan. Tom. iv. p. 26.

This may be accepted as a mark of the Gallican origin of a Collect, and as a proof that it is, or at least was originally, addressed to Christ. It is an abbreviation of a termination which in one of its fullest forms stood thus : 'Salvator mundi, qui cum Patre et Spiritu Sancto vivis, dominaris, et regnas, Deus in saecula saeculorum.'[1] It is found in various abbreviated forms, and is frequently indicated in Gallican MSS. by the single word 'Salvator,'[2] or even by its first syllable 'Sal.'[3] In Celtic MSS. this termination is generally indicated by the two words 'Qui regnas.' In the Book of Deer we find the following Collect, evidently of Gallican origin, and in its full and original form : 'Deus, tibi gratias agimus, per quem mysteria sancta celebravimus, et a te sanctitatis dona deposcimus, miserere nobis, Domine, Salvator mundi, Qui regnas in saecula saeculorum. Amen.'[4] This Collect occurs again in the Book of Dimma,[5] and in the Stowe Missal,[6] with the Gallican phrase 'Salvator mundi' left out, and its address to Christ so far obscured. It occurs again in the Book of Mulling[7] in a yet more Petrine shape, with its original address to Christ forgotten, and the 'Qui regnas,' &c. changed into 'Per Dominum nostrum,' &c. It is remarkable that it had already assumed its Petrine shape in the two places where it occurs in the *Missale Gothicum*,[8] an Old-Gallican Missal where Roman influence has made some strong marks.

Other examples of Celtic Collects addressed to Christ, and ending with the formula 'Qui regnas,' &c., may be seen in the Stowe Missal.[9]

§ 6. *Commemorations of Martyrs.* There are a considerable number of commemorations of Martyrs in the Bangor Antiphonary, viz. in [11], [52], [55], [61], [67], [87], [97], [101], [102], [103], [104], [124]. There is no commemoration of any other class of Saints, such as Confessors or Virgins. This conspicuous regard for martyrs in an early Irish liturgical document is curious, because the Irish Church before A.D. 700 had escaped the persecutions of heathendom, and had not produced martyrs. Martyrs, as such, are not invoked in the Litany or Diptychs of the Stowe Missal. On the other hand, in the Hibernensis one whole book (Liber xlix.) consisting of fifteen chapters, is entitled 'De Martyribus,' and is exclusively devoted to that subject, and in another Canon, attributed to St. Patrick (Liber xxix. cap. 7) a special penalty is attached to theft from a church where the remains of martyrs and saints are sleeping. Mr. T. Olden has referred to such Canons to prove the non-Irish and continental origin of much of the Hibernensis.[10]

But the frequent and pointed commemoration of martyrs in the Bangor MS. seems, like so many other peculiar features of the ancient Irish Office, to have been derived from Gaul

[1] From a 'Collectio post Prophetiam' in the *Missale Gothicum*, p. 34. See Bangor Antiphoner. [62.]
[2] *Missale Gothicum*, pp. 88 (*bis*) 110, &c.   [3] *Ibid.* p. 94.   [4] W. p. 165.
[5] W. p. 171.   [6] W. p. 225.   [7] W. p. 173.
[8] Missa cxxvi. p. 144 ; lxxx. p. 150. In the latter case it immediately precedes the Roman canon under the title of 'Missa Cotidiana Romensis,' the text of which, though lost here, may be supplied from the *Missale Vesontionense*, p. 206.
[9] W. pp. 207, 221 (where there is confusion between the First and Second Persons in the Trinity) 232.
[10] *Church of Ireland*, London, 1892, p. 154.

or from the East through Gaul, and to have been somewhat blindly adopted from a land of martyrs into the services of a church where martyrdom was either unknown up to the time in question, or of rare occurrence.

In the Divine Office of the East Syrian Church there is a Martyrs' Anthem in the daily evening and morning services. This anthem is of great length, beauty, and variety. St. George and St. Cyriacus with or without his mother Julitta are among the saints most frequently commemorated by name.[1]   In Armenia martyrs were specially commemorated on Saturday: 'Oportet vespere diei Sabbati agere Martyrum officium.'[2]

In early Gallican and Spanish monastic Rules there were special directions for the Feasts of Martyrs, e.g. ' In Martyrum Festivitatibus tres aut quatuor missae fiant.   Primam missam de Evangelio legite, reliquas de passionibus Martyrum.[3]   In Dominicis vero diebus vel Festivitatibus Martyrum, solemnitatis causa, singulae superaddantur Missae.'[4]

The following Eastern Canon is of special interest, partly because it associates the commemoration of martyrs with Saturdays and Sundays in Lent, partly because it is incorporated in the following way in the Irish Collection of Canons known as the *Hibernensis*.

' Sinodus Laudacensis [dicit]: Non oportet in Quadragesima natalitia Martyrum cele-brari, sed eorum sancta commemoratio in diebus Sabbatorum et Dominicorum convenit.'[5]

It is, however, just possible that ' Martyr' in the Bangor Book is equivalent to 'Confessor.' There is early Gallican authority for applying the former title to the latter.

The epitaph on the tomb of St. Martin described that saint as:

"' Confessor meritis, martyr cruce, apostolus actu."[6]

In the opening Prefatio of the "Missa S. Martini Episcopi' in the *Sacramentarium Gallicanum* it is said of that saint : " Hic vir, quem adnumerandum Apostolis, Martyribus adgregandum proxima ita in rem tempora protulerunt.   Dubium enim non est ut sit martyr in caelo qui fuit Confessor in saeculo ; cum sciamus non Martinum martyrio, sed martyrium defuisse Martino.[7]

Sulpicius Severus, writing to the deacon Aurelius on the death of St. Martin said : " Nam licet ei ratio temporis non potuerit praestare martyrium, gloria tamen Martyris non carebit, quia voto atque virtute et potuit esse martyr et voluit."[8]

And again :

' Sed quamquam ista [i.e. supplicia] non tulerit, implevit tamen etiam sine cruore martyrium.'[9]

[1] A. J. Maclean, *East Syrian Daily Offices*, London, 1894, pp. xiv. xvi. 109, 181, &c.
[2] Synod of Tovin. Can. 17. A.D. 719. Johannes Ozniensis, *Opera omnia*, Venice, 1834, pp. 64-5.
[3] *Regula S. Aureliani ad Monachos*, Holst. Pt. ii. p. 68. *Ad Virgines*, Holst. Pt. iii. p. 44.
[4] *Regula S. Isidori*, cap. vii. Holst. Pt. iii. p. 124.
[5] *Hibernensis*, Lib. xlix. cap. 7.   The reference is to the fifty-first Canon of the Council of Laodicea.   Mansi, *Concil.* Tom. ii. col. 571.
[6] E. Le Blant, *Nouveau Recueil des Inscriptions Chrétiennes de la Gaule antérieures au viii⁰ siècle*. Paris, 1892, p. 457.   The editor is indebted to Mons. Le Blant for the four following liturgical and patristic quotations.
[7] Page 304. Muratori, *Liturgia Rom. Vetus*, Venetiis, mdccxlviii. Tom. ii. col. 891.
[8] Sulpicius Severus, *Epistola ad Aurelium Diaconum*, P.L. Tom. xx. col. 179.
[9] *Ibid.* col. 180.

St. Maximus of Turin says :

" Martyr Latine testis dicitur, ac quotiescunque bonis actibus mandatum Christi facimus, toties Christo testimonium perhibemus. Unde et crux Domini non illa tantum dicitur quae passionis tempore ligni affixione construitur, sed et illa quae totius vitae curriculo cunctarum disciplinarum virtutibus cooptatur."[1]

This Gallican view of what constitutes a martyr seems to have been reproduced in Ireland. St. Patrick is included among the martyrs in the *Book of Obits of Christ Church, Dublin*,[2] ' unde etiam animo et summa intentione persecutiones sustinendo martyr effectus.' His claim to the title is thus explained and justified in the septima vita published by Colgan : " Nec incongrue martyrem dixeris, qui crucem Christi in corde ac corpore continuo gestavit, qui continuo cum Magis, cum Regibus ac Principibus idolatris, et cum daemonibus conflictando, corpus suum mille mortis generibus obiecit, ac ad ea subeunda cor semper habuit paratum ; et sic viventem Domino semper se exhibuit hostiam."[3]

We have felt it due to our readers to place this possible interpretation of the term ' martyr' before them. Nevertheless, the language in which martyrs and martyrdom are described in some of the Bangor Collects, e.g. in [67], [101], is too graphic and realistic to admit of this interpretation being accepted, in our opinion, as the true one.

§ 7. *Version of Holy Scripture employed.* Scriptural passages of varying length occur chiefly in the form of Canticles or Anthems. They are taken from the following nine books of Holy Scripture : Exodus, Deuteronomy, Psalms, Daniel, St. Matthew,. St. Luke, St. John, Acts, Revelation. Two passages, viz., the first anthem in [34], and the fifteenth anthem in [99], also occur in the Book of Judith. But in Judith, as in the Bangor Antiphonary, they are quotations from the Books of Psalms and Exodus respectively. Judith, therefore, is not entitled to a place in the above list.

These scriptural extracts exhibit a mixed text, partly Vulgate, partly Old-Latin, with the intermixture of readings apparently not found elsewhere.

The following tables will illustrate this statement.

EXODUS xv. 1–19 [5] fol. 7r. p. 8.

The variations of reading between B and V throughout this passage are so numerous that the best way to exhibit them will be by printing the two texts throughout in parallel columns, italicizing the variations in B. The third column contains authorities for the B text, and Old-Latin variations therefrom, as given by P. Sabatier, *Bibliorum Sacrorum Latinae Versiones Antiquae seu Vetus Italica*, Parisiis, 1751. Where no variation of text is marked it may be concluded that the text of the Old-Latin authorities quoted agrees with B.

The following are the authorities made use of by Sabatier in those portions of the Old Testament text with which we have to deal. A meagre account of them is given in his Praefatio, capp. lxxiv–lxxix. We refer to them by the aid of Arabic and Roman numerals. 1. The Versio antiqua of Sabatier, a conflated text from MS. and printed sources selected by him for the purpose of its construction ; 2. Codex Colbertinus (used as the main text in the

[1] Maximus Taurinensis, *Homilia*, lxxxii. *De Sanctis martyribus.* P.L. Tom. lvii. coll. 429–30.
[2] Dublin, 1844, p. 97. [3] *Trias Thaumaturga*, Lovanii, 1647, p. 168.

Gospels); 3. Corbeiensis; 4. olim Reginae Sueciae nunc Vaticanus; 5. Remensis; 6. S. Michaelis super Mosam, Vulgo St. Mihiel; 7. Psalterium Romanum a Thomasio editum, *Opera Omnia*, Romae, 1747, Tom. ii. p. 303 ; 8. Mozarabicum ; 9. Corbeiense ; 10. Sorbonicum i.; 11. Sorbonicum ii.; 12. S. Salabergae ; 13. S. Germani ; 14. Missale Romanum ; 15. Missale Mozarabicum ; 16. Breviarium Mozarabicum; i. Augustinus; ii. Ambrosius; iii. Hieronymus; iv. Vigilius Tapsensis; v. Gaudentius Brixianus; vi. Lucifer Calaritanus ; vii. Arnobius; viii. Hilarius; ix. Prosper; x. Cyprianus.

Verse.	B.	Verse.	V.	Verse.	Old-Latin authorities for and variations from B text as given by Sabatier.
1	Cantemus Domino, gloriose enim *honorificatus* est, equum et ascensorem *projecit* in mare.	1	Cantemus Domino, gloriose enim magnificatus est, equum et ascensorem dejecit in mare.	1	[a] glorificatus 6 ; magnificatus 1. i. iii. [b] equitem i. [c] dejecit 1, 6.
2	*Adiutor et protector fuit mihi* in salutem ; *hic* Deus meus et *honorificabo* eum, Deus patris mei, et exaltabo eum.	2	Fortitudo mea et laus mea Dominus, et factus est mihi in salutem, iste Deus meus et glorificabo eum, Deus patris mei et exaltabo eum.	2	[a] factus est i. ii. [b] mihi fuit 3, 16 add Dominus 16. [c] iste 1 *hic* –eum 5, 7, 10, 14. [d] glorificabo 1.
3	Dominus *conterens bella,* Dominus nomen *est illi.*	3	Dominus quasi vir pugnator ; omnipotens nomen ejus.	3	[a] pugnas 1. [b] ei 3, 5, 7.
4	Currus Pharaonis et exercitum ejus projecit in mare, *electos ascensores, ternos statores, demersit in rubrum mare.*	4	Currus Pharaonis et exercitum ejus projecit in mare ; electi principes ejus submersi sunt in mari rubro.	4	[a] Faraonis 1, 3. 5, 7. [b] fortitudinem iii. [c] ascensor est 12. [d-d] sternutantes (for ternos statores) 10 sternit (for ternos) 16 stratores 16, i. [e] projecit iii. [f-f] rubro mari 1, 10, 12 rubrum i.
5	*Pelago cooperuit* eos, *devenerunt* in profundum *tamquam* lapis.	5	Abyssi operuerunt eos, descenderunt in profundum quasi lapis.	5	[a] pelagus 7, 10, 11, pelagusque 16. [b] operuit 11, 16. [c] merserunt 3, 11, dimersi sunt 16.
6	Dextera tua, Domine, *glorificata* est in *virtute,* dextera manus tua, Domine, *confringet* inimicos.	6	Dextera tua, Domine, magnificata est in fortitudine, dextera tua, Domine, percussit inimicum.	6	[a] tuae 6. [b] confregit 1, 3, 5, 6, 7, 16.
7	Et *per multitudinem majestatis* tuae *contrivisti* adversarios, misisti iram tuam, *et comedit* eos *tamquam* stipulam.	7	Et in multitudine gloriae tuae deposuisti adversarios tuos, misisti iram tuam quae devoravit eos sicut stipulam.	7	[a-a] prae multitudine 16. [b] gloriae 1. 11. [c] contribulasti 1, conteruisti 10, 12, 16, conteruisti 11, contenuisti 3. [d] comedisti 3.
8	Et *per spiritum iracundiae* tuae *divisa est aqua ; gelaverunt tamquam murus aquae, gelaverunt fluctus* in medio mari.	8	Et in spiritu furoris tui congregatae sunt aquae ; stetit unda fluens, congregatae sunt abyssi in medio mari.	8	[a-a] spiritu 11, ii. [b] irae 1, 3, 13, i. iv. [c] omit 12. [d] mare 4, maris 7, 10.
9	Dixit inimicus : *Persequens* comprehendam, *partibor* spolia, *replebo animam meam interficiam gladio meo,* dominabitur manus mea.	9	Dixit inimicus : Persequar et comprehendam, dividam spolia ; implebitur anima mea, evaginabo gladium meum, interficiet eos manus mea.	9	[a] persequar et 11. [b] add et before dominabitur 16.

Verse.	B.	Verse.	V.	Verse.	Old-Latin authorities for, and variations from B text as given by Sabatier.
10	*Misisti spiritum tuum,*[a] et[b] *cooperuit*[c] eos mare[d]; *merserunt*[e] *tamquam* plumbum in aqua[f] *validissima*[f].	10	Flavit spiritus tuus, et operuit eos mare; submersi sunt quasi plumbum in aquis vehementibus.	10	[a] meum 7, 13. [b] omit 16. [c] operuit 11. [d] omit 16. [e] descenderunt 1, 3, i. ii; mersisti 4; mersi sunt 12; dimersi sunt 16; demersi sunt iii; miserunt 11. [f-f] aquam validissimam 1, 3, 13.
11	Quis similis *tibi* in *diis*, Domine? quis similis *tibi*,[a] *gloriosus in sanctis, mirabilis*[b] *in majestatibus*, faciens *prodigia*[c]?	11	Quis similis tui in fortibus, Domine? quis similis tui, magnificus in sanctitate, terribilis atque laudabilis, faciens mirabilia?	11	[a] omit 3, 5, 7, 12. [b] omit 13. [c] magnalia 16.
12	Extendisti *dexteram tuam*, et[a] devoravit[b] eos terra.	12	Extendisti manum tuam, et devoravit eos terra.	12	[a] omit 3, i. [b] transvoravit i.
13	*Gubernasti*[a] *justitiam tuam* populo *tuo hunc* quem *liberasti; exhortatus es in virtute* tua, *in refrigerio sancto tuo*.[a]	13	Dux fuisti in misericordia tua populo quem redemisti; et portasti eum in fortitudine tua, ad habitaculum sanctum tuum.	13	[a-a] Gubernasti in justitia tua populum tuum hunc quem redemisti; exhortatus es in virtute tua in requie sancta tua 1, 6 (omitting in justitia tua), 13. Gubernasti justitia tua populum hunc quem liberasti; exhortatus es in virtute tua et in refectione sancta tua 3 (with justitiam tuam for justitia tua and est for es), 5, 7, 10, 12 (justitiam tuam). Gubernasti justitia tua populum quem liberasti, consolatus es virtute tua, in refectione sancta tua 16.
14	Audierunt *gentes*, et *iratae*[a] sunt; dolores *comprehenderunt*[b] *inhabitantes*[c] Philisthim[d].	14	Ascenderunt populi et irati sunt, dolores obtinuerunt habitatores Philisthim.	14	[a] irati 12. [b] apprehenderunt 11, 16. [c] habitantes 1, 13, habitatores i. [d] Filistim 14.
15	Tunc *festinaverunt duces* Edom, *et principes Mohabitarum*[a]; *apprehendit eos*[b] *timor*[c]; *tabuerunt*[d] omnes *inhabitantes*[e] Chanaan.	15	Tunc conturbati sunt principes Edom, robustos Moab obtinuit tremor, obriguerunt omnes habitatores Chanaan.	15	[a] Mohabitum 16. [b] illos 1, 13, 16. [c] tremor 4, 5, 7, 10, i. [d] fluxerunt 1, 13, 16; defluxerunt 3, 11. [e] habitantes 13.
16	*Decidat*[a] super eos *timor* et *tremor magnitudinis*[b] *brachii* tui; fiant *tamquam* lapis[c] donec *transeat*[d] populus tuus. Domine, *usque dum*[e] *transeat*[f] populus tuus, Domine,[g] *hunc*,[h] quem *liberasti*.[i]	16	Irruat super eos formido et pavor in magnitudine brachii tui; fiant immobiles quasi lapis, donec pertranseat populus tuus Domine donec pertranseat populus tuus iste, quem possedisti.	16	[a] cecidit 1; incumbat i. [b] magnitudine 1; a magnitudine 16. [c] lapides 13, i. [d] pertranseat 1. [e] donec for usque dum i. [f] pertranseat 3, 5, 10, 12, 16. [g] omit 3, 5, 7, 10, 12, i. [h] hic 3, 5, 7, 10, 12, 13 i; iste 16. [i] adquisisti 1, 7, 13, i. vi.

Verse.	B.	Verse.	V.	Verse.	Old-Latin authorities for, and variations from B text as given by Sabatier.
17	*Induces*[a] *plantans*[b] eos[c] in *montem*[d] hereditatis tuae, *in praeparata*[e] *habitatione tua,*[e] *quam*[f] *praeparasti,* Domine, *sancti-monium*[g] tuum,[h] Domine,[i] quod[k] *praeparaverunt*[l] manus tuae.[m]	17	Introduces eos, et plantabis in monte hereditatis tuae, firmissimo habitaculo tuo quod operatus es, Domine, sanctuarium tuum, Domine, quod firmaverunt manus tuae.	17	[a] inducens 1, 3, 13, ii; induc 5, (*prima manu*, induces *secunda manu*) 7, 12. [b] plantato 1, 3, 13, ii; planta 5; plantas 12; et planta 7, 11, 16. [c] eum 16. [d] monte 4, 11. [e-e] praeparatam habitationem tuam 1, 3, 13, i; praeparato habitaculo tuo 5. 7, 11, 12; praeparatum habitaculum tuum ii. [f] quod 5, 7, 11, 12. [g] add tibi 16: sanctificationem 1; sanctuarium 11, 16. [h] omit 1, 3, 13. [i] omit 16. [k] quam 1, 13. [l] paraverunt 1, 13; praeparavit 12. [m] tua 12.
18	Domine,[a] *tu*[b] *regnas*[c] in aeternum, et *in saeculum saeculi,*[d] *et adhuc.*[e]	18	Dominus regnabit in aeternum et ultra.	18	[a-a] Dominus regnans in aeternum et super saeculum et adhuc 11. [b] qui 1, 3, 5, 7, 8, 12, 13. [c] pugnas 6. [d] omit 1, 3, 5, 7, 10.
19	*Quoniam*[a] *intravit*[b] *equitatus* Pharaonis cum curribus[c] et *ascensoribus*[d] in mare; et *induxit*[e] *Dominus*[e] *super eos*[e] aquas[f] maris; filii autem Israel *abierunt*[g] per siccum[h] *per*[i] *medium mare.*[i]	19	Ingressus est enim eques Pharao cum curribus et equitibus ejus in mare: et reduxit super eos Dominus aquas maris; filii autem Israel ambulaverunt per siccum in medio ejus.	19	[a] quia 1, 5, 7, 10, 12, 13, 16. [b] introiit 1, 3; introivit 5, 7, 10, 11, 12, 16: introibit 13. [c] quadrigis 3, 5, 7, 10, 12, 16. [d] adduxit 1, 13, i. [e-e] super eos Dominus 1, 5, 7, 10, 12, 16, i. [f] aquam 3. [g] transierunt 1; ambulaverunt 3, 5, 7, 10, 11, 12, 16, i. [h] aridam 11. [i-i] in medio mari 1, 3, 11, 13.

N.B.—Part of verse 19 occurs again in [99] anthem 19, fol. 32*v*. p. 30.

DEUT. xxxii. 1–43.
[1] fol. 1*r*. p. 1.

This song of Moses is unfortunately mutilated, but enough (more than half) has been preserved to enable us to draw a fair inference as to the whole. It presents in the main a Vulgate text, yielding, however, the following fifteen textual variations, some of which appear to be unique.

Verse.	B.	V.	Old-Latin authorities for, and variations from B text as given by Sabatier.
2	in	ut	
11	*deest*	et	
13	et	ut	
,,	oleum	oleumque	et oleum 1, 3, 5, 7, 10, 12, 16, vii.

Verse.	B.		V.	Old-Latin authorities for, and variations from B text as given by Sabatier.
15	*deest*	{	dereliquit Deum factorem suum	
21	*deest*	{	in eo qui non erat Deus et irritaverunt	
22	devorabit		devorabitque	devorabit iii ; comedet 3, 5, 7, 12, 16 ; et consumet 3 ; manducabit 4.
24	a		*deest*	
31	Deus		dii	
„	insensati		judices	1, 5, 7, 10, 11, 12, 16 ; insipientes iv.
32	{ propago eorum ex gomorrha	{	de suburbanis gomorrhae	1, 4, 5, 10, 16, iii. iv.
35	*deest*		et	
37	ubinam		ubi	
41	et		*deest*	
43	in saecula saeculorum		*deest*	

PSALMS.

Forty-one passages are quoted from the Book of Psalms. No passage consists of more than one verse except the first and thirteenth passages which comprise two verses each. In thirty of these passages B and V agree, in eleven there is a difference ; so that the B text in the Psalms must be described as mainly but not exclusively Vulgate.

In this list a cross (×) signifies identity of text.

Ps.		No.	B.	V.	Old-Latin authorities for B text as given by Sabatier.
v.	2, 3	[116.5]	×	×	
„	4	[116.6]	et	*deest.*	
„	11	[47]	×	×	
x H.	16	[99.13]	ⅹ	×	
xi.	8	[44]	×	ⅹ	
xvi.	8	[43] [119]	×	×	
xxii.	4	[109]	×	×	
xxvii.	1	[53]	×	×	
xxvii.	9	[41]	saeculum	aeternum	1, 3, i.
xxviii.	11	[45]	×	×	
xxx.	2	[117]	×	×	
xxxiii.	9	[110]	quam	quoniam	
xxxvii.	22, 23	[117]	×	×	
xl.	3	[42] [118]	× .	×	
xliii.	26	[51*]	×	×	
xlv.	8	[53]	×	×	
l.	3	[56]	×	×	
lxix.	2	[40*] [117]	×	×	
lxxviii.	8	[40]	×	ⅹ	
lxxxvii.	4	[116.7]	×	×	
			×	×	
lxxxix.	1	[98] [105]	×	×	
„	13	[105]	misericordiam tuam	misericordia tua	1, 3, 8.
„	14	[107]	×	×	

f 2

Ps.	No.		B.	V.	Old-Latin authorities for B text as given by Sabatier.
lxxxix.	16	[106]	×	×	
,,	17	[108]	×	×	
cv.	6	[34]	×	×	
cvi.	6	[51]	×	×	
cxi.	9	[50]	×	×	
cxvii.	25	[48]	×	×	
cxviii.	103	[113]	×	,×	
,,	165	[34]	×	×	
,,	171	[111]	In labiis meis meditabor hymnum cum docueris me ego iustitias respondebo.	Eructabunt labia mea hymnum cum docueris me justificationes tuas.	
cxx.	7	[42]	×	×	
,,	,,	[118]	custodet.	custodit	
,,	8	[42][118]	×	×	
cxxii.	3	[116.4]	nobis.	nostri.	1.7
cxxiii.	8	[51*]	×	×	
cxxxi.	9	[41*]	induentur iustitia.	induantur iustitiam	justitia 3 i. vii. ix.
,,			deest.	exultent	
cxxxvii.	8	[46]	×	×	
cxliv.	2	[116.1]	cotidie	per singulos dies	
,,			benedicimus	benedicam	
,,			laudamus	laudabo	
,			aeternum	saeculum	3, 7, 8. ix.
cxlviii.	1	[100]	{ De caelis Dominum laudate	{ Laudate Dominum de caelis.	
cl.	3	[100]	×	×	

DANIEL iii. 26, 57–88.

The Old-Latin text is mainly followed in the case of the Book of Daniel, and the Old-Latin order of verses is followed where it differs from the order in the Vulgate.

[116.3] fol. 33v. p. 31.

Chapter.		B.	V.	Authorities for B text as given by Sabatier.
iii.	26	×	×	

[99.16.18] fol. 32r.v. p. 30.

iii.	57	Dei Dominum	Domini Domino	
,,	,,	hymnum dicite.	laudate	1, 4, 16.

[6.] fol. 8v. p. 8.

iii.	57	*Vide supra.* 'Dominum' for 'Domino,' and 'hymnum dicite' for 'laudate' are retained throughout this Canticle.		
,,	58	Domini	*deest*	
,,	60	super caelos	quae super caelos sunt	
,,	61	potentias	virtutes	
,,	63	Domini	*deest*	
,,	64	*deest*	omnis	4. 10.

Chapter.		B.	V.	Authorities for B text as given by Sabatier.
iii.	66	calor	aestus	
,,	68	tenebrae et lumen	lux et tenebrae	4, 10.
,,	69	aestas	aestus	
,,	70	pruina	glacies	4, 10.
,,	71	fulgor	fulgura	
,,	74 {	omnia nascentia terrae	universa germinantia in terra	4, 10, 13. 4, 13.
,,	76	aquarum	deest	
,.	79	bilue	cete	
,,	81	bestiae et iumenta {	omnes bestiae et pecora	1.
,,	83	benedicite Israhelite	benedicat Israel	
,,	89	not belonging to the original text.		

[99.14] fol. 32r. p. 30.

,,	87 {	Sancti et humiles corde benedicite Domini Dominum.	Benedicite sancti et humiles corde Domino.	

St. Matthew vi. 10–13.

[36] fol. 19v. Page 21.

St. Matt.		B.	V.	Authorities for B text as given by Wordsworth and White.[1]
vi.	11	cotidianum	supersubstantialem	C D E ℱᵐ L T. W.
,,	12	remitte	dimitte	ℱᵖᵍ R.
,,	13	patiaris nos induci	nos inducas	D. R.
,,	,,	deest	Amen.	cor. vat. (et mg.)

St. Luke i. 68-80.

[4] Foll. 6r., 10r., pp. 7, 8.

The extracts from this Gospel, like the extract above from St. Matthew's Gospel, exhibit a mixed text with several variations from the Vulgate.

St. Luke.		B.	V.	Authorities for the B text as given by Wordsworth and White (with additional references to KK = Camb. Univ. Lib. MS. KK 124.)
i.	69	domu	domo	D ℱ L Q R V.
,,	70 {	sanctorum prophetarum suorum qui ab eo [i.e. euo or aeuo] sunt	sanctorum qui a saeculo sunt prophetarum ejus	D G Q (ino) R. (ℱ₁) q r.
,,	71	et liberabit i.e. liberavit nos ab	salutem ex	D G Q R gat KK. b c ff₂ l (de) g r aur.
,.	,,	nos oderunt	oderunt nos	A G L Q R X KK.
,,	72	sancti sui	sui sancti	C G T c q KK.
,,	74	manibus	manu	D ℱ I L Q R gat KK. R. W.
,,	77	meorum	eorum	D ℱ J L M Q.
.,	79	et umbra	et in umbra	D ℱ L Q R gat.
,,	80	in spiritu	spiritu	Q R W.
,,	,,	ad diem	in diem	Q R KK.
,,	,,	et Israhel	ad Israel	

---

[1] *Novum Testamentum Domini nostri Jesu Christi Latine secundum Editionem S. Hieronymi.* Ad Codicum MSS. fidem recensuit Iohannes Wordsworth, S.T.P. Episcopus Sarisburiensis. In operis societatem adsumpto Henrico Iuliano White, A.M. Fasc. I. Euangelium secundum Matthaeum. Fasc. II. Euangelium secundum Marcum. Fasc. III. Euangelium secundum Lucam. Fasc. IV. Euangelium secundum Iohannem, Clarendon Press, Oxford, 1805.

St. Luke ii. 14.

[116] Fol. 33*r*. p. 31.

St. Luke.	B.	V.	Authorities for the B text as given by Wordsworth and White (with additional references to KK = Camb. Univ. Lib. MS. KK 124.)
ii. 14	in excelsis	in altissimis	D 𝔓 G L O R *gat a f l r q δ aur. Iren*, secundum usum liturgicum.

St. John's Gospel vi. 59.

[114] Fol. 33*r*. p. 31.

St. John.	B.	V.
vi. 59	uiuus.	*deest.*
„ „	ex eo	hunc panem

Acts vii. 59.

[46] Fol. 21*r*. p. 23.

As this forms part of a short collect, it may perhaps be regarded as an adaptation rather than a quotation.

Acts.	B.	V.	Old-Latin authority for B text as given by Sabatier.
vii. 59	Deus uirtutum	*deest.*	
„ „	in	*deest.*	

Apocalypse vii. 14.

[102] Fol. 32*v*. p. 30.

The single verse quoted from the Apocalypse exhibits two variations from the Vulgate text.

Apoc.	B.	V.	Old-Latin authority for B text as given by Sabatier.
vii. 14	Magna tribulatione	tribulatione magna	x.
„ „	candidas eas fecerunt	dealbaverunt eas	x.

The lists above contain many instances in which the reading of the Bangor text is different from the reading of the Textus receptus of the Vulgate. Some of these variations are of very slight importance, and may be even merely variations of orthography. For most of them some other MS. authority, especially that of British MSS. is forthcoming.

It may be said that the type of text in the Bangor Antiphonary is that which is common to the Irish and North British group of MSS. and in almost every case, at least as far as the New Testament is concerned, can be paralleled from MSS. of that group. This group is marked by a conservation of Old-Latin readings in a text which is largely or mainly Vulgate.

In estimating the weight to be attached to the presence of Old-Latin readings as against Vulgate readings in liturgical MSS. it should not be forgotten that the Old-Latin has up to the present day succeeded in partially retaining its position in the *Missale* and *Breviarium Romanum*, and, mainly through them, in the *Graduale* and *Antiphonarium Romanum* as well. Old-Latin readings survive there in the Pater noster, Gloria in Excelsis, and elsewhere. The *Psalterium Romanum* of St. Jerome has been retained in 'Venite exultemus Domino,' and in general in the special Office Books of the Vatican basilica, where the Clementine recension of the Vulgate text has never been introduced.

§ 8. In conclusion the Editor wishes to reiterate his thanks to those to whom indebtedness was expressed at the end of the introduction to Part I. adding to that list the names of the Rev. H. J. White, M.A.; Rev. J. H. Bernard, D.D.; Rev. Benedict Zimmerman, O.C.D.; Mr. W. M. Lindsay; Mr. J. Lupton; and the Rev. T. A. O'Reilly, O.S.F. Librarian of the Franciscan Convent, Merchants' Quay, Dublin, for enabling him, at some inconvenience to the authorities, to see the copy of the Irish Liber Hymnorum belonging to that convent.

CORRIGENDA.

PART I.

Page ix, line 6, *transpose* and *to after* 517.
  „ x, „ 22, *for* Camanus *read* C[ol]manus.
  „ xii, note 1, *for* Royal MS. 2 A. xx. *read* Harl. MS. 2965.
  „ xx, line 20, *omit* (See p. xx.)
  „ xxx, 2nd col., line 5, *for* cantate *read* cantemus.
Fol. 1r., line 12, *for* redddes *read* reddes.
  „ 9r., „ 1, *omit* dicite.
  „ 15r., col. 1, line 23, *for* insignsi *read* insignis.
  „ 27r., line 9, *for* iter *read* ita et.
  „ 36v., col. 2, line 9, *for* camanus *read* c[ol]manus

PART II.

Page x, note 1, line 4, *after* sixth *add* or seventh.
  „ 28 in [96], line 3, *for* cerbero *read* cerebro.
  „ 35, col. 1, line 17, *after* Reg. *add* 2.
  „ 53, „ 2, „ 20, *omit* M.
  „ 70, „ 1, „ 17, *omit* M'.
  „ 79 in note, „ 6, *for* iuuentium *read* uiuentium.

AMENDED TEXT

OF

THE ANTIPHONARY OF BANGOR.

ANTIPHONARIUM BENCHORENSE.

[Fol. 1r.] In nomine Dei summi.[1]

[1.] CANTICUM MOYSI.

1. Audite, cœli, quæ loquor ; audiat terra verba oris mei. 2. Concrescat ut [MS. in] pluvia doctrina mea, fluat [ut] ros eloquium meum, quasi imber [super] herbam, et quasi stillæ super gr[amina.] 3. Quia nomen Domini invocabo. d[ate magni]ficentiam Deo nostro. 4. Dei perfecta [sunt opera, et omnes viæ] ejus judicia.

Audite.

Deus fidelis, et absque ulla iniq[uitate, justus et] rectus. 5. Peccaverunt ei, [et non filii ejus in sor]dibus,

Audite.

Generati[o prava atque perversa.] 6. Hæceine reddis D[omino, popule stulte et] insipiens ? numquid [non ipse est pater tuus] qui possedit te, et fec[it, et creavit te ?

Audite.]

7. Memento dier[um antiquorum, cogita genera]tio[n]es singula[s ; interroga patrem tuum, et annun]ti[abit] tibi ; [majores tuos, et dicent tibi.

Audite.

8. Quando dividebat Altissimus gentes, quando separabat filios Adam, constituit terminos populorum juxta numerum filiorum Israel. 9. Pars autem Domini populus ejus, Jacob funiculus hereditatis ejus.

Audite.

10. Invenit eum in terra deserta, in loco horroris, et vastæ solitudinis ; circumduxit eum, et docuit, et custodivit quasi pupillam oculi sui.

Audite.]

[Fol. 1v.] 11. Sicut aquila provocans ad volandum pullos suos, [et] super eos volitans expandit alas suas, et as[su]mpsit eum, atque portavit in humeris suis.

Audite.

12. [Dominus] solus dux ejus fuit, et non

B

erat cum eo deus [alienus.] 13. Constituit
eum super excelsam terram, [ut come]deret
fructus agrorum, et sugeret [mel de petr]a,
oleum[que] de saxo durissimo.
Audite.
14. [Butyrum de a]rmento, et lac de ovibus,
cum adipe [agnorum et arie]tum filiorum
Basan ; et hircos [cum medulla tritici,] et
sanguinem uvæ biberet [meracissimum.]
Audite.
15. [Incrassatus est dilec]tus, et recalci-
travit in[crassatus, impinguatus] dilatatus
[dereliquit Deum factorem suum] et recessit
[a Deo salutari suo. 16. Provocaver]unt
eum in diis ali[enis] et in [abominationib]us
[ad] iracundiam concitave[runt.
Audite.
17. Immolave]runt demo[niis. et non Deo,
diis quos ignora]bant ; [no]vi [recentesque
venerunt quos non coluerunt patres eorum.
Audite.
18. Deum qui te genuit dereliquisti, et
oblitus es Domini creatoris tui. 19. Vidit
Dominus, et ad iracundiam concitatus est.
quia provocaverunt eum filii sui et filiæ.
20. Et ait, Abscondam faciem] [Fol. 2r.]
meam ab eis, et considerabo novissima
eorum.
Audite.
Generatio enim perversa est, et infideles
filii. 21. Ipsi me provocaverunt in vanita-
tibus suis, et ego provocabo eos in eo qui
non est populus, et in gente stulta irritabo
illos.
Audite.
22. Ignis succensus est in furore meo, et
ardebit usque ad inferni novissima ; devorabit terram cum germine suo, et montium
fundamenta comburet.
Audite.
23. Congregabo super eos mala, et sagittas
meas complebo in eis.   24. Consumentur
fame, et devorabunt eos aves a morsu amaris-
simo ; dentes bestiarum immittam in eos,

cum furore trahentium super terram, atque
serpentium.
[Audite.]
25. Foris vastabit eos gladius, et intus
p[avor,] juvenem simul ac virginem, lac[ten-
tem cum] homine sene.
Audite.
26. Dixi : [Ubinam sunt ?] cessare [faciam
ex hominibus memoriam eorum.   27. Sed
propter iram inimicorum distuli ; ne forte
superbirent hostes eorum, et dicerent, Manus
nostra excelsa, et non Dominus, fecit hæc
omnia.
Audite.
28. Gens absque consilio est, et sine pru-
dentia. 29. Utinam saperent, et intelli-
gerent, ac novissima] [Fol. 2v.] providerent !
30. Quomodo persequatur unus mille, et
duo fugent decem millia.
Audite.
Nonne ideo, quia Deus suus vendidit eos,
et Dominus conclusit illos ? 31. Non enim
est Deus noster ut Deus eorum, et inimici
nostri sunt insensati.
Audite.
32. De vinea Sodomorum vinea eorum, et
propago eorum ex Gomorrha ; uva eorum
uva fellis, et botrus amarissima.   33. Fel
draconum vinum eorum, et venenum aspidum
insanabile.
Audite.
34. Nonne hæc condita sunt apud me, et sig-
nata in thesauris meis ? 35. Mea est ultio, ego
retribuam in tempore, ut labatur pes eorum.
Audite.
Juxta est dies perditionis, et adesse fes-
tinant [t]empora. 36. Judicabit Dominus
populum suum, et in ser[vis su]is miserebitur.
Audite.
Videbit quod [infirmata] sit manus, et clausi
quoque defecerunt, [residuique con]sumpti
sunt. 37. Et dicet : Ubinam sunt [dii
eorum in quibus habebant fiduciam ?]
Audite.

38. [De quorum victimis comedebant adipes, et bibebant vinum libaminum : surgant, et opitulentur vobis, et in necessitate vos protegant.
Audite.
39. Videte quod ego sim solus, et non sit alius Deus præter me : ego occidam, et ego vivere faciam :] [Fol. 3r.] percutiam, et ego sanabo, et non est qui de manu mea possit eruere.
Audite.
40. Levabo ad cœlum manum meam, et dicam : Vivo ego in æternum. 41. Et si acuero ut fulgur gladium meum, et arripuerit judicium manus mea : reddam ultionem hostibus meis, et his qui oderunt me retribuam.
Audite.
42. Inebriabo sagittas meas sanguine, et gladius meus devorabit carnes, de cruore occisorum, et de captivitate, nudati inimicorum capitis.
Audite.
43. Laudate gentes populum ejus, quia sanguinem servorum ulciscetur ; et vindictam retribuet in hostes eorum, et propitius erit terræ populi sui in sæcula sæculorum.
Audite.

[2.] HYMNUS SANCTI HILARII DE CHRISTO.

     i. Hymnum dicat turba fr[atrum,]
         Hymnum cantus person[et,]
         Christo regi concinent[es]
         Laud[es demus debitas.]

     ii. Tu Dei d[e corde verbum,
         Tu via, tu veritas,
         Jesse virga tu vocaris,
         Te leonem legimus.]

[Fol. 3v.]
     iii. Dextra Patris, mons, et agnus,
         Angularis tu lapis,
         Sponsus idem vel columba,
         Flamma, pastor, janua.

     iv. In prophetis inveniris
         Nostro natus sæculo,
         Ante sæcla tu fuisti
         Factor primi sæculi.

     v. Factor cœli, terræ factor,
         Congregator tu maris,
         Omniumque tu creator
         Quæ Pater nasci jubet.

     vi. Virginis receptus membris,
         Gabriele nuntio,
         [Cr]escit alvus prole sancta,
         [Nos mon]emur credere

     vii. [Rem novam nec ante] visam
         [Virginem puerper]am.
         [Tunc Magi stellam secu]ti
         [Primi adorant parvulum,

     viii. Offerentes thus et aurum,
         Digna regi munera ;
         Mox Herodi nuntiatum ;
         Invidens potentiæ]

     ix. Tum jubet parvos necari,
         Turbam fecit martyrum,
         Fertur infans occulendus
         Nili flumen quo fluit ;

     x. Qui refertur post Herodem
         Nutriendus Nazareth,
         Multa parvus, multa adultus
         Signa fecit cœlitus,

     xi. Quæ latent et quæ leguntur,
         Coram multis testibus,
         Prædicans cœleste regnum
         Dicta factis approbat.

     xii. Debiles fecit vigere,
         Cæcos luce illuminat,
         Verbis purgat lepræ morbum,
         Mortuos resuscitat.

xiii. Vinum quod deerat hydriis
     Mutari aqua jubet,
     Nuptiis mero retentis
     [Propinat]o populo.

xiv. [Pane quino pisc]e bino
     [Quinque pascit mil]lia,
     [Refectis fragmenta cœnæ
     Ter quaternis corbibus.]

[Fol. 4r.]

xv. Turba ex omni discumbente
    Jugem laudem pertulit,
    Duodecim viros probavit.
    Per quos vita discitur.

xvi. Ex quibus unus invenitur
     Christi Judas traditor.
     Instruuntur missi ab Anna
     Proditoris osculo.

xvii. Innocens captus tenetur,
      Nec repugnans ducitur,
      Sistitur falsis, grassantur
      Offerentes Pontio.

xviii. [Discutit objecta Præses,
       Nullum crimen invenit,
       Sed cum turba Judeorum
       Pro salute Cæsaris]

xix. Dicerent Christum negandum,
     Turbis Sanctus traditur,
     Impiis verbis grassantur,
     Sputa, flagra sustinet.

xx. Scandere crucem jubetur
    Innocens pro noxiis,
    Morte carnis quam gerebat
    Mortem vicit omnium.

xxi. Tum Deum clamore magno
     [Patr]em pendens invocat,
     [Mors secuta] membra Christi
     [Laxat stricta vincul]a.

xxii. Vela templi scissa pendent,
      Nox obscurat sæculum ;
      Excitantur de sepulchris
      Dudum clausa corpora.

xxiii. Affuit Joseph beatus ;
       Corpus myrrha perlitum
       Linteo rudi ligatum
       Cum dolore condidit.

xxiv. Milites servare corpus
      Annas princeps præcipit,
      Ut videret si probaret
      Christus quod spoponderat.

xxv. Angelum Dei trementes
     Veste amictum candida
     Qui candore claritatis
     Vellus vicit sericum.

xxvi. Demovit saxum sepulchro
      Surgens Christus integer.
      Hæc vidit Judæa mendax,
      Hæc negat cum viderit.

xxvii. F[eminæ p]rimum monent[ur
       Salvatorem vivere,
       Quas salutat ipse mœstas,
       Complet tristes gaudio.]

[Fol. 4v.]

xxviii. Seque a mortuis paterna
        Suscitatum dextera
        Tertia die redisse
        Nuntiat apostolis.

xxix. Mox videtur a beatis
      Quos probavit fratribus,
      Quod redisset ambigentes,
      Intrat clausis januis.

xxx. Dat docens præcepta legis,
     Dat divinum Spiritum,
     Spiritum Dei perfectum,
     Trinitatis vinculum.

xxxi. Præcipit totum per orbem
    Baptizari credulos,
    Nomen Patris invocantes,
    Confitentes Filium.

xxxii. Mystica fide revelat
    Tinctos Sancto Spiritu
    Fonte tinctos innovatos
    Filios factos Dei.

xxxiii. Ante lucem turba [fratrum]
    Concin[amus gloriam,
    Qua docemur nos futuros
    Sempiterna sæcula.]

xxxiv. Galli cantus, galli plausus,
    Proximum sentit diem,
    Nos canentes et precantes
    Quæ futura credimus.

xxxv. Majestatemque immensam
    Concinemus uniter,
    Ante lucem nuntiemus
    Christum Regem sæculo.

xxxvi. Ante lucem nuntiemus
    Christum Regem sæculo,
    Qui in illum recte credunt
    Regnaturi cum eo.

xxxvii. Gloria Patri ingenito,
    Gloria Unigenito,
    Simul cum Sancto Spiritu,
    In sempiterna sæcula.

[3.] HYMNUS APOSTOLORUM UT ALII DICUNT.

i. Precamur Patrem
    Regem omnipotentem,
    Et Jesum Christum,
    Sanctum quoque Spiritum.
    Alleluia.

ii. Deum in una
    Perfectum s[ubstantia,]
    Trinum [in tribus
    Adorandum personis.]

[Fol. 5r.]
iii. Universorum
    Fontis jubar luminum
    Æthereorum
    Et orbi lucentium.

iv. Hic enim dies
    Velut primogenitus
    Cœli ab arce
    Mundi moli micuit.

v. Sic verbum caro
    Factum a principio
    Lumen æternum
    Missum Patre sæculo.

vi. Illeque proto
    Vires adimens chao
    Tum improviso
    Noctem pepulit mundo.

vii. Ita veterno
    Iste hoste subacto
    Polum nodoso
    Solvit mortis vinculo.

viii. Tenebræ super
    Ante erant abyssum
    [Qu]am radiaret
    [Prim]us dies dierum.

ix. Hic quum prodiret
    Vera lux mortalia
    Contexit alta
    Corda ignorantia.

x. Eodem die
    Rubrum, ut aiunt, mare
    Post tergum liquit
    Liberatus Israel.

xi. Per hoc docemur
Mundi acta spernere,
Et in deserto
Virtutum consistere.

xii. Summerso sævo
Cincri canunt æmulo
Certatim Deo
Laudes duci igneo.

xiii. Sicque erepti
Nequam jubemur fretis
Laudare Deum
Explosis inimicis.

xiv. Et sicut ille
Lucis fit initium
Ita et iste
Salutis exordium.

[Fol. 5v.]
xv. Locatur primus
In tenore diei,
Secundus vero
In calore fidei.

xvi. In fine mundi
Post tanta mysteria
Adest Salvator
Cum grandi clementia.

xvii. Tamque aperte
Elementa prætendunt
Quam vatum ora
Lucide concelebrant.

xviii. Natus ut homo
Mortali in tegmine
Non deest cœlo
Manens in Trinitate.

xix. Vagit in pannis,
Veneratur a magis,
Fulget in stellis,
Adoratur in cœlis.

xx. Statura vili
Continetur præsepi,
Cujus pugillo
Potest orbis concludi.

xxi. Primumque signum
Portendit discipulis
Aquæ conversæ
In sapore nectaris.

xxii. Tum per prophetam
Completur ut dictum,
" Saliet claudus
Ut cervus " perniciter.

xxiii. Planaque fatur,
Absoluto vinculo,
Lingua mutorum
Imperante Domino.

xxiv. Surdi sanantur,
Cæci atque leprosi,
Funere truso
Suscitantur mortui.

xxv. Totidem panes
Quinque dividit virum
Saturaturus
Procul dubio millibus.

xxvi. Post tantas moles
Divinæ clementiæ
Exosus ille
Stimulo invidiæ.

xxvii. Qui invidere
Et odere animam
Pro inimicis
Prorogans [precatus est.]

[Fol. 6r.]
xxviii. Adversus eum
Initur conisilum
Qui magni dictus
Consilii est nuntius.

xxix. Accedunt ei
Ut latroni cum gladiis
Furem æternis
Tradituro æstibus.

xxx. Tandem humano
Traditur judicio,
Mortali rege
Damnatur perpetuus.

xxxi. Cruci confixus
Polum mire concutit,
Lumenque solis
Tribus obtendit horis.

xxxii. Saxa rumpuntur,
Velum scinditur templi,
Vivi consurgunt
De sepulchris mortui.

xxxiii. Corrosum nodis
Annis fere millibus
Extricat senis
Inferi feralibus.

xxxiv. [Et] protoplastum
[Probr]osa soboli
Abjecta mali morte
Sæva ultrice.

xxxv. Quemque antiquum
Paradiso incolam
Recursu suo
Clementer restituit.

xxxvi. Exaltans caput
Universi corporis
In Trinitate
Locavit ecclesiam.

xxxvii. In hoc cœlitus
Jubet portas principes
Regi cum sociis
Æternales pandere.

xxxviii. Errantem propriis
Evehens centesimam
Supernis ovem
Humeris ovilibus.

xxxix. Quem expectamus
Affuturum judicem
Justum cuique
Opus suum reddere.

xl. Rogo, quam tantis
Talibusque donariis
Vicem condigne
Possumus rependere ?

| Fol. 6v.]

xli. Quid tam mortales
Tentamus micrologi
Narrare quivit
Quæ nullus edicere ?

xlii. Solum oramus
Hoc, idemque maximum ;
Nostri æterne
Miserere, Domine.
Alleluia.

[4.] BENEDICTIO SANCTI ZACHARIÆ.

68. Benedictus Dominus Deus Israel, quia visitavit, et fecit redemptionem plebis suæ ; 69. Et erexit cornu salutis nobis, in domo David pueri sui.

70. Sicut locutus est per os sanctorum prophetarum suorum, qui ab ævo sunt ; 71. Et liberavit nos ab inimicis nostris, et de manu omnium qui nos oderunt.

72. Ad faciendam misericordiam cum patribus nostris, et memorari testamenti sancti sui.

73. Jusjurandum, quod juravit ad Abraham patrem nostrum daturum se nobis.

74. Ut sine timore, de manibus inimicorum nostrorum liberati, serviamus illi ; 75. In

sanctitate et justitia coram ipso, omnibus diebus nostris.

76. Et tu, puer, propheta Altissimi vocaberis, præibis enim ante faciem Domini parare vias ejus.

77. Ad dandam scientiam salutis plebi ejus, in remissionem peccatorum eorum ;

78. Per viscera misericordiæ dei nos[tri,] in quibus [Fol. 10r.] visitavit nos oriens ex alto.

79. Illuminare his qui in tenebris et umbra mortis sedent, ad dirigendos pedes nostros in viam pacis.

80. Puer autem crescebat, et confortabatur in spiritu, et erat in desertis usque ad diem ostensionis suæ ad Israel.

[5.] CANTICUM [MOYSI.]

[Fol. 7r.] 1. Cantemus Domino, gloriose enim honorificatus est, equum et ascensorem projecit in mare. 2. Adjutor et protector fuit mihi in salutem ;

Hic Deus meus, et honorificabo eum, Deus patris mei, et exaltabo eum. 3. Dominus conterens bella, Dominus nomen est illi.

4. Currus Pharaonis et exercitum ejus projecit in mare, electos ascensores, ternos statores, demersit in rubrum mare.

5. Pelago cooperuit eos, devenerunt in profundum tamquam lapis. 6. Dextera tua, Domine, glorificata est in virtute, dextera manus tua, Domine, confringet inimicos.

7. Et per multitudinem majestatis tuæ [Fol. 7v.] contristi adversarios, misisti iram tuam, et comedit eos tamquam stipulam.

8. Et per spiritum iracundiæ tuæ divisa est aqua ; gelaverunt tamquam murus aquæ ; gelaverunt fluctus in medio mari.

9. Dixit inimicus ; Persequens comprehendam, partibor spolia, replebo animam meam,

interficiam gladio meo, dominabitur manus mea.

10. Misisti spiritum tuum, et cooperuit eos mare ; merserunt tamquam plumbum in aqua validissima.

11. Quis similis tibi in diis, Domine ? quis similis tibi, gloriosus in sanctis, mirabilis in majestatibus, faciens prodigia ?

12. Extendisti dexteram tuam,[Fol.8r.] et devoravit eos terra. 13. Gubernasti justitiam tuam populo tuo hunc quem liberasti ;

Exhortatus es in virtute tua in refrigerio sancto tuo. 14. Audierunt gentes, et iratæ sunt ; dolores comprehenderunt inhabitantes Philisthim.

15. Tunc festinaverunt duces Edom, et principes Mohabitarum ; apprehendit eos timor ; tabuerunt omnes inhabitantes Chanaan.

16. Decidat super eos timor et tremor magnitudinis brachii tui ; fiant tamquam lapis, donec transeat populus tuus, Domine, usque dum transeat populus tuus, Domine, hic [MS. hunc] quem liberasti.

[Fol. 8v.] 17. Induces plantans eos in montem hereditatis tuæ, in præparata habitatione tua, quam præparasti, Domine, sanctimonium tuum, Domine, quod præparaverunt manus tuæ.

18. Domine, tu regnas in æternum, et in sæculum sæculi, et adhuc. 19. Quoniam intravit equitatus Pharaonis cum curribus et ascensoribus in mare ; et induxit Dominus super eos aquas maris ; filii autem Israel abierunt per siccum per medium mare.

[6.] BENEDICTIO [TRIUM] PUERORUM.

57. Benedicite omnia opera Domini Dominum : hymnum dicite, et superexaltate eum in sæcula.

59. Benedicite cœli Domini Dominum : hymnum dicite, et superexaltate eum in sæcula.

[Fol. 9r.] 58. Benedicite angeli Domini Dominum : hymnum dicite, et superexaltate eum in sæcula.

60. Benedicite aquæ omnes super cœlos Dominum : hymnum dicite, et superexaltate eum in sæcula.

61. Benedicite omnes potentiæ Domini Dominum: hymnum dicite, et superexaltate eum in sæcula.

62. Benedicite sol et luna Dominum : hymnum dicite, et superexaltate eum in sæcula.

63. Benedicite stellæ cœli Domini Dominum : hymnum dicite, et superexaltate eum in sæcula.

64. Benedicite imber et ros Dominum : hymnum dicite, et superexaltate eum in sæcula.

65. Benedicite omnes spiritus Dominum : hymnum dicite, et superexaltate eum in sæcula.

66. Benedicite ignis et calor Dominum : hymnum dicite, et superexaltate eum in sæcula.

71. Benedicite noctes et dies Dominum : hymnum dicite, et superexaltate eum in sæcula.

72. Benedicite tenebræ et lumen Dominum : hymnum dicite, et superexaltate eum in sæcula.

67. Benedicite frigus et æstas Dominum : hymnum dicite, et superexaltate eum in sæcula.

70. Benedicite pruina et nives Dominum : hymnum dicite, et superexaltate eum in sæcula.

73. Benedicite fulgura et nubes Dominum : hymnum dicite, et superexaltate eum in sæcula.

74. Benedicat terra Dominum : hymnum dicat, et superexaltet eum in sæcula.

75. Benedicite montes et colles Dominum : hymnum dicite, et superexaltate eum in sæcula.

76. Benedicite omnia nascentia terræ Dominum : hymnum dicite, et superexaltate eum in sæcula.

[Fol. 9v.] 78. Benedicite maria et flumina Dominum : hymnum dicite, et superexaltate eum in sæcula.

77. Benedicite fontes aquarum Dominum : hymnum dicite, et superexaltate eum in sæcula.

79. Benedicite beluæ, et omnia quæ moventur in aquis Dominum: hymnum dicite, et superexaltate eum in sæcula.

80. Benedicite omnes volucres cæli Dominum : hymnum dicite, et superexaltate eum in sæcula.

81. Benedicite bestiæ et jumenta Dominum : hymnum dicite, et superexaltate eum in sæcula.

83. Benedicite Israelitæ Dominum : hymnum dicite, et superexaltate eum in sæcula.

82. Benedicite filii hominum Dominum : hymnum dicite, et superexaltate eum in sæcula.

84. Benedicite sacerdotes Domini Dominum : hymnum dicite, et superexaltate eum in sæcula.

85. Benedicite servi Domini Dominum : hymnum dicite, et superexaltate eum in sæcula.

86. Benedicite spiritus et animæ justorum Dominum : hymnum dicite, et superexaltate eum in sæcula.

87. Benedicite sancti et humiles corde Dominum : hymnum dicite, et superexaltate eum in sæcula.

88. Benedicite, Anania, Azaria, Misael, Dominum : hymnum dicite, et superexaltate eum in sæcula.

89. Benedicamus Patrem, et Filium, et Spiritum Sanctum, Dominum : hymnum dicamus, et superexaltemus eum in sæcula.

c

[Fol. 10v.]

[7.] Hymnus in die Dominica.

Laudate pueri Dominum : laudate nomen Domini. 1. Te Deum laudamus : te Dominum confitemur.

2. Te æternum Patrem omnis terra veneratur. 3. Tibi omnes angeli, tibi cœli, et universæ potestates.

4. Tibi Cherubin et Seraphin incessabili voce proclamant : 5. Sanctus, Sanctus, Sanctus, Dominus Deus Sabaoth.

6. Pleni sunt cœli et universa terra honore gloriæ tuæ.

7. Te gloriosus apostolorum chorus. 8. Te prophetarum laudabilis numerus.

9. Te martyrum candidatus laudet exercitus. 10. Te per orbem terrarum sancta confitetur ecclesia.

11. Patrem immensæ majestatis. 12. Venerandum tuum verum unigenitum Filium. [Fol. 10v.] 13. Sanctum quoque Paraclitum Spiritum. 14. Tu rex gloriæ, Christe.

15. Tu Patris sempiternus es Filius. 16. Tu ad liberandum mundum suscepisti hominem.

Non horruisti Virginis uterum. 17. Tu, devicto mortis aculeo, aperuisti credentibus regna cœlorum.

18. Tu ad dexteram Dei sedens in gloria Patris. 19. Judex crederis esse venturus.

20. Te ergo quæsumus, nobis tuis famulis subveni, quos pretioso sanguine redemisti.

21. Æterna [Aeternam MS.] fac cum sanctis [in] gloria [gloriæ MS.] munerari.

22. Salvum fac populum tuum, Domine, et benedic hæreditati tuæ. 23. Et rege eos, et extolle illos usque in sæculum.

24. Per singulos dies benedicimus te. 25. Et laudamus nomen tuum in æternum, et in sæculum sæculi. Amen.

26. Fiat, Domine, misericordia tua super nos, quemadmodum speravimus in te.

[8.] Hymnus quando communicant sacerdotes.

i. Sancti venite,
Christi corpus sumite,
Sanctum bibentes
Quo redempti sanguinem.

ii. Salvati Christi
Corpore et sanguine,
A quo refecti
Laudes dicamus Deo.

[Fol. 11r.]

iii. Hoc sacramento
Corporis et sanguinis
Omnes exuti
Ab inferni faucibus.

iv. Dator salutis
Christus, Filius Dei
Mundum salvavit
Per crucem et sanguinem

v. Pro universis
Immolatus Dominus
Ipse sacerdos
Existit et hostia.

vi. Lege præceptum
Immolari hostias,
Qua adumbrantur
Divina mysteria.

vii. Lucis indultor
Et salvator omnium
Præclaram sanctis
Largitus est gratiam.

viii. Accedant omnes
Pura mente creduli,
Sumant æternam
Salutis custodiam.

ix. Sanctorum custos,
Rector quoque Dominus,
Vitæ perennis
Largitor credentibus

x. Cœlestem panem
Dat esurientibus,
De fonte vivo
Præbet sitientibus.

xi. Alpha et Omega,
Ipse Christus Dominus
Venit, venturus
Judicare homines.

[9.] HYMNUS QUANDO CEREUS BENEDICITUR.

i. Ignis creator igneus,
Lumen donator luminis,
Vitaque vitæ conditor,
Dator salutis et salus.

ii. Ne noctis hujus gaudia
Vigil lucerna deserat,
Qui hominem non vis mori
Da nostro lumen pectori.

iii. Ex Ægypto migrantibus
Indulges geminam gratiam,
Nubis velamen exhibes,
Nocturnum lumen porrigis.

Fol. 11v.]

iv. Nubis columna per diem
Venientem plebem protegis,
Ignis columna ad vesperum
Noctem depellis lumine.

v. E flamma famulum provocas,
Rubum non spernis spineum,
Et cum sis ignis concremans
Non uris quod illuminas.

vi. Fuco depasto nubilo
Tempus decoctis sordibus
Fervente Sancto Spiritu
Carnem lucere ceream.

vii. Secretos jam condens favi
Divini mellis halitus
Cordis repurgans intimas
Verbo replesti cellulas.

viii. Examen ut fœtus novi
Ore prælectum spiritu
Relictis cœlum sarcinis
Quærit securis pinnulis.

ix. Gloria Patri ingenito,
Gloria Unigenito,
Simul cum Sancto Spiritu,
In sempiterna sæcula.

[10.] HYMNUS MEDIÆ NOCTIS.

i. Mediæ noctis tempus est,
Prophetica vox admonet,
Dicamus laudes ut Deo
Patri semper ac Filio,

ii. Sancto quoque Spiritui ;
Perfecta enim Trinitas
Uniusque substantiæ
Laudanda nobis semper est.

iii. Terrorem tempus hoc habet,
Quo cum vastator angelus
Ægypto mortem intulit,
Delevit primogenita.

iv. Hæc justis hora salus est,
Quod ibidem tunc angelus
[MS. Et quos idem tunc angelus]
Ausus punire non erat,
Signum formidans sanguinis.

C 2

Fol. 12r.]

12 HYMNUS IN NATALI MARTYRUM, VEL SABBATO AD MATUTINAM.

Fol. 12r.]

v. Ægyptus flebat fortiter
Tantorum diro funere;
Solus gaudebat Israel
Agni protectus sanguine.

vi. Nos verus Israel sumus,
Lætamur in te, Domine,
Hostem spernentes et malum
Christi defensi sanguine.

vii. Ipsum profecto tempus est
Quo voce evangelica
Venturus sponsus creditur,
Regni cœlestis conditor.

viii. Occurrunt sanctæ virgines
Obviam tunc adventui,
Gestantes claras lampades,
Magno lætantes gaudio.

ix. Stultæ vero remanent, quæ
Extinctas habent lampades,
Frustra pulsantes januas,
Clausa jam regni regia.

x. Quare vigilemus sobrii,
Gestantes mentes splendidas,
Adventui ut Jesu
Digne curramus obviam.

xi. Noctisque medio tempore
Paulus quoque et Sileas
Christum vincti in carcere
Collaudantes soluti sunt.

xii. Nobis mundus hic carcer est;
Te laudamus, Christe Deus,
Solve vincla peccatorum
In te, Sancte, credentium.

xiii. Dignos nos fac, rex hagie,
Futuri regni gloriæ,
Æternis ut mereamur
[Fol. 12v.]
Te laudibus concinere.

xiv. Gloria Patri ingenito,
Gloria Unigenito,
Simul cum Sancto Spiritu
In sempiterna sæcula.

[11.] HYMNUS IN NATALI MARTYRUM, VEL
SABBATO AD MATUTINAM.

i. Sacratissimi martyres summi Dei,
Bellatores fortissimi Christi regis,
Potentissimi duces exercitus Dei,
Victores in cœlis Deo canentes
Alleluia.

ii. Excelsissime Christe cœlorum Deus,
Cherubin cui sedes cum Patre sacra,
Angelorum ibi et martyrum fulgens
chorus,
Tibi sancti proclamant
Alleluia.

iii. Magnifice tu prior omnium passus
crucem,
Qui devicta morte refulsisti mundo,
Ascendisti ad cœlos ad dexteram Dei,
Tibi sancti proclamant
Alleluia.

iv. Armis spiritalibus munita mente
Apostoli sancti te sunt secuti,
Qui cum ipsam crucis paterentur mor-
tem
Tibi sancti canebant
Alleluia.

v. Christe, martyrum tu es adjutor potens
Prœliantium sancta pro tua gloria,
Qui cum victores exirent de hoc sæculo
Tibi sancti canebant
Alleluia.

vi. Illustris tua, Domine, laudanda virtus
Quæ per Spiritum Sanctum firmavit
martyres,
Qui consternerent zabulum et mortem
vincerent,
Tibi sancti canebant
Alleluia.

[Fol. 13r.]
vii. Manu Domini excelsa protecti
Contra diabolum steterunt firmati,
Semper Trinitati fidem toto corde ser-
vantes
Tibi sancti canebant
Alleluia.

viii. Vere regnantes erant tecum, Christe
Deus,
Qui passionis merito coronas habent,
Et centenario fructu repleti gaudent,
Tibi sancti proclamant
Alleluia.

ix. Christi Dei gratiam supplices obse-
cremus,
Ut in ipsius gloriam consummemur
Et in sanctam Jerusalem civitatem Dei
Trinitati cum sanctis dicamus,
Alleluia.

[12.] HYMNUS AD MATUTINAM IN
DOMINICA.

i. Spiritus divinæ lucis gloriæ
Respice in me, Domine.

ii. Deus veritatis,
Domine Deus Sabaoth,
Deus Israel,
Respice in me, Domine.

iii. Lumen de lumine,
Referemus Filium Patris,
Sanctumque Spiritum in una substantia.
Respice in me, Domine.

iv. Unigenitus et primogenitus
A te obtinemus
Redemptionem nostram.
Respice in me, Domine.

v. Natus es Sancto Spiritu
Ex Maria Virgine,
In id ipsum in adoptionem
Filiorum, qui tibi
Procreati ex fonte vivunt.
Respice in me, Domine.

vi. Heredes et coheredes
Christi tui, in quo
Et per quem cuncta creasti,
[Fol. 13v.]
Quia in prædestinatione
A sæculis nobis est
Deus Jesu, qui nunc cœpit,
Respice in me, Domine.

vii. Unigenito ex mortuis
Deo obtinens corpus,
Claritatem Dei, manens
In sæcula sæculorum
Rex æternorum,
Respice in me, Domine.

viii. Quia nunc cœpit qui semper fuit,
Naturæ tuæ Filius,
Divinæ lucis gloriæ tuæ,
Qui est forma et plenitudo
Divinitatis tuæ frequens,
Respice in me, Domine.

ix. Persona unigeniti
Et primogeniti
Qui est totus a toto
Diximus lux de lumine,
Respice in me, Domine

x. Et Deum verum a Deo
Vero sese confitemur
Tribus personis
In una substantia,
Respice in me, Domine.

[13.] Hymnus Sancti Patricii magistri
           Scotorum.

  i. Audite omnes amantes
     Deum sancta merita
     Viri in Christo beati,
     Patricii episcopi,
     Quomodo bonum ob actum
     Similatur angelis,
     Perfectamque propter vitam
     Æquatur apostolis.

 ii. Beata Christi custodit
     Mandata in omnibus,
     Cujus opera refulgent
     Clara inter homines,
     Sanctumque cujus sequuntur
     Exemplum mirificum,
     Unde et in cœlis Patrem
     Magnificant Dominum.

iii. Constans in Dei timore
     Et fide immobilis,
     Super quem ædificatur
     Ut Petrum ecclesia,
     Cujusque apostolatum
[Fol. 14r.]
     A Deo sortitus est,
     In cujus portæ adversum
     Inferni non prævalent.

 iv. Dominus illum elegit
     Ut doceret barbaras
     Nationes, et piscaret
     Per doctrinæ retia,
     Et de sæculo credentes
     Traheret ad gratiam,
     Dominum qui sequerentur
     Sedem ad æth   eream.

  v. Electa Christi talenta
     Vendit evangelica,
     Quæ Hibernas inter gentes
     Cum usuris exigit,

     Navigii hujus laboris
     Tum operæ pretium
     Cum Christo regni cœlestis
     Possessurus gaudium.

 vi. Fidelis Dei minister,
     Insignisque nuntius,
     Apostolicum exemplum
     Formamque præbet bonis,
     Qui tam verbis quam et factis
     Plebi prædicat Dei,
     Ut quem dictis non convertit
     Factu provocet bono.

vii. Gloriam habet cum Christo
     Honorem in sæculo,
     Qui ab omnibus ut Dei
     Veneratur angelus,
     Quem Deus misit ut Paulum
     Ad gentes apostolum,
     Ut hominibus ducatum
     Præberet regno Dei.

viii. Humilis Dei ob metum
     Spiritu et corpore,
     Super quem bonum ob actum
     Requiescit Dominus,
     Cujusque justa in carne
     Christi portat stigmata,
     Et cujus sola sustentans
     Gloriatur in cruce.

 ix. Impiger credentes pascit
     Dapibus cœlestibus,
     Ne qui videntur cum Christo
     In via deficiant,
     Quibus erogat ut panes
     Verba evangelica,
     Et cujus multiplicantur
     Ut manna in manibus.

  x. Kastam qui custodit carnem
     Ob amorem Domini,
     Quam carnem templum paravit
     Sanctoque Spiritui,

[Fol. 14v.]

A quo constanter cum mundis
Possidetur actibus,
Quam et hostiam placentem
Vivam offert Domino.

xi. Lumenque mundi accensum
Ingens evangelicum,
In candelabro levatum,
Toto fulgens sæculo,
Civitas regis munita
Supra montem posita,
Copia in qua est multa,
Quam Dominus possidet.

xii. Maximus namque in regno
Cœlorum vocabitur
Qui quod verbis docet sacris
Factis adimplet bonis ;
Bono præcedit exemplo
Formamque fidelium,
Mundoque in corde habet
Ad Deum fiduciam.

xiii. Nomen Domini audenter
Annunciat gentibus,
Quibus lavacri salutis
Æternam dat gratiam,
Pro quorum orat delictis
Ad Deum quotidie,
Pro quibus ut Deo dignas
Immolatque hostias.

xiv. Omnem pro divina lege
Mundi spernit gloriam,
Qui cuncta ad cujus mensam
Æstimat quisquilia,
Nec ingruenti movetur
Mundi hujus fulmine,
Sed in adversis lætatur
Cum pro Christo patitur.

xv. Pastor bonus et fidelis
Gregis evangelici,

Quem Deus Dei elegit
Custodire populum,
Suamque pascere plebem
Divinis dogmatibus,
Pro qua ad Christi exemplum
Suam tradit animam.

xvi. Quem pro meritis Salvator
Provexit pontificem,
Ut in cœlesti moneret
Clericos militia,
Cœlestem quibus annonam
Erogat cum vestibus,
Quod in divinis impletur
Sacrisque affatibus.

xvii. Regis nuntius invitans
Credentes ad nuptias,
[Fol. 15r.]
Qui ornatur vestimento
Nuptiali indutus.
Qui cœleste haurit vinum
In vasis cœlestibus,
Propinatque Dei plebem
Spiritale poculum.

xviii. Sacrum invenit thesaurum
Sacro in volumine,
Salvatorisque in carne
Deitatem pervidet,
Quem thesaurum emit sanctis
Perfectisque meritis,
Israel vocatur hujus
Anima videns Deum.

xix. Testis Domini fidelis
In lege catholica,
Cujus verba sunt divinis
Condita oraculis,
Ne humanæ putreant carnes
Esæque a vermibus,
Sed cœlesti saliantur
Sapore ad victimam.

xx. Verus cultor et insignis
Agri evangelici,
Cujus semina videntur
Christi evangelia,
Quæ divino serit ore
In aures prudentium,
Quorumque corda ac mentes
Sancto arat spiritu.

xxi. Xps [*i.e.* Christus] illum sibi elegit
In terris vicarium,
Qui de gemino captivos
Liberat servitio,
Plerosque de servitute
Quos redemit hominum
Innumeros de zaboli
Absolvit dominio.

xxii. Ymnos cum Apocalypsi
Psalmosque cantat Dei,
Quosque ad ædificandum
Dei tractat populum,
Quam Legem in Trinitate
Sacri credit nominis,
Tribusque personis unam
Docetque substantiam.

xxiii. Zona Domini præcinctus
Diebus ac noctibus
Sine intermissione
Deum orat Dominum,
[Fol. 15*v*.]
Cujus ingentis laboris
Percepturus præmium
Cum apostolis regnabit
Sanctus super Israel.

Patricius episcopus
Oret pro nobis omnibus,
Ut deleantur protinus
Peccata quæ commisimus.

Patricii laudes semper dicamus,
Ut nos cum illo semper vivamus.

[14] HYMNUS SANCTI COMGILLI ABBATIS
NOSTRI.

Recordemur justitiæ
Nostri patroni fulgidæ
Comgilli sancti nomine,
Refulgentis in opere,
Adjuti Dei flamine,
Sancto claroque lumine
Trinitatis celsissimæ,
Cuncta tenentis regmine.
Quem Deus ad ætherea
Conduxit habitacula
Ab angelis custodita
Permansura in sæcula.

i. Audite pantes ta erga
Allati ad angelica
Athletæ Dei abdita,
A juventute florida
Aucta in legis pagina,
Alta Sancti per viscera,
Apta fide justitia,
Ad Dei ducta gaudia,
Alti allata merita
Affatim concordantia,
Ab angelis &c.

ii. Bonam vitam, justitiam,
Benignitatem floridam,
Caritatem firmissimam,
Deo primo adhibitam,
Juxta mandatum solidam,
In regno præstantissimam,
Proximis sæpe debitam,
Corde sereno placitam,
Efficiebat cognitam
In futuro fructiferam,
Quem Deus &c.

iii. Contemptum mundialium
Voluntatum præsentium
Vitiorum firmissimum
Infirmos devastantium,

Verborum cogitaminum
Parte læva versantium,
Continebat per viscerum
Secreta vigilantium.
                    Ab angelis &c.

iv. Doctus in Dei legibus
Divinis dictionibus,
Dilatus sanctis opibus
Deo semper placentibus,
Dedicatus in moribus,
Dei Stephanus hagius
Docebat sic et cæteros
Dicta docta operibus.
                    Quem Deus &c.

[Fol. 16r.]

v. Elegit a primordio
Quod erat in principio
Æternum verbum paterno
Eructatum sanctissimo
Corde verum altissimo
Carum eidem lucido
Pignus præclaro animo
Constans opere placido.
                    Ab angelis &c.

vi. Fulgebat alti fulgore
Solis vice in vertice
Rutilantis meridie
Fidei claritudine,
Confirmatus ex viscere
In Dei semper fidere.
Confidens sanctimoniæ
Præcipuo munimine.
                    Quem Deus &c.

vii. Gaudium Sancti Spiritus
Habebat in visceribus,
Regnum quod est sublimibus
Deo dignum et fortius,
Gladium quoque Spiritus,
Levatum ad nequissimos,

Quo prosterneret superbos,
Tenens sanctis in manibus.
                    Ab angelis &c.

viii. Humilis, sanctus, benignus,
Probus in Dei legibus,
Humanus, justus, commodus,
Laudabilis in moribus,
Hilaris vultu, sobrius,
Caritatis in floribus
Decoratus, ordinibus
Factus palam mortalibus.
                    Quem Deus &c.

ix. In Scripturis eruditus,
Inspiratus divinitus,
In Sacramentis providus,
Canonicis affatibus
Veteris, Novi actibus
Testamenti præfulgidus,
Fervens spiritu, placidus,
Deo carus, et piissimus.
                    Ab angelis &c.

x. Kalcavit mundum subdolum
Karitatis per studium
Kastitatis firmissimum,
Contemnens omne vitium,
Inserens agrum floridum,
Pectus adornans lucidum,
Divinum habitaculum
Trino nomine sancitum.
                    Quem Deus &c.

[Fol. 16v.]

xi. Lampadem sapientiæ
Constituit in pectore,
In thesauro scientiæ
Condito Dei munere;
Inflammatus magnopere
Luce veræ justitiæ,
Exaltatus munimine
Legis, spiritus, litteræ.
                    Ab angelis &c.
                                        D

xii. Magnum apprendit bradium
Æterna vita condignum,
Adeptus sanctum præmium
Post laborem firmissimum,
Cujus perfectum meritum
Vocamus in auxilium,
Ut mereamur omnium
Vitiorum excidium.
Quem Deus &c.

xiii. Notus sanctorum cœtibus,
Abbatum in ordinibus,
Monachorum militibus,
Anchoretarum sensibus,
Synodum sanctis plebibus,
Immo vir apostolicus,
Clarus cunctis in sortibus,
Adauctus in sublimibus.
Ab angelis &c.

xiv. O petram solidissimam
In fundamento positam!
O contemptorem omnium
Rerum nequam præsentium!
O ducem sanctum militum
Domino militantium!
O tironem fortissimum
Domino totum deditum!
Quem Deus &c.

xv. Positus muri ferrei
Vice in luce populi,
Dissipare, disperdere,
Cuncta mala destruere,
Ædificare, plantare
Bona tota in commune,
More sancti Hieremiæ
Constituti in culmine.
Ab angelis &c.

xvi. Quis contempsit præsentia
Hujus ævi decidua,
Quis ascendit ad superna
Toto animo gaudia,

Quis volebat in æthera
Carne volare posita,
Qualiter iste talia
Adeptus sancta merita?
Quem Deus &c.

[Fol. 17r.]
xvii. Rexit sanctam ecclesiam
Catholicam per regulam,
Retinens fidem solidam
Malam contra nequitiam,
Suam exercens animam
Sanctæ legis per paginam,
Cujus, exopto, gratia
Mihi adornet animam!
Ab angelis &c.

xviii. Sapiens suos internos
Sanctos elevans oculos
Deducebat ad superos
Capite sancto intentos,
Parte sancta in dextera
Collocans sua viscera,
Centurionis opera
Habens sancta per studia.
Quem Deus &c.

xix. Tulit suam memoriam
Ad mansionem supernam,
Caram Deo et floridam
Suam exercens animam,
Contemnens terram subdolam,
Vanam omnem insaniam
Domans, [pergens] cum Abraham
Ad terram illam optimam.
Ab angelis &c.

xx. Vitam æternam fulgida
Adeptus est sub corona,
Ubi assumet præmia
Permansura in sæcula,
Comitaturus agmina
Angelorum præcipua,
Inquirens semper talia,
Vigilans in ecclesia.
Quem Deus &c.

xxi. Xpm [*i.e.* Christum] orabat magis-
trum,
Summum ornans obsequium,
Xpi [*i.e.* Christi] gerens officium
Actum per apostolicum.
Hujus sequens vestigium,
Ducens Deo exercitum
In sanctum habitaculum
Trinitatis lectissimum.
Ab angelis &c.

xxii. Ymnum Deo cum cantico
Immolabat altissimo,
Diei noctis circulo
Orans sæpe cum triumpho.
Nunc cantavit sub numero
Canticum novum Domino.
Junctus choro angelico
Summo sanctus in jubilo.
Quem Deus &c.

[Fol. 17*v*.]
xxiii. Zona cinctus justitiæ,
Castitatis eximiæ,
Mundo opertus sindone
In signo castimoniæ
Feminalia lucidæ
Habens toto ex viscere,
Cujus sancto pro opere
Reddetur merces condigne.
Quem Deus ad ætherea
Conduxit habitacula
Ab angelis custodita
Permansura in sæcula.

Per merita et orationes sancti Comgilli abbatis nostri omnes nos, Domine, in tua pace custodi.

[15.]   HYMNUS SANCTI CAMELACI.

i. Audite bonum exemplum
Benedicti pauperis
Camelaci Cumiensis
Dei justi famuli.

ii. Exemplum præbet in toto
Fidelis in opere,
Gratias Deo agens,
Hilaris in omnibus,

iii. Jejunus et mansuetus
Kastus hic servit Deo,
Lætatur in paupertate,
Mitis est in omnibus,

iv. Noctibus atque diebus
Orat Dominum suum ;
Prudens, justus, ac fidelis,
Quem cognati diligunt.

v. Regem Dominum aspexit
Salvatoremque suum :
Tribuit huic æternam
Vitam cum fidelibus.

vi. Xps [*i.e.* Christus] illum insinuavit
Patriarchæ Abrahæ,
Yn Paradiso regnavit
Cum sancto Lazaro.

[16.]   COLLECTIO AD SECUNDAM.

Esto nobis protector in ista die, Domine, sancte Pater, omnipotens æterne Deus, et miserator et misericors, et auxiliator et dux nobis, et illuminator cordium nostrorum. Custodi, Domine, cogitationes, serm[o]nes, opera, ut possimus placere in conspe[ctu] tuo, Domine, et perficere voluntatem tuam, et [am]bulare in via recta toto nostræ vitæ t[em-pore.]

[Fol. 18*r*.]
[17.]   ITEM ALIA AD SECUNDAM.

Te oramus, Altissime,
Exorto solis lumine,
Christo oriens nomine,
Adesto nobis Domine,
Qui regnas in sæcula.
D 2

[18.]   AD TERTIAM.

Christi per horam tertiam
Deprecamur clementiam,
Uti nobis perpetuam
Suam tribuat gratiam,
          Qui regnas, &c.

[19.]   AD SEXTAM.

Tuis parce supplicibus
Sexta hora orantibus,
Qua fuisti pro omnibus,
Christe, in cruce positus,
          Qui regnas, &c.

[20.]   AD NONAM.

Exaudi preces omnium
Nona hora orantium,
In qua, Christe, Cornelium
Visitasti per angelum,
          Qui regnas, &c.

[21.]   AD VESPERTINAM.

Vespertino sub tempore
Te invocamus, Domine,
Nostris precibus annue,
Nostris peccatis ignosce,
          [Qui regnas, &c.]

[22.]   COLLECTIO AD INITIUM NOCTIS.

Noctis tempus exigimus
Christe, in tuis laudibus;
Misereris omnibus
Te ex corde precantibus,
          Qui regnas, &c.

[23.]   AD NOCTURNAM.

Jesu, clementer visita
Nocte orantes media,
Qua divina potentia
Petri solvisti vincula,
          Qui regnas, &c.

[24.]   AD MATUTINAM.

Deus, subveni omnibus
Te ter sanctum laudantibus,
Unumque confitentibus
Sacris hymnorum cantibus,
          Qui regnas, &c.

[25.]   ITEM AD MATUTINAM.

Gallorum, Christe, cantibus
Te deprecor sonantibus,
Petri ut quondam fletibus
Nostris intende precibus,
          Qui regnas, &c.

[Fol. 18a.]

[26.]   ITEM ALIA AD MATUTINAM.

Deus, qui pulsis tenebris
Diei lucem tribuis,
Adventum veri luminis
Tuis effunde famulis,
          Qui regnas, &c.

[27.]   ✠ ITEM AD SECUNDAM.

Exaudi nos, Domine, supplices tuos, qui in
hac hora prima diei referimus tibi gratias
Domino Deo nostro, qui nos redemisti de
tuo sancto sanguine, ut preces ac petitiones
nostras vice primitiarum tibi oblatas pie
clementerque suscipias, Qui regnas, &c.

[28.]   AD HORAM TERTIAM.

Tibi subnixis precibus Christo Domino
supplicamus, qui in hora tertia diei Spiritum
Sanctum apostolis orantibus emisisti, ejusdem
gratiæ participationem nobis poscentibus
jubeas concedi, Qui regnas, &c.

[29.]   AD HORAM SEXTAM.

Omnipotens æterne Deus, qui nobis mag-
nalia fecisti, sexta hora crucem sanctam

ascendisti, et tenebras mundi illuminasti, sic
et corda nostra illuminare digneris, Qui
regnas, &c.

[30.]   AD HORAM NONAM.

Nona agitur diei hora ad te, Domine,
directa supplicatione, qua cultoribus tuis
divina monstrantur miracula, nostra quoque
eorum imitatione corda illumina, Qui regnas, &c.

[31.]   AD VESPERTINAM.

Vespertina oratio nostra ascendat ad aures
divinæ majestatis tuæ, et descendat benedictio tua, Domine, super nos, quemadmodum
speravimus in te, Qui regnas, &c.

[Fol. 19r.]
[32.]   AD INITIUM NOCTIS.

Deus, qui inextricabiles tenebras illuminas
noctium, densitatem caliginis illustrans, corda
nostra in opere mandatorum tuorum te
oramus, Domine, custodias, Qui regnas, &c.

[33.]   AD INITIUM NOCTIS.

Evolutis nunc diei temporibus, nocturnisque spatiis supervenientibus, Dei misericordiam deprecemur, ut suppleti divinis sensibus
tenebrarum operibus renuntiare possimus,
Qui regnas, &c.

[34.]   AD PACEM CELEBRANDAM.

[Ant.] Injuste egimus, [iniquitatem feci-
mus.]
[Collectio.] Redemisti nos, Domine Deus
veritatis, in tuo sancto sanguine, nunc adjuva
nos in omnibus, Jesu Christe, Qui regnas, &c.

[Ant.] Pax multa diligentibus [legem
tuam ; et non est illis scandalum].
[Collectio.] Pax tua, Domine, rex cælestis,
permaneat semper in visceribus nostris, ut
non timeamus a timore nocturno, Qui
regnas, &c.

[35.]   INCIPIT SYMBOLUM.

Credo in Deum Patrem omnipotentem,
invisibilem, omnium creaturarum visibilium et
invisibilium conditorem.

Credo et in Jesum Christum, Filium ejus
unicum, Dominum nostrum, Deum omnipotentem, conceptum de Spiritu Sancto, natum
de Maria Virgine, passum sub Pontio Pilato,
qui crucifixus et sepultus descendit ad inferos,
[Fol. 19v.] tertia die resurrexit a mortuis,
ascendit in cœlis, seditque ad dexteram Dei
Patris omnipotentis, exinde venturus judicara
vivos ac mortuos.

Credo et in Spiritum Sanctum, Deum
omnipotentem, unam habentem substantiam
cum Patre et Filio. Sanctam esse ecclesiam
catholicam, abremissam peccatorum, sanctorum communionem, carnis resurrectionem.

Credo vitam post mortem, et vitam æternam
in gloria Christi. Hæc omnia credo in
Deum. Amen.

[36.]   ORATIO DIVINA.

Pater noster, qui es in cœlis, sanctificetur
nomen tuum. Adveniat regnum tuum. Fiat
voluntas tua sicut in cœlo et in terra. Panem
nostrum cotidianum da nobis hodie. Et
remitte nobis debita nostra, sicut et nos
dimittimus debitoribus nostris. Et ne
patiaris nos induci in temptationem. Sed
libera nos a malo.

[37.]   AD NOCTURNAM.

Per horam mediæ noctis tunc gavisi sunt
angeli de nativitate Domini nostri Jesu
Christi ; [Fol. 20r.] ita et nos lætari debemus in tua pace, omnipotens Deus, Qui
regnas, &c.

[38.]   AD MATUTINAM.

Tu es, Domine, illuminator caliginum,
conditorque elementorum, remissor crimi-
num ; misericordia tua, Domine, magna est
super eos qui te toto corde requirunt.
Majestas tua, Domine, mane nos exaudiat,
et deleat delicta nostra quæ tibi non sunt
abdita, Qui regnas, &c.

[39.]   ITEM AD MATUTINAM.

Tu es spes et salus. Tu es vita et virtus.
Tu es adjutor in tribulationibus. Tu es
defensor animarum nostrarum, Deus Israel,
in omnibus, Qui regnas, &c.

[40.]   ORATIO COMMUNIS FRATRUM.

[*Ant.*] Ne memineris iniquitatum nostrarum antiquarum ; cito anticipent nos
misericordiæ tuæ, quia pauperes facti sumus
nimis.

[*Oratio.*] Adjuva nos, Deus salutaris
noster, propter gloriam nominis tui. Domine,
libera nos, et propitius esto peccatis nostris
propter nomen tuum. Ne tradas bestiis
animam confitentem tibi. Animas pauperum
tuorum ne obliviscaris in finem. Respice in
testamentum tuum, Domine, [Qui regnas,
&c.]

[Fol. 20v.]
[40*.]   [PRO PECCATIS NOSTRIS.]

[*Ant.*] Deus, in adjutorium meum intende.
Domine, ad adjuvandum me festina.

[*Oratio.*] Festina, Domine, liberare nos
ex omnibus peccatis nostris, [Qui regnas,
&c.]

[41.]   PRO BAPTIZATIS.

[*Ant.*] Salvum fac populum tuum, Domine,
et benedic hereditati tuæ ; et rege eos et
extolle illos usque in sæculum.

[*Oratio.*] Miserere, Domine, ecclesiæ
tuæ catholicæ, quam redemisti in tuo sancto
sanguine, Qui regnas, &c.

[41*.]   [PRO SACERDOTIBUS.]

[*Ant.*] Exsurge, Domine, in requiem tuam,
tu et arca sanctificationis tuæ.
Sacerdotes tui induentur justitia, et sancti
tui [exultent.]

[*Oratio.*] Lætentur in te, Domine, omnes
sancti tui, qui sperant in te in omni veritate.
[Qui regnas, &c.]

[42.]   PRO ABBATE.

[*Ant.* i.] Dominus conservet eum, et vivificet eum, et beatum faciat eum in terra.

[*Ant.* ii.] Dominus custodiat te ab omni
malo ; custodiat animam tuam Dominus.

[*Ant.* iii.] Dominus custodiat introitum
tuum, et exitum tuum, ex hoc, nunc, et usque
in sæculum.

[43.] [PRO FRATRIBUS.]

[*Ant.*] Custodi nos, Domine, ut pupillam
oculi, sub umbra alarum tuarum protege
nos.

[*Oratio.*] Protegere et sanctificare digneris omnibus, omnipotens Deus, Qui regnas,
&c.

[44.]   PRO FRATERNITATE.

[*Ant*] Tu, Domine, servabis nos, et cus-
todies nos a generatione hac et in æternum.

[*Oratio.*] Exaudi orationes nostras pro fratribus nostris, ut illis Deus misereris, [Qui
regnas, &c.]

[Fol. 21r.]
[45.] PRO PACE POPULORUM ET REGUM.

[*Ant.*] Dominus virtutem populo suo
dabit ; Dominus benedicet populo suo in
pace.

[*Oratio.*] Pacem præstare digneris omnibus, omnipotens Deus, Qui regnas. &c.

[46.] PRO BLASPHEMANTIBUS.

[*Ant.*] Domine, misericordia tua in sæculum, opera manuum tuarum ne despicias.

[*Oratio.*] Domine Deus virtutum, ne statuas illis hoc in peccatum, [Qui regnas &c.]

[47.] PRO IMPIIS.

[*Ant.*] Judica illos, Deus, decidant a cogitationibus suis, [secundum multitudinem impietatum eorum expelle eos, quoniam] irritaverunt te, Domine.

[*Oratio.*] Confundantur illi qui confidunt in se. et non nos, Domine, qui confidimus in te, [Qui regnas, &c.]

[48.] PRO ITER FACIENTIBUS.

[*Ant.*] O Domine, salvum fac, O Domine, bene prosperare.

[*Oratio.*] Prosperitatem itineris præsta tuis famulis, Qui [regnas, &c.]

[49.] [PRO GRATIAS AGENTIBUS.]

[*Ant.*] Confiteantur tibi, Domine. omnia opera tua, et sancti tui confiteantur tibi.

[*Oratio.*] Tibi gratias agunt animæ nostræ pro innumeris beneficiis tuis, Domine, Qui regnas, &c.

[50.] PRO ELEEMOSYNARIIS.

[*Ant.*] Dispersit, dedit pauperibus ; justitia ejus manet in sæculum sæculi, cornu ejus exaltabitur in gloria.

[*Oratio.*] Eleemosynas facientibus in hoc mundo retribue, Domine, in regno tuo sancto, [Qui regnas, &c.]

[Fol. 21*v*.]

[51.] PRO INFIRMIS.

[*Ant.*] Et clamaverunt ad Dominum cum tribularentur, et de necessitatibus eorum liberavit eos.

[*Oratio.*] Tribue, Domine, tuis famulis sanitatem mentis et corporis, [Qui regnas, &c.].

[51*.] [PRO CAPTIVIS.]

[*Ant.* i.] Exsurge, Domine, adjuva nos, et redime nos propter nomen tuum.

[*Ant.* ii.] Adjutorium nostrum in nomine Domini.

[*Oratio.*] Salvare nos digneris per invocationem sancti tui nominis, Qui regnas, &c.

[52.] DE MARTYRIBUS.

Deus, qui sanctis et electis tuis coronam martyrii præstitisti, te oramus, Domine, ut eorum meritis obtineamus veniam, qui tantam gloriam non meremur, Qui regnas &c.

[53.] [PRO TRIBULANTIBUS.]

[*Ant.* i.] Ad te, Domine, clamabo ; deus meus, ne sileas a me.

[*Ant.* ii.] Dominus virtutum nobiscum, susceptor noster Deus Jacob.

[*Oratio.*] Adjutor noster Deus Jacob, miserere nobis, Domine, Qui [regnas, &c]

[54.] COLLECTIO.

Sanctus in sanctis, Agnus immaculatus, gloriosus in cœlis, mirabilis in terris, præsta nobis, Domine, secundum magnam misericordiam tuam, Deus, quæ te petimus et oramus, Qui regnas, &c.

[55.] AD MARTYRES.

Æternum virtutis tuæ nomen, omnipotens Deus, oramus, uti nos martyrum et omnium sanctorum tuorum meritis socios, fide pares, [Fol. 22*r*.] devotione strenuos, passione consimiles, in resurrectione felicium facias coæquari, Qui regnas, &c.

[56.] [PRO PŒNITENTIBUS.]

[*Ant.*] Miserere mei, Deus, secundum magnam [misericordiam tuam.]

[*Oratio.*] Tribue, Domine, veniam petentibus te ex fide secundum magnam misericordiam tuam, Deus, Qui regnas, &c.

[57.] ✠ AD NOCTURNAM.

Media nocte clamore facto, [da] ut nos inveniamur parati sponso, Qui regnas. &c.

[58.] AD MATUTINAM.

Deus, Deus noster, ad te de luce vigilare debemus, et tu excita de gravi somno, et libera de sopore animas nostras, ut in cubilibus nostris compungamur, et tui esse memores mereamur, Qui regnas, &c.

[59.] AD MATUTINAM.

Tu es spes et salus. Tu es vita et virtus. Tu es adjutor in tribulationibus. Tu es defensor animarum nostrarum, Deus Israel, in omnibus, Qui regnas, &c.

[60.] AD MATUTINAM.

O qui in altis habitas, et humilia respicis in cœlo, et in terra, in mari et in omnibus abyssis, de profundo cordis te deprecamur ut firmes manus nostras ad prœlium, et digitos nostros ad bellum, quo possimus in matutino interficere omnes peccatores terræ nostræ, ac nos indeficienter mereamur esse templum sanctum tuum, Christe, Qui regnas, &c.

[Fol. 22*v*.]
[61.] DE MARTYRIBUS.

Deus, qui sanctos tuos cum mensura probas, et sine mensura glorificas, cujus præcepta finem habent, et præmia terminum non habent, exaudi per illorum merita preces nostras, et tribue ut eorum patrocinia adjuvent nos ad fidei profectum, ad bonorum operum fructum, ad prosperitatis bonum, ad salubritatis commodum, ad religionis cultum, ad divini timoris augmentum, per Dominum nostrum Jesum Christum, Filium tuum, qui est rex regum, et Dominus dominantium, et gloria futurorum, regnans et permanens una cum æterno Spiritu Sancto in sæcula sæculorum.

[62.] ✠ COLLECTIO POST CANTICUM.

Deus, qui exeunti ex Ægypto populo tuo maria divisisti, et suspensis utrinque marginibus in specie muri erigi fluentia jussisti, animas quoque nostras a diluvio peccatorum liberare digneris, ut transire vitiorum gurgitem valeamus, hoste contempto, [Fol. 23*r*.] Salvator mundi, qui cum æterno Patre vivis, dominaris, ac regnas, cum Spiritu Sancto, in sæcula sæculorum.

[63.] COLLECTIO POST BENEDICTIONEM PUERORUM.

Exaudi preces nostras, omnipotens Deus, et præsta ut sicut in decantato hymno beata puerorum instituta sectamur, ita tuo munere peccatorum laqueis absoluti æterni ignis non ambiamur incendiis, Salvator mundi, Qui cum Patre vivis, &c.

[64.] COLLECTIO POST TRES PSALMOS. IN FINE.

Te Dominum de cœlis laudamus, tibi ut canticum novum cantare mereamur. Te Dominum in sanctis tuis venerabiliter deprecamur, ut omnia vota nostra suscipias, peccata dimittas, Salvator mundi, Qui regnas, &c.

[65.] COLLECTIO POST EVANGELIUM.

Exsultantes gaudio pro reddita nobis hujus diei luce omnipotenti Deo laudes gratiasque referamus, ipsius misericordiam obsecrantes, ut diem dominicæ resurrectionis nobis sollemniter celebrantibus pacem, et tranquillitatem, [Fol. 23v.] lætitiam præstare dignetur, ut a vigilia matutina usque ad noctem clementiæ suæ favore protecti, exsultantes lætitia perpetua gaudeamus, per Dominum nostrum Jesum Christum sanctum.

[66.] SUPER HYMNUM.

Sancte Domine, illuminatio et salus vera credentibus, resurrectio dominicæ claritatis, illumina cor nostrum, ut Trinitatis scientia, et Unitatis cognitione, filii lucis, et membra Christi, ac templum Sancti Spiritus esse mereamur, Qui regnas in sæcula sæculorum.

[67.] DE MARTYRIBUS.

Hi sunt, Domine, qui felici cruore perfusi, dum blandientem mundi hujus illecebram gloriosa passione despiciunt, mortem morte vicerunt, considerantesque tenebras hujus lucis certo termino ac fine ruituras, sumpserunt de pœna vitam, et de morte victoriam. Rogamus te, Christe, ut eorum precibus adjuvari mereamur, quorum consortes esse non possumus, per te, Christe, Qui cum Patre vivis, dominaris, et regnas.

[68.] SUPER CANTEMUS DOMINO GLORIOSE.

[Fol. 24r.]

✠ Deus, qui cotidie populum tuum jugo Ægyptiæ servitutis absolvis, et per fluenta spiritalis lavacri in terram repromissionis devicto hoste transducis ; da nobis de vitiorum impugnatione victoriam, ut devictis tenebris nostris deducas hereditatem in sanctuarium, quod præparaverunt manus tuæ, Salvator mundi, Qui cum æterno, &c.

[69.] SUPER BENEDICTIONEM TRIUM PUERORUM.

Sancte Domine et gloriose, mirabilium et virtutum effector, qui tribus pueris inter supplicia constitutis quartus assistis, cui factum facile est ignium temperare naturam, et vim quodammodo exustantium coercere flammarum, ut inter incendia frigidi hymnum tibi canentes cum magna victoria exultarent, eandem nunc, Domine, ad liberandos ac protegendos nos dona virtutem, Salvator mundi, [Qui regnas, &c.].

[70.] SUPER LAUDATE DOMINUM DE CŒLIS.

Quem cuncta canunt elementa Dominum laudent. [Fol. 24v.] Cujus confessio sacra eadem in cœlo et terra, et pignora Sion, novum Tonanti dicite hymnum, facturi judicium nefandis in fine conscriptum perstrepite diversis spiritalis melodiæ modis, ut Christum collaudent spiritus per sæcula omnes, Qui cum Patre vivit, &c.

[71.] ✠ SUPER CANTICUM.

Deus, qui impiam Ægyptum denis corruptionibus mulctas, et diviso mari planum iter populo præstas, preces exaudi quæsumus nostras, et nos nostris taliter hostibus salva, Salvator mundi, Qui regnas, &c.

[72.] POST BENEDICTIONEM TRIUM PUERORUM.

Deus, qui pueris fide ferventibus fornacis flammam frigidam facis, et tribus invictis morte devicta quartus assistis, precamur nobis æstibus carnis talem virtutem præstes adustis, per te, Jesu Christe, Qui regnas, &c.

E

[73.] Post laudate dominum de
cœlis.

Deus noster, Deus omnium animarum, te
adoramus, ut in hac vigilia sollemnitatis
admissa pervenire præstes, quousque tenebræ
[Fol. 25r.] iniquitatis nostræ convertantur in
lumine, sicut sol in meridie splendescit,
Salvator mundi, Qui regnas, &c.

[74.] Post evangelium.

Dominicam, nostræ resurrectionis initium,
venerantes, Trinitati Deo nostro debitas
laudes et grates unito referamus affectu,
obsecrantes misericordiam ejus, ut nobis
Domini et Salvatoris nostri beatæ resurrectionis participium tam in spiritu quam
etiam in corpore concedat, Qui cum Patre
vivit, &c.

[75.] Post hymnum.

Respice, Domine, ad preces nostras, qui
infirmitates visitasti humanas, et tuam nobis
sanctificationem largire et immortalitatem,
Christe, Qui regnas, &c.

[76.] ✠ Item post canticum.

Summerso in mari Pharaone liberatur
Israel : nos quoque per baptismi gratiam, et
crucis triumphum ab omni malo quæsumus
liberari per te, Christe, [Qui regnas, &c.]

[77.] Item post benedicite.

Deus, qui tres pueros de fornace eripuisti,
[Fol. 25v.] sic nos eripias de suppliciis inferni,
Qui regnas in sæcula, &c.

[78.] Post laudate Dominum de
cœlis.

Te laudamus, Domine, cum sanctis tuis
ut preces nostras suscipere digneris, Qui
regnas, &c.

[79.] Post evangelium.

Resurgentem in hoc diluculo Dominum
deprecamur, ut et nos in vitam æternam
resurgamus, per omnia sæcula sæculorum.

[80.] Post hymnum.

Resurrectionem tuam, Christe, veneramur,
per quam in æternum salvari mereamur, per
omnia sæcula.

[81.] ✠ [Post canticum.]

Christe Deus, qui in salutem populi tui
Israel adjutor et protector fuisti, quem per
siccum mare ab Ægypto duxisti, salva nos
hoc modo ab jugo peccati, Qui regnas in
sæcula, &c.

[82.] Post hymnum trium puerorum.

Te enim, omnipotens Deus, benedicimus
jure. Qui tres pueros liberasti ab igne, nos
quoque de supplicio mortis æternæ propter
misericordiam tuam eripe, Qui regnas, &c.

[83.] Post laudate Dominum de
cœlis.

Deus altissime, rex angelorum,
Deus, laus omnium elementorum,
Deus, gloria et exultatio sanctorum,
[Fol. 26r.] Custodi animas servorum tuorum,
Qui regnas in sæcula [sæculorum.]

[84.] Post evangelium.

Canticis spiritalibus delectati hymnos,
Christe, consonantes canamus tibi, quibus tua
majestas possit placari, oblata laudis hostia
spiritali, Qui tecum vivit, &c.

[85.] Item post evangelium.

Diluculo lucis, auctore resurgente, exsul-
temus in Domino, devicta morte, quo peccata
possimus semper obire, vitæque ambulemus in
novitate, Qui tecum vivit, &c.

[86.]   Post hymnum.

Lux orta est in luce prima, exordio dierum antiquo facta, Unigenitus tuus, Domine, qui nostra abluere venit per crucem peccata, Qui tecum vivit, &c.

[87.]   De martyribus.

Triumphalium memores martyrum tuorum, qui pro te toleravere vexilla passionum, precamur, ut per sancta merita ipsorum nostrorum veniam mereamur peccatorum, Qui regnas, &c.

[Fol. 26v.]

[88.]   ✠ Post cantemus.

Plebs Israel in figuram nostri liberatur in transitu maris; nos, ergo, per gratiam baptismi libera tu ab exitiis mundi, Qui regnas, &c.

[89.]   Post benedicite.

Ut tres pueros in flamma salvasti descensu in fornacem cœlestis nuntii, sic nos per angelum magni consilii liberare digneris ab igne inferni, Qui regnas, &c.

[90.]   Post laudate Dominum de cœlis.

Deus, quem exercitus canit cœlorum,
Quemque Ecclesia laudat sanctorum,
Quem hymnizat spiritus universorum,
Miserere, obsecro, omnium nostrorum,
Qui regnas [in sæcula sæculorum.]

[91.]   ✠ Super cantemus.

Cantemus tibi, Domine exercituum, Christe, orantes ut quemadmodum exemisti dilectum populum tuum captivitatis acerrimæ jugo, iter demonstrante eis nubis columna [Fol. 27r.] per diem, eadem ignis quoque per noctem:

Finditur ergo mare dextera lævaque in abruptum; digestis aggeribus stupens unda solidatur; tuus populus navigat plantis. Mira res! iter ejus nec eques potest sequi nec ratis. Maria tympanum quatit, hymnus iste canitur, grex peculius tuetur. Ita et nos ab insectatione veteris inimici, et ab omni periculo mundi liberare digneris, Salvator mundi, Qui cum æterno Patre vivis, dominaris, ac regnas, una cum æterno Spiritu Sancto in sæcula sæculorum.

[92.]   Super benedictionem trium puerorum.

[Fol. 27v.]

Tres Hebræi venerabiles numero, sacramento muniti, ætate teneri, sed fidei soliditate robusti, amore divinæ religionis regis adorare imaginem contempserunt, utpote qui ipsum contempserant regem, qui ira sufflatus solito septies amplius caminum jussit incendi, ac pice et stuppa armatum citari incendium æstuantibus globis. Erubescit quoque ipsum alienis ignibus cœlum. Illo præcipitantur insontes, ibidemque te, propter quem præcipitantur, inveniunt, Christe. Taliter nos et ex tyranni intellectualis furore, et ab ingenito igne digneris liberare, Salvator mundi, Qui cum æterno Patre vivis, &c.

[Fol. 28r.]

[93.]   Post laudate dominum de cœlis.

Laudent te, Domine, angeli, virtutes, sidera, potestates, et quæ ortum suum tibi debent officio tuæ laudationis exultent; ut per universitatis harmoniam tibimet concinentem fiat ut in cœlo ita et in terra voluntas tua. Sit tibi, precamur, Domine, beneplacitum in populo tuo, ut per exaltationes tuas in ejus faucibus collocatas, maneat in singulis et verbi tui armatura, qua doceas, et vitæ nostræ veritas, qua semper aspicias, et salus qua mansuetos exaltes, quia secundum

E 2

multitudinem magnitudinis tuæ te laudamus,
Domine, gratia laudationis ostensæ [Fol. 28v.]
immolatione per psalterium, mortificatione
per tympanum, congregatione per chorum,
exultatione per organum, jubilatione per
cymbalum, ut semper misericordiam tuam
habere mereamur, Christe, Salvator mundi,
Qui cum æterno Patre vivis, &c.

[94.] ✠ SUPER CANTEMUS DOMINO.

Domine, qui Cinchrim fugientes tueris bis
senas per invisa tribus æmulum itinera, prius
fluctibus in binis montium utrimque redactis
celsorum, ceu jugis abrupte arentibus talis
æquore murum, quasi et de petra lymphas
producens; mergatur ergo ut olim piorum
supplicium hostis æterni, quæsumus, statores
curruum, quod est cujus affatus, [Fol. 29r.]
actusque cum cogitatu celeri nequam sit
Pharaoni ; rex Israelem verum, quæ unda
salvat, ut Christo carmina canat per sæcula,
Qui cum Patre vivit, &c.

[Fol. 30r.]
[95.] VERSICULI FAMILIÆ BENCHUIR.

  i. Benchuir bona regula,
       Recta, atque divina,
       Stricta, sancta, sedula,
       Summa, justa, ac mira.

 ii. Munther Benchuir beata,
       Fide fundata certa,
       Spe salutis ornata,
       Caritate perfecta.

iii. Navis numquam turbata,
       Quamvis fluctibus tonsa,
       Nuptiis quoque parata
       Regi Domino sponsa.

 iv. Domus deliciis plena,
       Super petram constructa,
       Necnon vinea vera
       Ex Ægypto transducta.

  v. Certe civitas firma,
       Fortis, atque unita,
       Gloriosa, ac digna,
       Supra montem posita.

 vi. Arca Cherubin tecta,
       Omni parte aurata,
       Sacro-sanctis reperta,
       Viris quatuor portata.

vii. Christo regina apta,
       Solis luce amicta,
       Simplex, simulque docta,
       Undecumque invicta.

viii. Vere regalis aula,
       Variis gemmis ornata,
       Gregisque Christi caula
       Patre summo servata.

 ix. Virgo valde fecunda
       Hæc, et mater intacta,
       Læta ac tremebunda,
       Verbo Dei subacta.
[Fol. 30v.]
  x. Cui vita beata
       Cum perfectis futura,
       Deo Patre parata
       Sine fide mansura.
       Benchuir bona regula.

[96.] COLLECTIO SUPER HOMINEM QUI
              HABET DIABOLUM.

Domine, sancte Pater, omnipotens æterne
Deus, expelle diabolum et gentilitatem ab
homine isto, de capite, de capillis, de cerbero,
de vertice, de fronte, de oculis, de auribus,
de naribus, de labiis, de ore, de lingua, de
sublingua, de faucibus, de gutture, de collo,
de corde, de corpore toto, de omnibus
compaginibus membrorum suorum, intus et
deforis, de ossibus, de venis, de nervis, de
sanguine, de sensu, de cogitationibus, de
verbis, de omnibus operibus suis, de virtute,
[Fol. 31r.] de omni conversatione ejus, hic,

et in futuro. Sed operetur in te virtus Christi, in eo qui propassus est ut vitam æternam mereamur, per Dominum nostrum Jesum Christum Filium suum, &c.

[97.]   ORATIO DE MARTYRIBUS.

✠ Deus qui martyribus tuis largitus es regnum, nobis autem peccantibus veniam præstare digneris. Hi coronam suam passione per fidem meruerunt ; nos autem pro iniquitatibus et prævaricationibus nostris remissionem a te et misericordiam postulamus per te, Jesu, Christe, &c.

[98.]   INCIPIT ANTIPHONA IN NATALI DOMINI,
SUPER DOMINE REFUGIUM.
AD SECUNDAM.

[Fol. 31v.]

✠ Ab hodierno die nox minuitur, dies crescit, concutiuntur tenebræ, lumen augetur, et, in lucro lucis nocturna dispendia transferuntur.

[99.]   INCIPIUNT ANTIPHONÆ SUPER CANTEMUS ET BENEDICITE.

[1. *Super Cantemus.*]

✠ Educti ex Ægypto patres nostri et pertransierunt pedibus Rubrum Mare, [et] dixerunt laudem Domino nostro.

[2. *Super Benedicite.*]

Tres pueri in caminum missi sunt,
Et non timuerunt
Flammam ignis, [et] dixerunt
Laudem Domino nostro.

[3. *Super Cantemus.*]

Filii Hebræorum penetraverunt,
Israelitæ plebes transierunt
Per siccum mare, [et] laudem dixerunt.

[4. *Super Benedicite.*]

Tres pueri te orabant,
De medio ignis ad te clamabant,
Ex una voce hymnum dicebant.

[5. *Super Cantemus.*]

Gloriosus in sanctis, mirabilis in majestatibus, faciens prodigia.

[6. *Super Benedicite.*]

Benedicamus Deum Patrem, et Filium, et Spiritum Sanctum, Dominum.
[Fol. 32r.]

[7. *Super Cantemus.*]

Dextram lævamque Moyses aspexit,
Viam regalem populum eduxit,
Ad littus maris usque perduxit.

[8. *Super Benedicite.*]

Fornacis flammas pueri contempserunt,
Christo jugiter immolaverunt,
Viam iniquam dereliquerunt.

[100.]   SUPER LAUDATE DOMINUM DE CŒLIS.

De cœlis Dominum laudate, psalterium jucundum immolate, laudate eum in sono tubæ.

[99.]   [ANTIPHONÆ SUPER CANTEMUS ET BENEDICITE.]

[9. *Super Cantemus*]

Pharao demersus est in Rubrum Mare ; Moyses pertransit in sicco pede maria, [et] dixit, Deo cantate.

[10. *Super Benedicite.*]

Tres pueri in caminum conjecti
Verbo cogentis regis iniqui
Canebant hymnum domino regi.

[11. *Super Cantemus.*]

Gubernasti, Domine, populum tuum per Rubrum Mare.

[12. *Super Benedicite.*]

Tres pueri cantabant una voce de medio ignis ardentis flammæ.

[13. *Super Cantemus.*]

Domine, tu regnas in æternum, et in sæculum sæculi, et adhuc.

[14. *Super Benedicite.*]

Sancti et humiles corde benedicite Domini Dominum.

[15. *Super Cantemus.*]

Dominus conterens bella ; Dominus nomen est illi.

[16. *Super Benedicite.*]

Benedicite omnia opera Dei Dominum.

[Fol. 32*v.*]

[17. *Super Cantemus.*]

✠ Cantemus Domino, gloriose enim magnificatus est.

[18. *Super Benedicite.*]

Hymnum dicite, et superexaltate eum in sæcula.

[19. *Super Cantemus.*]

.Filii autem Israel abierunt per siccum per medium mare.

[20. *Super Benedicite.*]

Benedicamus Deum Patrem, et Filium, et Spiritum Sanctum, Dominum.

[101.]   DE MARTYRIBUS.

Post ignes et laminas,
Cruces atque bestias,
Sancti cum magno triumpho
Vehuntur in regnum
Et in refrigerium.

[102.]   ITEM ALIA DE MARTYRIBUS.

Hi sunt qui venerunt ex magna tribulatione, et laverunt stolas suas, et candidas eas fecerunt in sanguine Agni.

[103.]   DE MARTYRIBUS.

In memoria martyrum tuorum,
Domine, adesto precibus servorum tuorum, Christe.

[104.]   DE MARTYRIBUS.

In invocatione sanctorum martyrum.
Miserere, Deus, supplicum tuorum.

[105.] SUPER DOMINE REFUGIUM IN DOMINICO DIE.

✠ Convertere, Domine, usquequo ? et deprecabilis esto super servos tuos.

[106.]   ITEM ALIA.

Respice in servos tuos, et in opera tua, Domine.

[107.]   ITEM ALIA.

Repleti sumus mane misericordia tua.

[108.]   ALIA COTIDIANA.

Sit splendor Domini Dei nostri super nos.

[109.]   ✠ AD COMMUNIONEM.

Corpus Domini accepimus, et sanguine ejus potati sumus. Ab omni malo non timebimus, quia Dominus nobiscum est.

[Fol. 33*r.*]

[110.]   ITEM ALIA.

Gustate et videte, Alleluia, quam suavis est Dominus. Alleluia.

[111.]   ITEM ALIA.

In labiis meis meditabor hymnum, Alleluia,
cum docueris me ego justitias respondebo.
Alleluia.

[112.]   ALIA.

Hoc sacrum corpus Domini et Salvatoris
sanguinem sumite vobis in vitam perennem.
Alleluia.

[113.]   ITEM ALIA.

Quam dulcia faucibus meis eloquia tua,
Domine. [Alleluia.]

[114.]   ITEM ALIA.

Hic est panis vivus qui de cœlo descendit,
Alleluia. Qui manducat ex eo vivet in
æternum. Alleluia.

[115.]   ITEM ALIA.

Refecti Christi corpore et sanguine tibi
semper, Domine, dicamus, Alleluia.

[116.] ✠ AD VESPERUM ET AD MATUTINAM.

Gloria in excelsis Deo, et in terra pax
hominibus bonæ voluntatis.

Laudamus te, benedicimus te, adoramus te,
glorificamus te, magnificamus te, gratias
agimus tibi, propter magnam misericordiam
tuam, Domine, rex cœlestis, Deus, Pater
omnipotens.

Domine, Fili unigenite, Jesu Christe,
Sancte Spiritus Dei, et omnes dicimus,
Amen.

Domine, Fili Dei Patris, Agne Dei, qui
tollis peccatum mundi, miserere nobis.

Suscipe orationem nostram, qui sedes ad
dexteram Dei Patris, miserere nobis.

Quoniam tu solus sanctus, tu solus Dominus, tu solus gloriosus cum Spiritu Sancto in
gloria Dei Patris. Amen.

[Fol. 33v.]   [Antiphonæ.]

(1.) Cotidie benedicimus te, et laudamus
nomen tuum in æternum et in sæculum sæculi.
Amen.

(2.) Dignare, Domine, die ista sine peccato
nos custodire.

(3.) Benedictus es, Domine, Deus patrum
nostrorum, et laudibile et gloriosum nomen
tuum in sæcula. Amen.

(4.) Miserere nobis, Domine, miserere
nobis.

(5.) Verba mea auribus [percipe, Domine,
intellige clamorem meum. Intende voci
orationis meæ, rex meus] et Deus meus.

(6.) Mane et exaudies vocem meam.

(7.) Mane oratio mea præveniet te, Domine.

(8.) Diebus atque noctibus, horis atque
momentis, miserere nobis, Domine.

(9.) Orationibus ac meritis sanctorum
tuorum miserere [nobis, Domine].

(10.) [Orationibus ac meritis] angelorum
archangelorum, patriarcharum, prophetarum,
miserere nobis, Domine.

(11.) [Orationibus ac meritis] apostolorum, martyrum, et confessorum, atque
universi gradus sanctorum, miserere [nobis,
Domine.]

(12.) Gloria et honor Patri, et Filio, et
Spiritui Sancto, et nunc, et semper, et in
sæcula sæculorum. Amen.

[Fol. 34r.]
[117.] AD HORAS DIEI ORATIO COMMUNIS.

[Ant. i.] In te, Domine, speravi; non
confundar in æternum. In justitia tua libera
me, et eripe me.

[Ant. ii.] Domine Deus meus, ne disces-
seris a me; intende in adjutorium meum, Domine salutis meæ.

[Ant. iii.] Deus, in adjutorium meum
intende; Domine, ad adjuvandum me festina.

[*Oratio.*] Festina, Domine, liberare nos ex omnibus peccatis nostris, [Qui regnas, &c.]

[118.] ORATIO PRO ABBATE NOSTRO.

[*Ant.* i.] Dominus conservet eum, et vivificet eum, et beatum faciat eum in terra.

[*Ant.* ii.] Dominus custodiat te ab omni malo ; custodiat animam tuam Dominus,

[*Ant.* iii.] Dominus custodiat introitum tuum, et exitum tuum, ex hoc, nunc, et usque in sæculum.

[119.]   COMMON OROIT DUN.

[*Ant.*] Custodi nos, Domine, ut pupillam oculi, sub umbra alarum tuarum protege nos.

[*Oratio.*] Protegere et sanctificare digneris [nos] omnes, omnipotens Deus, [Qui regnas, &c.]

Pater noster, &c.

[Fol. 34*v.*]

[120.]   AD MATUTINAM.

Deus, Deus noster, ad te de luce vigilare debemus, et tu excita de gravi somno, et libera de sopore animas nostras, ut in cubilibus nostris compungamur, et tui esse memores mereamur, Qui regnas, &c.

[121.]   AD HORAM NONAM.

Convenientes, fratres dilectissimi, ad orationem nonam, in quo tempore latro confessus est, et regnum paradisi pollicetur ei, ita et nos, Domine, confitemur peccata nostra, ut regnum cœlorum consequamur, et vitam æternam mereamur, Qui regnas, &c.

[Fol. 35*r.*]

[122.]   AD SECUNDAM.

Domine, sancte Pater, omnipotens æterne Deus, qui diem clarificas, et in lumine luminas, misericordiam tuam, Domine, ne

auferas a nobis ; redde nobis lætitiam salutaris tui, et spiritu principali confirma nos, ut oriatur lucifer in cordibus nostris, per te, Jesu Christe, Qui regnas, &c.

[123.] POST LAUDATE PUERI DOMINUM IN
                    DOMINICO DIE.

Te Patrem adoramus æternum.

Te sempiternum Filium invocamus.

Teque Spiritum Sanctum in una divinitatis substantia manentem confitemur.

Tibi uni Deo in Trinitate debitas laudes et gratias referimus, ut te incessabili voce laudare mereamur, per æterna sæcula sæculorum.

[124.]   DE MARTYRIBUS.

Sancti et gloriosi, mirabiles atque potentes, martyres, quorum in operibus gaudet Dominus, et in congregatione lætatur, intercessores optimi, et fortissimi protectores, mementote nostri semper in conspectu Domini, ut Domini mereamur auxilium, Qui regnas, &c.

[Fol. 35*v.*]

[125.]   ITEM ALIA POST LAUDATE.

Te Patrem adoramus æternum.

Te sempiternum Filium invocamus.

Teque Spiritum Sanctum in una divinitatis substantia manentem confitemur.

Tibi Trinitati laudes et gratias referimus.

Tibi uni Deo incessabilem dicimus laudem.

Te Patrem ingenitum,

Te Filium unigenitum,

Te Spiritum Sanctum a Patre et Filio procedentem corde credimus.

Tibi inæstimabili, incomprehensibili, omnipotens Deus, gratias agimus, Qui regnas in sæcula, &c.

[126.]   ITEM ALIA SUPER LAUDATE.

Te, Pater rerum, jure laudamus.
Te in omni loco fatemur et colimus.
Tibi famulatu spontaneo ministramus.
Exaudi nos, et præsta ea quæ rogamus,
Qui regnas, &c.

[Fol. 36r.]
[127.]   AD CEREU[M] BENEDICE[NDUM.]

In nocte tu fuisti columna ignis, Domine,
ad defendendam plebem tuam a facie Pharaonis, et exercitus ejus ; ita [et] digneris,
Domine, emittere Spiritum tuum Sanctum
de throno flammeo gemmatoque terribili tuo
ad custodiendam plebem tuam.   In ista
nocte scuto fidei defendas nos, ut non
timeamus a timore nocturno, Qui regnas in
sæcula, &c.

[128.] [POST LAUDATE PUERI DOMINUM.]

[Te Patrem adoramus æternum.
Te sempiternum Filium invocamus.
Te] que Spiritum Sanctum in una divini-
[tatis substantia m]anentem confitemur.
Tibi[uni Deo in Trinitate d]ebitas laudes
et gratias [referimus, ut te i]ncessabili voce
laudare [mereamur, per æterna sæcula
sæculorum.]

[Fol. 36v.]
[129.] [IN] MEMORIAM ABBATUM NOSTRORUM.

i. Sancta sanctorum opera
  Patrum, fratres, fortissima,
  Benchorensi in optima
  Fundatorum ecclesia,
  Abbatum eminentia,
  Numerum, tempora, nomina,
  Sine fine fulgentia,
  Audite magna merita,
      Quos convocavit Dominus
      Cœlorum regni sedibus.

ii. Amavit Christus Comgillum,
  Bene et ipse Dominum,
  Carum habuit Beognoum,
  Domnum ornavit Ædeum,
  Elegit sanctum Sinlanum,
  Famosum mundi magistrum,
      Quos convocavit Dominus
      Cœlorum regni sedibus.

iii. Gratum fecit Fintenanum
  Heredem almum inclitum,
  Illustravit Maclaisreum
  Kaput abbatum omnium,
  Lampade sacræ Seganum
  Magnum scripturæ medicum.
      Quos [convocavit Dominus
      Cœlorum regni sedibus.]

iv. Notus vir erat Berachus,
  Ornatus et Cumenenus,
  Pastor Columba congruus,
  Querela absque Aidanus,
  Rector bonus Baithenus,
  Summus antistes Critanus,
      Quos [convocavit Dominus
      Cœlorum regni sedibus.]

v. Tantis successit C[o]lmanus,
  Vir amabilis omnibus,
  Xpo [i.e. Christo] nunc sedet supremus
  Ymnos canens. Quindecimus
  Zoen ut carpat Cronanus,
  Conservet eum Dominus.
      Quos convocabit Dominus
      Cœlorum regni sedibus.

vi. Horum sanctorum merita
  Abbatum fidelissima
  Erga Comgillum congrua
  Invocamus altissima,
  Uti possimus omnia
  Nostra delere crimina,
  Per Jesum Christum, æterna
  Regnantem in sæcula.

[FINIS.]

F

NOTES.

[For the meaning of the abbreviations and signs used in these notes, see the beginning of the Introduction.]

[1]

'In nomine Dei summi.' This short and pious motto which is written on the upper margin of the opening page of the Bangor Antiphonary seems to have been especially, if not exclusively, used by Irish scribes. It occurs at the commencement of the portion of an Irish sermon inserted in the middle of Lib. xxi. cap. 24. of an eighth century copy of the Hibernensis at Cambray. (H. Wasserschleben, *Die Irische Kanonensammlung*, Leipzig, 1885, p. 70.) The 'Capitularis descriptio' at the commencement of the Chartres MS. of the 'Hibernensis' opens with the same words. (H. Bradshaw, *The early collection of Canons known as the Hibernensis*, Cambridge, 1893, p. 50.) So does the Hibernensis itself in the same MS. (*Ibid.* p. 58.) It is found as a heading on Fol. 5*v*. of the Irish *Libellus Precum*, Harl. MS. 7653 (see Appendix) also on fol. 46*r*. of MS. Reg. A. xx. where it may be reckoned among the signs of Irish influence on that Northern English MS. Also at the head of one of the Charters in the Cartulary of the Celtic monastery of Landevenec. (Ed. A. de la Borderie, Rennes, 1888. p. 164.)

'Canticum Moysi.' This Song of Moses taken from Deut. xxxii. 1-43 is part of daily ἔρθρον in the Greek Divine Office. It is used at Lauds on some Sundays in the Mozarabic Breviary; at Lauds on Saturday in the Roman, etc., and Monastic Breviaries. In the latter a 'Divisio' is marked at verse 22, 'Ignis successus est in furore.' In the Ambrosian Breviary it is used at Lauds instead of 'Benedictus' on Sundays in Advent, on Christmas Day, the Feasts of the Circumcision and of the Epiphany.

Analogy would therefore point to this Canticle being used at Bangor at Mattins, and if our theory of the use of this MS. is correct, at Mattins on Saturdays and Sundays.

On the other hand, this is the only canticle throughout the Antiphonary of Bangor which is provided with a refrain. The repetition of the first word 'Audite' as a catchword at frequent intervals shows that the first verse, or part of it, was repeated in the course of its recitation, as the Invitatorium 'Adoremus Dominum,' prefixed to 'Venite exultemus,' is repeated several times in the course of that Canticle at the commencement of Nocturns in the Roman Breviary, and as 'Nunc dimittis' is farced in the Roman Missal at the distribution of candles on Candlemas Day by the repetition of its last verse after each verse of the Canticle including 'Gloria Patri.' These are the only survivals of farced Canticles or Psalms in the Roman rite of the present day. This fact suggests the inference that this 'Canticum Moysi' was part of Nocturns, as distinguished from Lauds, at Bangor, and that it occupied a position corresponding to the position of 'Venite exultemus.' But no similar use of this Canticle is known to exist or to have existed anywhere. It must also be noticed that there is no refrain in S. where the Canticle is, as usual in later MSS. written in verses, and not, as here, in paragraphs, often consisting of more than one verse.

Indeed we do not think that the inference is a true one. For although [1.] is the only Canticle in B in which the opening word of the refrain is written down, yet it will be noticed that every other Canticle, except 'Benedicite omnia opera' [6] which has an original refrain of its own, is written, not in verses, but in paragraphs of irregular length, like 'Audite coeli,' and we believe that they were all intended to be used, like 'Audite coeli,' responsorially not antiphonally. A cantor or cantors recited the Canticle, the body of monks or the congregation present breaking in again and again with some appointed refrain. If so, this must be regarded as a mark of the great antiquity of the Bangor Book; the responsorial way of reciting Canticles and Psalms having given way almost everywhere, at a very early date, to the antiphonal, but being still retained at Bangor in the seventh century.

For the history of the gradual supersession of the responsorial mode of reciting or chaunting by the antiphonal see P. Batiffol (*Histoire du Bréviaire Romain*, Paris, 1893, p. 42.)

In the Divine office of the East Syrian Church an anthem is intercalated between all the verses of certain Psalms on Sundays and Feasts of our Lord. (A. J. Maclean, *East Syrian Daily Offices*, London, 1894, pp. 152, 154.) In the Greek Divine office on Easter Even there is an anthem to each verse of Psalm 118. (*Triodion*, Venice, 1863, pp. 398–407.)

The lost portions of this Canticle have been restored within square brackets from the Vulgate. The restoration of an 'Audite' within such brackets is of course a conjectural addition to the Vulgate text. For *variae lectiones* see Introd. § 7. The readings of S. are noted below.

Verse 2 for 'ut' S. reads 'in' as in MS. text.

" 5 for 'atque' S. reads 'et.'

" 11 for 'volandum' S. reads 'ualandum.'

" 13 after 'oleum' S. omits 'que.'

" 15 for 'dilectus' S. reads 'dilectatus.'

" " [dereliquit . . . suum] the absence of these four words is not due to any defect in the skin, but to deliberate omission from the text. They are also omitted in S. where, however, the words 'et reliquit deum factorem suum' are added after 'salutari suo.' There is no room for such an addition in the missing portion of B.

" 16 [ad] iracundiam. These two words are omitted in the main text, but the words, 'et in iracu[n]dia[m]' have been written on the margin.

" 17 for 'demoniis' S. reads 'demonibus.'

" " for 'coluerunt' S. reads 'nouerunt.'

" 22 S. omits 'que,' as B.

" 24 S. adds 'a' after 'aves,' as B.

" " From the double stop after 'serpentium,' and the capital F at the beginning of the next line we infer that an 'Audite' has been torn off at the end of this verse.

" 28 S. omits 'est.'

" 30 for 'fugent' S. reads 'fugiant.'

" 35 for 'labatur' S. reads 'lauatur' [i.e. labatur.]

" 36 for 'residuique' S. reads 'et residui.'

" 37 for 'dicet' S. reads 'dicent.'

" 38 for 'quorum' S. reads 'corum' [i.e. quorum.]

" " for 'surgant' S. reads 'surgent.'

" 39 for 'vivere' S. reads 'uiuificare.'

" 43 S. omits 'in saecula saeculorum.'

[2]

Title. The title to this Hymn in this MS. is the earliest authority for attributing its composition to St.

Hilary. Cassander printed it from a very ancient MS. containing the 'Regula S. Benedicti,' and a 'Libellus Hymnorum.' He does not enable us to identify the MS., but the Hymn is there described as 'incerto auctore.' (*Hymni Ecclesiast. in Opp.* Paris, 1616, pp. 149, 186.) Muratori is disinclined to believe that the Hymn is the composition of St. Hilary on the ground of its want of finish and polish. 'Majorem fortasse elegantiam desiderabunt nonnulli ut eum sancto Hilario adscribant.' (M. p. 125.)

Daniel prints it among the 'Hymni ἀδέσποτοι' circa saec. vi–ix conscripti' (Dan. Tom. i. p. 191.) Dr. Julian inclines to the opinion that it is an anonymous poem of the sixth century. (*Dict. of Hymnology*, London, 1892, p. 642, § v.) Bede, as quoted below, describing the metre of this Hymn calls it 'ille hymnus pulcherrimus,' but he makes no mention of its being the composition of St. Hilary, and his silence on that point seems to prove that either he did not know of, or did not accept, its reputed authorship.

The Hilary to whom this Hymn is ascribed in B. is no doubt St. Hilary of Poictiers, who died in 368. This is explicitly stated in the Latin preface to the same Hymn in L.H. 'Hilarius, Episcopus et princeps civitatis que dicitur Pictavis fecit hunc Ymnum Christo,' etc. (p. 15) and a similar statement as to its authorship is in the Latin Preface to it in L.H.* (p. 20.)

Although Hilary's 'Liber Hymnorum' is lost, and there are no hymns extant which can with absolute certainty be assigned to him, yet there is good and early authority for his reputation as a Hymn-writer. The Fourth Council of Toledo, A.D. 633, speaks of and defends Hymns as then used in church, 'quos beatissimi auctores Hilarius et Ambrosius ediderunt.' (Canon 13. Mansi, *Concil. Ampliss. Collec.* Tom. x. p. 622.) And St. Isidore of Seville, who died in 636, says : 'Sunt autem divini Hymni, sunt et humano ingenio compositi. Hilarius autem Gallus, episcopus Pictaviensis, eloquentia conspicuus, carmine floruit primus. Post quem Ambrosius episcopus, &c.' (Isidorus Hispalensis, *de Eccles. Officiis*, lib. i. cap. 6.)

These quotations in no wise prove that the Bangor Antiphonary is right in attributing this hymn to St. Hilary. Indeed while on the one hand they give some ground for such attribution, on the other hand they suggest the possibility of a popular hymn being assigned to a well-known author, as in the cases of 'Te Deum laudamus' and 'Quicumque vult.'

There are some internal indications of the date of composition in the Hymn itself, but not of a very precise character.

In stanza xxxii the hymn runs :

'Ante lucem turba fratrum.

Concinemus gloriam.'

Daniel thought that he detected here an illustration of the words of Pliny : "quod Christiani essent soliti stato die ante lucem convenire carmenque Christo quasi Deo dicere." (Dan. Tom. iv, p. 31.) And that the above lines indicated a very primitive date for the composition of the Hymn, and that they even suggested or corroborated the tradition of a very early connexion between the churches of Asia Minor and Britain! But the reference is evidently not to the nocturnal meetings of the earliest Christians in times of heathen persecution, but to the 'nocturns' or midnight and early morning devotions of the monastic orders. The phrase 'turba fratrum' also occurs in stanza i. and, though capable of a more general interpretation, probably refers to the crowd of monks in the monastery of Bangor or elsewhere.

'Gallicantus' in stanza xxxiv. may be a liturgical term. The title or rubric to 'Aeterne rerum conditor' and to this hymn 'Hymnum dicat' is 'Incipiunt Hymni nocturni post mediam noctem ad primum gallicantum' in the Cod. MS. Vetustiss. Reg. Sueciae n. 12 nunc Alex. II. (Thomasius, *Opp. omnia.* Ed. Vezzosi, Romae 1747, t. ii. p. 404.) The first mass for Christmas Day in the Sarum Missal is entitled 'Ad missam in Gallicantu.' All these expressions may point to a date after the establishment and organization of monasticism in Western Christendom, that is to say, to a date not earlier than the fifth, and possibly not earlier than the sixth, century. The ascription of this hymn, therefore, to St. Hilary of Poictiers, seems to be at least a century too early.

In stanza x. there is an allusion to the miracles wrought by our Saviour in His youth. This points to an acquaintance with the apocryphal gospel of the Childhood, a Gnostic production of the second century which became widely disseminated. A Latin translation of it is known to exist in a fifth century palimpsest MS. at Vienna. (Smith and Wace, *Dict. of Christ. Biog.* vol. ii. p. 704.)

Metre. Bede quotes this hymn in his work, *De Arte Metrica,* as an example of 'trochaic tetrameter metre.' His words are these : "Metrum trochaicum tetrametrum, quod a poetis Graecis et Latinis frequentissime ponitur, recipit locis omnibus trochaeum, spondeum omnibus praeter tertium. Currit autem alternis versiculis ita ut prior habeat pedes quatuor, posterior pedes tres et syllabam. Hujus exemplum est totus ille hymnus pulcherrimus.

"'Hymnum dicat turba fratrum, hymnum cantus

personet, Christo regi concinentes laudes demus debitas.'

"In quo aliquando et tertio loco prioris versiculi spondaeum reperies, ut 'Factor caeli, terrae factor,' 'verbis purgat leprae morbos.'" (Beda. *De Arte Metrica,* § 23. P.L. Tom. xc. col. 173.) The lines (versiculi) are trochaic dimeter acatalectic, and trochaic dimeter catalectic alternately.

But we do not propose to discuss at length here or elsewhere the metre of this and other Hymns of the early Irish Church. Those who are interested in the subject are referred to valuable disquisitions thereon by Dr. J. H. Todd (L.H. pp. 47–9), and Zeuss (*Grammatica Celtica,* Berlin, 1871, pp. 936–62.)

Use. There is no direction in the Bangor MS. as to the place where, or the time when, this hymn was to be used. The Rule of St. Ailbhe of Emly (ob. 542) ordered that it should be sung when the bell was rung for the Canonical Hours :

"The Hymnum Dicat should be sung

"At striking the bell for Canonical hours,

"All wash their hands carefully,

"The brethren assume their habit."

(J. O'Laverty, *Historical Account of the Diocese of Down and Connor,* Dublin, 1884, vol. ii. p. 116.)

The Irish Preface to this hymn in L.H. (pp. 151, 162) states that it was composed by St. Hilary after dinner, and suggests its post-prandial use.

There can be little doubt however that here it is intended for use at Nocturns or Matins.

Stanza.	Line.	
I		The missing words in this stanza and elsewhere in this hymn are supplied from L.H.
„	1	The mutilated fourth word in this line, lengthened out into 'fidelium' by M. is evidently 'fratrum.' The second letter 'r' is quite legible in the MS. and a dissyllabic word is required by the metre.
„	3	The third word in this line must be 'concinentes,' which is the reading of L.H. M. reads 'concinentur,' which is untranslatable.
„	4	'laudem'—'debitam' L.H.
III	3	Cassander's text agrees with the Bangor MS. in reading 'uel,' but L.H. reads 'el,' i.e. El, the Hebrew name for God, as is there explained by the accompanying gloss .i. Deus.
V	1	'et terrae' L.H.
VI	3	L.H. reads 'albus,' which is only

Stanza.	Line.	
		another form of 'alvus,' through the interchange of 'u' and 'b.'
VII	2	'uirgine puerpera' L.H.
IX	3	'oculendus' L.H. 'occidendus' Cassander.
X	3, 4	See note to Title, *ad finem.*
XIII	2	'motari aquam,' MS. and L.H.
,,	3	Cassander, as printed by Dan. (Tom. i. p. 192) read 'moerore tentis' instead of 'mero retentis'; but the latter rendering is obviously the right one.
,,	4	'propinnando poculo' L.H. The MS. reading 'populo' may therefore be a mistake for 'poculo.' We have thought it best, however, to retain 'populo.' Compare 'Propinatque dei plebem Spiritale poculum.' [13] Stanza xvii. lines 7, 8.
XIV	3	'Et refert' L.H.
XVI	1	'quibus' must be treated as a monosyllable. L.H. reads 'quis' (for 'queis.') The shorter form is required by the metre.
,,	3	'instruentur' MS. 'instruuntur' L.H. 'instruentur' is probably due to an unclassical scribe imagining it to come from a verb 'instruëre.' Compare 'pendunt' in stanza xxii. line 1.
XVII	3, 4	In this verse M. reads 'grassantur'; L.H. reads 'grassatur' and 'offerendus.' The MS. text 'grasatur' and 'offerentes.'
XVIII	1–4	This verse is accidentally omitted in the MS. It is supplied here from L.H. For the curious mark on the margin of the MS. see Part I. Fol. 4*r.* note 3.
XIX	1	'necandum' L.H.
,,	3	'grasatur' MS. 'grassatur' L.H.
XXII	1	'pendunt' MS. 'pandunt' L.H. See note to XVI. 3.
XXIV	2	'Anna' MS. 'Annas' L.H.
,,	2	'praecepit' L.H. The grammar requires 'praecepit' but the metre 'praecipit.'
XXV	1	'quo' MS. and L.H.
XXVI	3	'mentax' L.H.
,,	4	'uideret' MS. followed by M. but the metre requires 'yiderit' which is also the reading of L.H.
XXIX	4	'ianuis clausis' MS. and L.H. but the

Stanza.	Line.	
		metre requires the transposition of these two words.
XXXI	1	'Praecepit' L.H. but 'praecipit' is preferable both metrically and grammatically.
,,	2	Cassander prints 'baptizare' a possible reading.
XXXII	1	'fratrum.' See note to Title.
,,	2	'Concinnemus' L.H. For the bearing of this verse on the date of the hymn see note to Title.
XXXIV	1	'Gallicantus.' See note to Title.
,,	3	'cantantes' L.H.
XXXVI	1, 2	'Ante lucem decantantes christo regi domino' L.H. See note to Title.
	3	L.H. prefixes 'et' to this line.
XXXVII	1–4	This doxology is not printed in Dan. In Cassander's edition, after which Daniel printed it, it is only represented by 'Gloria &c.'

The following three short anthems follow the last verse of this hymn in L.H. They are in the handwriting of the original scribe, though the style of letters is more angular than in the body of the hymn.

(1) Te decet ymnus deus in Sion et tibi reddetur uotum in hierusalem. (Ps. lxiv. 2.) So L.H.*

(2) Canticis spiritalibus dilectati ymnos christe consonantes canimus tibi quibus tua domine maiestas possit placari oblata deo laudis hostia spiritali per te christe ihesu saluator. To which L.H.* adds 'mundi qui.'

(3) Unitas in trinitate te deprecor domine ut me semper trahas totum tibi uotum nouere.

Of these Anthems:

(1) is found as an anthem in an eighth or ninth century fragment of an Irish 'Officium Defunctorum' at St. Gall, MS. 1395, printed in W. p. 80.

(2) occurs as an '[oratio] post Evangelium' on fol. 26*r.* of B. [84] p. 26.

(3) has not been hitherto found elsewhere. It is not in L.H.*

[3]

Title. The addition of the words 'ut alii dicunt,' omitted by M. may be taken to prove that even in the seventh century there was some doubt about the Apostolic authorship of this Hymn. We may compare them with the words 'commonly called' prefixed to the words

'The Creed of St. Athanasius' in the Anglican Book of Common Prayer.

The authorship of the Hymn is unknown. The following features of it incline us to the opinion that it is an Irish composition (1) The ruggedness of the metre. (2) The use of the word 'Cincris' (stanza xii.) (3) The introduction of Greek or Latinized Greek words, e.g. 'proto' (Stanza vi.) 'protoplaustum' (xxxiii.) 'migrologi' (xli.) Daniel thinks, and the author of the article on Latin Psalmody in Julian's *Dictionary of Hymnology* (p. 642) agrees with him, that this Hymn bears evident traces of being a translation from a Greek original. These traces consist (a) of a certain ruggedness, which is often the mark of a not over-skilful translator ; some verses being difficult to translate, as if the translator into Latin from a Greek original had not been quite sure of the meaning of that original, and (b) in the survival of the Greek or Latinized Greek words already alluded to.

No other MS. copy of this Hymn is known to exist. It was first printed in M., and Daniel reprinted Muratori's text in Dan. Tom. iv. p. 31.

This Hymn is mentioned in the second Vision of Adamnan, an Irish composition of the eleventh century, written shortly before 1096, and preserved in the *Lebar Brecc* (pp. 258ᵇ–259ᵇ.)

"In the time that is given to God for fasting and prayer it is wrong to think of aught save the benefit of the soul, both by preaching, and celebration, to wit, a hundred genuflexions with a 'Beati,' a 'Magnificat,' a 'Benedictus' and a 'Miserere mei Deus,' and a cross-vigil, and Patrick's Hymn, and the Hymn of the Apostles, and a smiting of hands, and a 'Hymnum dicat,' and Michael's Hymn, and a genuflexion thrice at the end of each Hymn, and they strike their breasts and say 'May mercy come to us,' &c."

No special day is mentioned in this passage, but the language of the Hymn points to its being specially intended as a commemoration of the Resurrection, and therefore for Easter-tide or Sunday use.

Metre. The Hymn consists of forty-two stanzas of four lines each. The lines are iambic penthemime, and trochaic dimeter catalectic alternately. Syllable-counting is a feature of all the lines here, and in all the other hymns, except [11] and [12]. All of them are rather rhythmic than quantitative.

Stanza.	Line.	
II	3, 4	No other copy of this Hymn being known to exist the words within square brackets have been supplied conjecturally.
IV	4	for 'moli' M. printed 'olim.'

Stanza.	Line.	
VI	1	'proto.' This Greek word occurs also in Adamnan's Life of St. Columba, "Hoc itaque protum virtutis documentum, &c." (Lib. ii. cap. 2. Edit. W. Reeves, Dublin, 1857, p. 105.) For other Greek words in B. see Part I. Introd. p. 19, § 14. See also note to [10] stanza xiii.
„	2	'cauo' MS.
VII	3	The 'p' at the end of 'polum' or at the beginning of 'nodoso' in this line in the MS. is probably only an instance of the tendency to insert this letter between 'm' and 'n,' which may be illustrated by such common forms as 'sollempnis,' 'columpna,' &c.
IX	1	for the MS. reading 'Hoc quam' one would have expected 'Hic quum.' The text has been altered accordingly.
XII	2	'Cincri.' This is the ablative of 'Cincris,' a name of Pharaoh. The eleventh king in the eighteenth dynasty of Egyptian kings, as given by Eusebius of Caesarea, was named 'Χεγχέρηϲ' 'Chencheres.' (*Chronicorum* Lib. ii. Migre, *Bib. Pat. Graec.* Tom. xiv. col. 333.) The name of the ninth king in the same dynasty is given as 'Achencheres,' and this note is added by Eusebius. "Hujus aetate Moses ducem se praebuit Hebraeis ex Aegypto excedentibus." (*Ibid.* col. 189.) The name is very rare in Latin. It occurs again in [94] line 1. It also occurs in a poem or hymn, of which two stanzas only are printed by Mone, from an eighth century, and, presumably, an Irish MS. at Reichenau (MS. No. 112, fol. 6.) Mone reads the word as 'cinerem,' and suggests that it is a clerical error for 'regem.'

> Katerva plebis
> sexcentum milium
> mare siccatum
> ovantes transeunt,
> carmen tunc dignum
> domino concinunt.
> Kaput retrorsum
> torquentes illico

Stanza. Line.

vident sepultum
cinerem (l. regem) cum curribus
demersum rubrum (l. rubri.)
maris in fluctibus.
(*Lateinische Hymnen des Mittelalters,*
Freiburg, 1853, Tom. i. p. 218.)
Muratori read the word 'cicni,' and
Daniel, printing after Muratori, offered
the explanation that Moses and
Miriam were called swans, because
they sang songs (Dan. Tom. iv. p. 34.)
In Harl. MS. 1023, fol. 63*v*. (a twelfth
century Irish Evangeliarium) there is a
list of the Kings of Egypt inserted,
which begins thus : 'Faro cineris rex
regnavit in aegipto, sub quo in aegipto
in captivitate filii israel fuerunt ; hic
item persequens filios israel in mari
rubro mersus est, et septem in aegipto
annis regnavit. Post cincrim farao
cerrest xii. annos regnavit, &c.'

XV   1   'loquatur' MS. but 'qu' is frequently
              written for 'c' in Irish MSS. and
              vice versâ.

XVII   3   'hora' MS. The grammar requires a
              plural noun.

XXIV   3   M. printed this line differently, dividing
              it thus,—Fune retruso—Daniel copied
              M. (Dan. Tom. iv. p. 32, line 95.)
              But there can be no doubt as to the
              right division of the words. The
              reference to death (funus) is intelli-
              gible ; the reference to a rope (funis)
              is not so readily understood.

XXV   3   'saturaturis' MS.

XXVII   1-4 This mutilated stanza is not easy to
              translate. We have altered 'odire'
              into 'odere' (= oderunt) as 'invi-
              dere' seems to stand for 'inviderunt.'
              Daniel proposes to alter and complete
              the verse thus :
                  'Cui invidere
                  Et oderunt, animam
                  Pro inimicis
                  Prorogans precatus est.'
              (Dan. Tom. iv. p. 34.)

XXVIII   4   See note to [89].

XXIX   4   Possibly for 'tradituro,' we ought to
              read 'tradituri.'

XXXI   4   'Obtondit' MS. 'o' being perhaps sub-
              stituted for 'e' in consequence of

Stanza. Line.

the next word beginning with 'o.'
[oris, MS.]

XXXIII   2   For the MS. 'annos' we have substi-
              tuted 'annis.' The other alternative
              would be to alter 'millibus' into
              'mille,' but the line would then be
              a syllable short.

XXXIV   1   For 'protoplastum' see note to Title.

         2   'Soboli' may be the ablative 'with his
              wicked progeny'; 'mali' must be the
              genitive after 'ultrice.'

XXXVIII 3, 4 'Supernis' 'Humeris.' It would be
              neater Latin if these two words were
              to change place, but there is not
              sufficient ground for disturbing the
              text.

XXXIX   3   The metre requires that 'cuique' should
              be treated as a trisyllable.

XL   4   Either 'possumus' is bad Latin for
              'possimus,' or the question must be
              treated as a direct one.

XLI   2   For 'micrologi' ('migrologi' MS.) see
              note to Title.

XLII   4   The 'alleluia' placed after the first and
              last verses of this hymn is suggestive
              of Easter-tide.

[4]

Title. If 'b' has been rightly expanded into 'Benedictio,' we have here a Title not known to exist elsewhere for this Canticle. See Part I. Fol. 6*r*. note 1.
Muratori printed the title as 'Canticum sancti Zachariae,'
but 'b' cannot possibly be an abbreviation for 'Canticum.'

This Canticle occurs also in L.H. (pp. 191–3), where
it is headed 'Benedictus Dominus,' and also in L.H.*
p. 33. The text in both is substantially identical with
the text in the Bangor Antiphonary, but omitting some
merely orthographical variations, the more important
various readings have been noted below.

For a comparison of the Bangor text with the Vulgate see Introd. § 7.

Use. We have no statement or indication here as
to the use or position of this Canticle. In the Greek,
Roman, (both secular and monastic,) and Ambrosian
Service books it is in daily use at ὄρθρος or Lauds, but
has no place in the Liturgy. In Mozarabic Service
books it is used occasionally both in the Divine Office
and in the Liturgy ; in the Divine Office on certain
Saints' Days 'In festis de uno justo' (P.L. lxxxvi. 870)

in the Liturgy and after the 'Officium' and before the 'Lectio prophetica,' on the Sunday of the Advent of St. John the Baptist, and, if Leslie's conjecture is right, on Easter Day (P.L. lxxxv. 478, 751). As to the Old-Gallican Church, information is wanting about the structure of its Divine Office, but the 'Benedictus' was used either at every Mass or at least on certain Festivals. The *Sacramentarium Gallicanum* has six 'Collationes post Prophetiam' (Benedictus) one for Advent, two for St. John the Baptist, and three for Sundays. Judging from the general purport of the Bangor Antiphonary, we conclude that it is placed here for use at Saturday and Sunday Mattins, and possibly, for daily use at the same office.

Verse 70 'eo' MS. This is probably a clerical error for 'euo' (aevo), the cursive interlinear 'u' having been accidentally omitted to be added by the scribe. 'aeuo' is the reading in L.H., 'euo' in L.H.*

" 71 For the opening 'et' L.H. reads 'ut.' 'liberabit' MS. 'liberauit' L.H. and L.H.*

" 72 'sui sancti' L.H. L.H.*

" 77 The 'meorum' of the MS. is an obvious error for 'eorum,' which is the reading of L.H. the opening 'm' having been suggested to the writer by the concluding 'm' of the preceding word. It is curious that 'meorum' should be also the reading of L.H.*

" 79 Before 'his' L.H.* inserts 'et'; 'uia' L.H.; L.H.*

" 80 Verse 80 is appended here to this Canticle as a sort of anthem. It is separated from the rest of the Canticle by an undulating ornamental line, as well as by a triple stop. The addition is very unusual. The only other MSS. or printed Service-books of any kind in which it is known to us to be found are L.H. and L.H.* We infer from this fact that the addition is an Irish peculiarity.

After 'desertis' L.H. adds 'locis.' For 'ad' before 'Israel' both B. and L.H.* read 'et.'

[5]

We come now to three inserted leaves of the MS. foll. 7, 8, 9, containing in their entirety two canticles, the 'Canticum Moysi' commencing 'Cantemus Domino,' &c., and the 'Benedictio trium puerorum' commencing 'Benedicite omnia opera.' These leaves are of the original skin, and are covered with the original hand-

writing, and are in every sense part of the original MS. It is evident that placed as they are now, in the middle of another Canticle, they are not in their proper place ; but neither an examination of the make up of the MS. (Pt. 1. p. xviii.) nor the consideration of its contents enables us to fix upon any position from which they have been displaced, and to which they must certainly have belonged. If we were to place them anywhere later on in the MS. we would place them after fol. 27, which contains on its *recto* the greater part of a collect 'super cantemus,' and on its *verso* a collect 'super Benedicite.' But we are driven to hold the theory that they were originally intended to be loose, and to be shifted backwards or forwards to that part of the MS. where the collect or anthem occurs which was to be used in connection with them.

Collects and anthems for both canticles are scattered up and down the MS. e.g. 'Super Cantemus Domino' on foll. 22v, 23r, 24v, 25r, 25v, 26v, 28v, 31v, 32r ; 32v ; 'Super Benedicite,' on foll. 23r, 24r, 24v, 25r, 25r, 26v, 27r, 31v, 32r, 32v.

If the question arises, 'Why are not the other four Canticles treated in the same way'? The answer is that there are no collects or anthems scattered up and down the pages of the MS. which belong to them. The 'Canticum Moysi' 'Audite coeli quae loquor' has its own single refrain repeated again and again. The 'Benedictio (Canticum) Zachariae' has a single verse, appended anthem-wise at its conclusion. 'Te Deum laudamus' has a single verse prefixed anthem-wise at its commencement. The three collects on Fol. 35 are an afterthought. 'Gloria in Excelsis' has twelve anthems written in close juxtaposition at its conclusion. None of these four Canticles have therefore the same need of being shifted which exists in the case of 'Cantemus Domino' and 'Benedicite omnia opera.' The difficulty in the way of accepting this theory is not an insuperable one, viz. that no other instance of such an arrangement is known to us.

This Canticle, 'A Song of Moses,' is taken from Exod. xv. 1–19. It is also contained in L.H.* p. 32. The text agrees mainly with the Old Latin. See Introd. § 7. It is written not in verses but in paragraphs, the conclusion of each paragraph being indicated by the use of a triple (:· or .. ,) and in one case of a quadruple stop (. . . ,) but no part of the Canticle is indicated for use as a refrain, to be repeated at the end of each paragraph, as in the case of [1.] refrains being provided in [99].

Use. In the absence of direct information as to the use of this Canticle we must be guided by analogy. It is not a part of any known Liturgy, though portions of it are used occasionally, as in the Tract after the fourth

G

Lection on Easter Even in the Roman Missal, and in the Tract and 'Prophetia' after the fifth Lection on the same day in the Mozarabic Missal. In the Divine Office it is said daily at Lauds (ὄρθρος) according to Greek usage; at Lauds on Thursday according to Roman usage both monastic and secular; at Easter-tide Lauds according to Mozarabic usage, and at Sunday Lauds according to Ambrosian usage. Old-Gallican usage is unknown, but it was probably identical with Mozarabic usage. It is most probable that at Bangor this Canticle was either used at Easter-tide Mattins, or at Sunday (and probably Saturday) Mattins, throughout the year in accordance with Mozarabic or Ambrosian precedent, so far as the Sunday is concerned.

Verse 1 equmt L.H.* deiecit L.H.*

,, 4 'electi principes eius submersi sunt in rubro mari' L.H.*

,, 3 This verse reappears as an anthem to this Canticle in [99] 15 on fol. 32r. p. 30.

,, 6 Confregit, L.H.*

,, 8 'Muros' MS. no doubt stands for 'murus,' which is the reading of L.H.*

,, 10 for 'merserunt' L.H.* reads 'submersi sunt.'

,, 11 Part of this verse reappears as an anthem for this Canticle in [99] No. 5, on fol. 32v. p. 29.

,, 13 We have printed this verse as it stands in the MS. ungrammatical though it be. A reference to Introd. § 7, shows that it is a mixture of Old Latin and Vulgate phraseology. For further information see Sabatier *in loco*. The reading in L.H.* is 'gubernasti iustitia tua populum tuum hunc quem liberasti.'

,, 15 for 'tabuerunt' L.H.* reads 'fluxerunt.'

,, 17 'habitationis tuae' MS.

,, 19 After the last verse L.H.* adds: "Deus patris mei et exaltabo eum. Dominus conterens bella, dominus nomen est illi": then immediately follows the Collect, "Deus qui exeunti ex aegipto &c." [62.]

[6]

Title. For the omission of the word 'trium' in the title see Part 1. fol. 8v. note 1. This Canticle is sometimes called the 'Hymnus (ymnus) trium puerorum,' as later on in this MS. [86], in the *Leofric Missal*, (Oxford, 1883, p. 3), &c.; but the title 'Benedictio trium Puerorum' is believed to be of great antiquity, and is said in Smith and Cheetham's *Dict. of Christian Antiqq.* vol. i. p. 187, to have been used by St. Bene-

dict, and by St. Fructuosus of Bragas, who died about 665; but we have been unable to verify this statement. It is found in the Utrecht Psalter (fol. 87v). No title is given in S. For its position in S. see List of Abbreviations.

This Canticle, as found in S. and L.H.* has substantially the same text and order and number of verses as here. In L.H.* an Irish Preface is prefixed to it, which has been printed with a translation in the *Revue Celtique*, vol. vi. pp. 264-5.

It is taken from Dan. iii. 57-88, with one additional verse.

Use. There being no rubric to regulate its use we are left to inference or conjecture on that point. In the Greek Divine Office it is used daily at ὄρθρος; in the Roman at Lauds on Sundays and Festivals; in the Mozarabic at Lauds on Sundays and Festivals, and daily in Lent: in the Ambrosian at Lauds on Sundays.

In the *Durham Ritual* it is ordered for general use in time of prosperity. "Et in omni tempore prosperitatis (glossed 'eðnisses') semper ymnum trium puerorum decanta." (Surtees Society, vol. for 1840, p. 184.)

This Canticle has also a recognised liturgical use, but in the West only. In the Roman rite it appears in the priests' 'Gratiarum actio post Missam,' and in an abbreviated form (Dan. iii. 52-3) with some additional matter on the four Ember Saturdays, though it has been cut down to a single verse in 'Sabbato iv. Temporum Pentecostes.' Originally the full 'Benedicite' was in use on all these four Saturdays, as may be seen by a reference to the *Leofric Missal* (Oxford, 1883, pp. 78, 114, 123, 129.)

In the Old-Gallican Liturgy it was in use after the Epistle, and in the Mozarabic Liturgy before the Epistle. In the latter it was ordered to be used not only on all Sundays and Festivals of Martyrs, but also at every Mass. (IV. Council of Toledo, A.D. 633, canon 14.)

On the whole it seems most probable that in B. it was intended for use at Mattins on Saturdays and Sundays, and possibly, as the nature of the Canticle suggests, and as the Mozarabic rite ordered, on Feasts of Martyrs.

The Vulgate numbering of the verses has been prefixed to each verse in the text of this Canticle, verse 89 being a Christian addition to a Jewish composition.

Verse 58 For 'angeli' L.H.* reads 'aquae,' an obvious clerical error.

,, 60 S. adds 'Domini' before 'Dominum.' So also in the following verses, 62, 63, 64, 67, 73, 74, 75, 76, 78, 80, 81, 83, 82, 86, 87.

,, 61 The reading of L.H.* is that of the amended text, 'potentiae.'

Verse 70 For 'nives' S. substitutes 'nubes.'
„   88 'annanias, zacharias,† misahel' S. after
        'annanias' add 'et' L.H.*
„   89 'Benedicam' S. Verse 89 now takes this
        form in Western Breviaries :

'Benedicamus Patrem, et Filium, cum Sancto Spiritu :
laudemus et superexaltemus in saecula,' to which is added
'Benedictus es, Domine, in firmamento coeli, et laudabilis, et gloriosus, et superexaltatus in saecula.'

After 89 L.H.* adds 'Sacerdotes domini benedicite
a'men' followed by 'Te enim, omnipotens deus
benedicimus iure' &c. as [82] as far as 'eripe,' inclusive ;
then instead of 'Qui regnas' come these words 'christe
audi nos ; oremus.'

[7]

Title. The title 'Hymnus in die Dominica' tells us
the day on which, but not the office at which, 'Te
Deum laudamus' was used at Bangor. It is silent as to
its authorship, which is too controverted a subject to
be discussed here, but for which the reader may be
referred to elaborate articles by our President, Dr. John
Wordsworth, Bishop of Salisbury (Julian's *Dictionary of
Hymnology*, London, 1892, pp. 1122, 1547), and to a
still more recent and very remarkable article on the
same subject by Dom G. Morin (*Revue Benedictine*,
Février, 1894) in which the authorship is ascribed to
Nicetas, Bishop of Remesiana in Dacia, c. 392-414,
Archbishop Ussher, describing an unidentified Psalter,
incidentally mentions that Irish tradition is in favour of
attributing the composition of this Hymn to 'Nicetius.'
"In Latino-Gallico quoque Psalterio circa tempora
Henrici .i. exarato inscribitur iste Hymnus 'sancti Niceti'
(Hibernicae nostrae traditioni satis consentanee) . . .
Latino-Gallicum illud Psalterium in bibliotheca Cotton-
iana vidimus." (*Whole Works*, Dublin, 1841-62, vol. vii.
p. 300.)

This Hymn is also found in L.H. and L.H.* In
L.H. it has the popular, but unhistorical mediaeval statement as to its origin prefixed to it : "Haec est laus
sanctae Trinitatis quam Augustinus sanctus et Ambrosius
composuit " (p. 196.)

There is no indication there of any day or season for
its use. The anthem 'Laudate pueri' &c. (Ps. cxii. 1.) is
there as here prefixed to the first verse.

Use. There is no known trace of the use of 'Te
Deum laudamus' in any Liturgy, Eastern or Western,
nor is there any ground here for connecting [7] with [8.]
It is likewise unknown in the Eastern Divine Office, but
in the Roman, Benedictine, and Ambrosian Breviaries it
is used on Sundays and Feasts of nine or twelve Lessons
in lieu of the Respond after the last Lesson in the

third Nocturn. In the Mozarabic Divine Office it is
used on Sundays and Festivals at Prime, where it is followed by 'Gloria in Excelsis' and the Creed (P.L. Tom.
lxxxvi. col. 944.) Old-Gallican usage is unknown, save
through allusions in ancient Gallican monastic Rules, &c.
e.g. according to the Rule of St. Caesarius of Arles (c. A.D.
527) it was said near the end of Mattins on Sundays.
"Omni Dominica sex missas facite, prima missa semper
resurrectio legatur ; dum resurrectio legitur nullus sedeat.
Perfectis missis dicite Matutinas, directaneo 'Exaltabo
te Deus meus et Rex meus' (Ps. cxliv.) Deinde
'Confitemini' (Ps. civ.) Inde 'Cantemus Domino'
(Exod. xv. 1-19.) 'Lauda anima mea Dominum' (Ps.
cxlv.) Benedictionem 'Laudate Dominum de coelis'
(Pss. cxlviii–cl.) 'Te Deum laudamus,' 'Gloria in
Excelsis Deo,' et Capitellum. Omni Dominica sic dica-
tur. (Can. xxi. Holst. Pt. ii. p. 56.) At Toulon it was
in daily use. See note to verse 16.

In the little later Rule of St. Aurelian of Arles (ob.
555), among other variations at Mattins, 'Magnificat' is
substituted for 'Te Deum laudamus.' (*Ibid.* p.66.)

We conjecture, therefore, that in the Bangor Antiphonary it is intended for use on Sundays (and perhaps
also on Saturdays and Feasts of Martyrs) at Mattins.
But see note to verse 16. See also [123] [125] and
[126].

For different texts of 'Te Deum laudamus' see the
Comparative Table in the Appendix. The textual variations of L.H.* are noticed below.

Verse 1 This anthem, taken from Ps. cxii. 1, is found
          prefixed to 'Te Deum laudamus' in L.H.
          and L.H.* It is also found prefixed to a
          different Hymn of praise in the Apostolic
          Constitutions. (Lib. vii. cap. 47.)
„   7 'hiruphin et saraphin' L.H.*
„   9 We have retained the MS. 'laudet' as a
          possible reading, but the present tenses
          before and after it make it almost certain
          that it is a clerical error for 'laudat.'
„   11 After 'maiestatis' L.H.* adds 'tuae.'
„   16 This which is also the reading of Harl. MS.
          7653, L.H. and L.H.* was not the Gal-
          lican reading in the seventh century, as
          appears by the following extract from a
          letter written c. 524-33 by Bishop Cyprian
          of Toulon to Bishop Maximus of Geneva :
              Sed in hymno, quem omnes ecclesia toto
          orbe receptum canit, cottidie dicemus.
          "Tu es rex gloriae christus ; tu patri
          sempiternus es filius," et consequenter
          subiungit "Tu ad liberandum suscepturus
          hominem non orruisti virginis uterum ; te

G 2

ergo, quaesumus, tuis famulis subveni, quos praetioso sanguine redimisti."

Printed from a seventh century MS. (Cod. 212) in the Cathedral Library at Cologne by Dr. W. Gundlach in the *Epistolae Aevi Merowingici* in the *Monumenta Germaniae*, Berlin, 1892, Tom. iii. pp. 434-6.

The mention here of the daily recitation of 'Te Deum' at Toulon is in contrast to its Sunday use at Bangor, and at Arles. See note to Title.

Verse 18 'sedens' may be a clerical error for 'sedes,' which is the reading of L H.*, as well as of the other early Irish texts, the 'sedis' in Harl. MS. 7533 being only a cacography for 'sedes.'

,, 20 The MS. 'sanguinem' is an impossible reading. It is no doubt a clerical error for 'sanguine,' which is the reading in L.H.* as well as of the other early Irish versions.

,, 21 It is not easy to say what is the true reading here. L.H.* adds 'tuis' after 'sanctis' and reads 'gloriam' for 'gloriae.'

,, 22 We have not discovered the meaning of the two groups of three points which follow 'domine' above and below the line, nor have we found any instance of similar punctuation or decoration elsewhere. See Part i. fol. 10v. note 3.

,, 25 The insertion of 'Amen' at this point is not found in L.H.* or elsewhere, but is peculiar to B. One suspects it of being a thoughtless insertion by a scribe, at the conclusion of words where an 'Amen' might naturally be expected to occur, but it may mark the actual termination at one period of the Hymn.

,, 26 After verse 26 in both L.H. and L.H.* there follows the Collect 'Te patrem adoramus aeternum,' &c. [123.]

[8]

This Hymn is evidently from its title a 'Communio' or 'Antiphona ad accedentes' to be used during the Communion of the Priests, of whom there would be many, headed by the Abbot himself, in such a monastery as Bangor. It may be compared with the following early Gallican Communion anthem preserved to us in the writings of St. Gregory of Tours: "Venite populi ad sacrum et immortale praesidium et libamen agendum. Cum timore et fide accedamus, manibus mundis

paenitentiae munus communicemus, quoniam propter nos Agnus Dei Patri sacrificium propositum est. Ipsum solum adoremus, ipsum glorificemus, cum angelis clamantes, Alleluia. (*De Mirac. S. Mart.* ii. 13) as quoted by Daniel (Tom. iv. p. 109) and by Margaret Stokes (*Six months in the Apennines*, London, 1892, p. 217.) I have been unable to verify the reference. It is interesting to find it still surviving in use in W.T. pp. xxvi and 19.

The following is the legend of the circumstances attending the original composition of this Hymn by angels, on the occasion of a singular meeting between St. Patrick and St. Sechnall. We quote the strange story as it is told in the Preface to St. Sechnall's (Secundinus) Hymn in the *Lebar Brecc*.

'. . . . . or this is the cause, namely, because of the provocation which Sechnall gave Patrick, to wit, "Patrick is a good man, were it not for one thing, namely, that he preacheth charity so little." So when Patrick heard that, he went to Sechnall in great wrath. It was then that Sechnall had finished mass, except going to Christ's Body, when he was told that Patrick had come to the place in great wrath against Sechnall. Then Sechnall left the oblation on the altar, and knelt unto Patrick. So Patrick drove the chariot over him, and God raised the ground around him, on this side and on that, so that (Patrick) hurt him not. "Why shouldst thou be (so) to me?" saith Sechnall. "What is that one thing," said Patrick, "thou saidst I did not fulfil? For if I fulfil not charity, I am guilty of breaking God's commandment. My God of doom knoweth that it is for sake of charity I preach not charity. For sons of life will come after me into this island, and they will need their service from men." "I did not know that," saith Sechnall, "that it was not from sluggishness thou didst so." Then the angel said to Patrick, "All that shall be thine." So then they made peace, Patrick and Sechnall, and while they were going round the cemetery they heard a choir of angels chanting at the offering in the church, and this is what they chanted, the hymn whose beginning is "Sancti venite Christi corpus" et reliqua. Wherefore from that time forward this hymn is sung in Ireland when one goes to Christ's Body.'

The above passage is translated by Mr. Whitley Stokes, and printed by him, together with the Irish text, in W. S., pp. 394-7.

The Hymn is familiar to most people in English dress, as translated by Dr. J. M. Neale, and contained in *Hymns Ancient and Modern*. It has been more recently inserted by Dr. E. H. Bickersteth, Bishop of Exeter, in the *Hymnal Companion*. It has also been incorporated into the Appendix of the *Church Hymnal of the*

Church of Ireland, which Appendix received the approval of the General Synod in 1891.

It consists of eleven quatrains or stanzas of four lines each. The lines are iambic penthemime, and trochaic dimeter catalectic alternately. It has been fancifully suggested that there are eleven stanzas in this Hymn because there were eleven Apostles who were present at the institution of the Eucharist and received it worthily.

Stanza. Line.

I   1   'Sancti.' Dr. Neale entirely omitted this word in his translation beginning ' Draw nigh and take the Body of the Lord ' (*Hymns Ancient and Modern*, No. 313) and Dr. Bickersteth mistranslated it in the following line, 'Come, take by faith the Body of your Lord' (*Hymnal Companion*, revised edition, London, 1880, No. 383.) The words 'by faith ' represent and translate, not the 'sancti' of verse i. but the 'creduli' of verse viii.

"   4   We have altered the last word ' sanguine' into 'sanguinem,' in accordance with grammatical requirement. Perhaps the horizontal line over its last syllable has been accidentally omitted. Perhaps it has been attracted into the case of the preceding 'quo.' It is curious that in the corresponding line in col. i. 'sanguinem ' has been written instead of ' sanguine.'

III   1-4   ' Hoc sacramento '&c. Dr. Neale did not translate this verse, misled, no doubt, by Daniel, who accidentally omitted it in his first printing of the Hymn, but who apologised for and explained the omission afterwards. (Dan. Tom. iv. p. 109.)

The expression 'ab inferni faucibus may be illustrated by the expression ' de suppliciis inferni' in [77.]

VIII   1   ' Accedunt' MS. almost certainly a clerical error for ' accedant.'

XI   1   'Alfa et ω' MS. In the only early extant Irish MS. of the Apocalypse this title of our Lord is written as it is here, the Alfa (for Alpha) in full, and the Omega as the small Greek letter (ω). So they are in the only liturgical passage known to the editor

in which they occur, viz., in a Mozarabic ' Post Nomina,' 'In Dominica ante Epiphaniam Domini.' (Book of Armagh, and P.L. Tom. lxxxv. col. 225.)

It is very likely that these symbols were stamped upon the Eucharistic wafer bread. The following canon was passed in a provincial synod held under John Comyn, Archbishop of Dublin in 1186.

' 4th. That the host, which represents the Lamb without spot, the Alpha and Omega, be made so white and pure, that the partakers thereof may thereby understand the purifying and feeding of their souls rather than their bodies.' (Sir Jas. Ware's *Works*, Dublin, 1764, vol. i. p. 316.)

The original Latin has perished, but it was in existence in Sir James Ware's time (1594–1666) in a very decayed state among the Archives of Christ Church, Dublin.

[9]

Title. We have altered the MS. ' coeria 'into ' cereus.' There seems to be no authority for such a form as ' coeria' or ' cerea.' The metre of the hymn is iambic dimeter acatalectic.

This Hymn is not found elsewhere. It is not certain from its title, nor from its contents, whether it was intended to be sung daily at the lighting of the lamps at the ' Hora Vespertina,' or the 'Lucernarium,' or whether it is connected with the benediction and lighting of the Paschal candle on Easter Even. A similar doubt has existed with regard to Prudentius' well-known Hymn 'Inventor rutili &c.' inscribed 'ad incensum lucernae.' (Dan. Tom. i. p. 132. Ducange *Glossarium* sub. voc. Cereus.) In mediaeval office books it is associated with the lighting of the Paschal candle on Easter Even, but this may be the solitary survival, in its most solemn form of a ceremonial used if not daily, at least frequently, in connection with the Lucernarium.

The following points seem to favour the connection of this Hymn [9] with Easter Even.

(a) The reference to the escape from Egypt in stanzas iii. and iv.

(b) The reference to the work of the bee in the manufacture of wax and honey in stanzas vi. vii. viii. This subject is worked out at great length in the preface for the ' Benedictio Cerei in Sabbato Sancto' in the older Missals. (See *Leofric Missal*, Oxford, 1883, p. 97. *Missale Gallicanum*, p. 185.)

(c) The possible reference to baptism in stanza vii. but the reference here may be to the adoption of the monastic life. The 'examen foetus novi' seems to us to be most naturally referred to the newly baptized.

The custom of lighting a special Paschal fire is of great antiquity. There is reference to the custom in Ireland more than two centuries before the Bangor Antiphonary was written. St. Patrick is described as lighting it in defiance of the edict of the pagan king Laoghaire.

"Sanctus ergo Patricius, sanctum pasca celebrans, incendit diuinum ignem, ualde lucidum et benedictum qui in nocte reffulgens a cunctis pene per planitiem campi habitantibus missus est." (Life of St. Patrick by Muirchu Maccu-Machtheni in *Book of Armagh*, Fol. 3. *b*. 2, printed in W. S. p. 279.)

There is also a reference to hallowed fire in the *Book of Lismore*, a fifteenth century compilation from earlier Irish MSS. (Whitley Stokes, *Lives of Saints, from the Book of Lismore*. Oxford, 1890, p. 277.)

This Paschal custom, originating in the Celtic Church, is believed to have spread thence to the Anglo-Saxon Church, and through the latter church to the continent of Europe. (L. Duchesne, *Origines du Culte Chrétien*, Paris, 1889, p. 240.) But some form of Paschal illumination was known in both Eastern and Western Europe at a very early date. (Smith and Cheetham, *Dict. of Christ. Antiqq.* vol. ii. p. 1564.)

Stanza.   Line.

VI   A friend has supplied the following translation or paraphrase of these three difficult verses:

'It is now time, while the dark bee-glue is eaten away (by the flame) that with all its filth burnt away by the (flame-like) warmth of the Holy Spirit, our flesh shall shine like wax.'

'Now storing up in our hearts the hidden breathings of the divine honey-comb, cleansing the inmost cells of the heart, thou hast filled them with the word.'

'As a swarm of new bees, leaving its burdens behind, on careless wings seeks with its face (i.e. in direct flight) the heaven which its (inner) spirit has selected.'

VII   1   'Secretis' MS.
VIII   3   'relectum' MS.
  „   1-4 'Examen &c.' This stanza is evidently corrupt. Daniel proposed to amend it thus:

'Examen ut foetus novi
Ortu praetectum, spiritu

Stanza.   Line.

          Retectum, coelum sarcicis
          Quaerat securis pinnulis.'
with this explanation, i.e. 'ut catechumeni coelum quod sarcicis jam ipso ortu vel peccato originis clausum est, nunc spiritus sancti gratia regenerati apertum certo ac felici cursu attingant.' (Dan. Tom. iv. p. 77.) But the English translation as given above is more literal, and involves no violent change of the MS. text.

IX   It will be noticed that this doxology is written in a fresher ink and by a different hand from the rest of the Hymn, but though the handwriting is different it is contemporaneous.

[10]

Title.   'Hymnus mediae noctis.'   'Mediae noctis tempus est,' &c.

This is a well-known hymn. It is sometimes printed as part of a long hymn, of which it forms a portion, commencing at the ninth verse. This long hymn is one of the three hymns given for 'medium noctis' in the Mozarabic Breviary. (P.L. Tom. lxxxvi. col. 931.) It consists of twenty-one stanzas, and begins thus :—

'Ihesu, defensor omnium,
Protector et mirabilis.'

It has been printed by Dan. (Tom. i. p. 46 ; Tom. iv. p. 26), to whose notes the reader is referred for information about MS. versions and printed texts. Daniel adduces proof from MS. authority as well as from internal evidence that the Hymns 'Ihesu defensor omnium' and 'Mediae noctis tempus est' are separate Hymns, which were erroneously printed together as one Hymn by Arevalus (in Lorenzana's reprint of Cardinal Ximenes' *Breviarium Gothicum*, Matrit. 1775, p. cxviii) and have therefore been frequently treated as one Hymn since his time.

Authorship.   The authorship of this Hymn is not touched upon in the Bangor MS. Instead of discussing the point fully, we will content ourselves here by saying, that Daniel is inclined to accept its Ambrosian authorship, not only on the external authority of the *Codex Rhenoviensis* (ninth century) but also and still more on account of the close resemblance both in thought and diction running through the Hymn to the following language used by St. Ambrose in his commentary on Ps. 118. "Docet te propheta quomodo teneas Dominum Jesum. 'Media nocte' surgebam ad confitendum tibi super judicia justitiae tuae." (*Expositio in Ps.* cxviii. vers. 6*1* ; P.L. Tom. xv. col. 1513.) See stanza i.

"Unde non otiose Paulus Apostolus et Silas trusi in carcerem, cum in nervo pedes haberent, media tamen nocte surgebant, mentis vestigio exorabant Dominum, et laudis sacrificium deferebant." (*Ibid.* col. 1515.) See stanza ii.

"Solet sponsus media nocte venire, cave ne te dormientem inveniat." (*Ibid.* col. 1516.) See stanza vii.

"Cave ne facem tuam non queas somnolentus accendere." (*Ibid.*) See stanza ix.

"Media nocte primogeniti Aegyptiorum liberi," &c *Ibid.* col. 1514.) See stanzas iii. iv. v.

There is a resemblance and correspondence here which certainly support the theory that this Hymn is the composition of St. Ambrose. It does not appear among the Hymns attributed to St. Ambrose by Luigi Biraghi (*Inni Sinceri e Carmi di Sant' Ambrogio,* Milano, 1862.) nor is it in the Ambrosian Breviary. There is nothing to suggest an Irish origin for the Hymn.

Use. This hymn was part of the 'Vigiliae Nocturnae.' According to the heading in the Mozarabic Breviary as well as in the Bangor Antiphonary it was for use at midnight. 'De medium noctis' (P. L. Tom. lxxxvi. col. 9, 32.) 'Mediae noctis' (Fol. 11v.) According to the Rule of St. Caesarius of Arles it was for use at the first nocturn ' Ad primum nocturnum.' (*Regula S. Caesarii ad Virgines,* Bolland. *Acta SS.* ad diem xii. Ianuarii § xi. No. 69, Tom. i. p. 736.) According to the *Codex Rhenoviensis* (ninth century) it was for use at Nocturns on Sunday, ' Dominicis diebus ad nocturnum.'

Metre. The Hymn consists of fourteen stanzas of four lines each. The metre is iambic dimeter acatalectic.

For 'variae lectiones' throughout this Hymn see Daniel *ut supra.*

Stanza.	Line.	
I	1-4	See note to Title.
II	1-4	do.
III-V		do.
IV	2	The MS. reading ' Et quos idem ' has not been retained. It seems to be just translatable. "Whom too the same angel then had not dared to punish," but the reading given by Thomasius 'ex Cod. Reg. Suec. et Cod. O.' "Quos ibidem" is to be preferred. (*Opera Omnia,* ed. Vezzosi, Romae, 1747, Tom. ii. p. 404.) The line might also be altered thus : ' Et iis quos tunc angelus.'
VI	1	' uero ' MS.

Stanza.	Line.	
VII	1-4	See note to Title.
IX	1-4	do.
XIII	1	'agie' MS. This Greek word in Latin letters occurs in the Hymn of St. Comgall [14] stanza v. line 6, and in the Hymn of S. Cumineus Longus line 44 (L. H. p. 80), and it has found its way into a Collect in the *Leofric Missal.* (Oxford, 1883, p. 176) : see also W.T. pp. 48, 49.

Other instances of Greek words introduced in a similar way into Latin texts are as follows, but the list makes no pretensions to be exhaustive. It is chiefly drawn from Celtic sources.

cata, Codex Usserianus, Irish sixth century, edited by T. K. Abbott, *Evangeliorum Versio Antehieronymiana,* Dublin, 1884. Pars prior p. (378) ; also in the headings of the Codex Bobiensis (*k*), a fifth century MS. of the gospels once belonging to St. Columbanus, edited by Dr. J. Wordsworth and others in *Old Latin Biblical Texts* (Oxford, 1886, pp. 3–53) ; in the *Peregrinatio Sylviae* (frequently.)

doxa, Sequence for Fer. iv. post Pentecosten (*York Missal,* Surtees Society, vol. lix. p. 157.)

karismata (W.T. p. 52.)

pneuma (W.T. pp. 14, 24, 41, 48, 52.)

sophia, 'Carmen de vita Sulgeni,' written in the eleventh century by Johannes, son of Sulgen. (H. & S. vol. i. p. 666.) Sequence for Sexagesima in the Anglo-Saxon *Tropary of Ethelred.* (Surtees Soc. vol. lx. p. 306 ; W.T. pp. 14, 48)

sophisma (W.T. p. 42) ; sother or soter (W.T. pp. 48, 49.)

sperma (W.T. p. 28) ; Theos (W.T. p. 49) ; ymon (W.T. p. 49.)

In Adamnan's *Life of St. Columba,* agonotheta, lithus, machera, omonimums, onoma, protus, sophia, xenium, &c. (Edit. Bp. W. Reeves, Dublin, 1857, p. 158, note n. and Glossary. See also W. p. 157 note.) The Lord's Prayer in Greek words and Greek characters is written on the last page of Codex A of this Life, and the colophon at the

Stanza.   Line.

end of the second book of the same codex is in Latin words but Greek characters. (Edit. Reeves *ut supra* pp. xiv. xx.)

In the *Book of Armagh* agon, anthropi, archidocos, &c. (W.S. pp. 298, 307, 312.) The Lord's Prayer in Latin words but Greek characters occurs on fol. 36r. and single words in Greek characters are found elsewhere in the same MS.

Whole passages of transliterated Greek words may be seen in Gerbert's *Monumenta Vet. Liturg. Aleman.* St. Blaise, 1779, Pars. ii. pp. 87, 88 ; in W.T. pp. 29, 60, 97, 192 ; the *Gelasian Sacramentary*, col. 540. In fact the older Western Liturgical MSS. of all kinds abound in them.

XIV   1–4   This doxology is only found here, not in the other MSS. of this Hymn.

[11]

Title.   This is a very rare Hymn, no other MS. text of it being known to us. It was reprinted, after Muratori, by Daniel (Tom. iv. p. 88) but without any suggestion as to its authorship or origin, and without any note or comment on its text. It does not bear upon the face of it any evidence of its birthplace or authorship, beyond this one general negative inference that a Hymn in honour of Martyrs is not likely to have originated in Ireland, and therefore must be an importation from outside Ireland, and most probably from Gaul or Spain. The metre is too irregular to fall under any classification. It is a rhythmic rather than a metrical poem.

'Matutina.'   See note to [24].

For the honour paid to martyrs, see Introd. § 6.

For the special observance of Saturdays, see Introd. §§ 2, 4.

Stanza.   Line.

I   4   The word 'Alleluia,' though only written after the first and last verses, was evidently intended to be repeated at the end of each verse of this Hymn. The sense and perhaps the metre require it. It has been inserted accordingly.

VI   2   'Qui' MS. But the grammar either

requires 'Quae' for 'Qui' or 'firmasti' for 'firmavit.'

VI   3   'zabulum.' For this form of the word see Part I, Introd. p. xxv. The same word occurs in W.T. p. 23.

[12]

Title.   This Hymn for use at Mattins on Sunday is found only in this MS. It does not exhibit sufficiently distinct characteristics to enable us to decide whether it is an Irish composition or an importation from the Continent ; but see note to stanza x. lines 3, 4.

The metre consists merely in breaking up sentences into clauses of fairly equal length. Its irregularity points rather to Ireland as the place of composition than to any workshop of more polished poetry.

The refrain is only written in full after the first and last verses, but the repetition of its catchword after each stanza, and the mark of abbreviation over it after the second stanza, imply its presence in full at the close of every verse.

Stanza.   Verse.

III   1   This phrase, like others which follow, connect this Hymn with the language of the Nicene Creed.

VI   1   Compare Rom. viii. 17.

 "   6   'qui nunc cepit.' These words do not seem to be required, and may be accidentally borrowed from the first line of stanza viii. 'Cepit' in both cases is evidently not the perfect of 'capio' but the present or perfect of 'coepio.'

IX   4   'Dixinus' hardly makes sense. 'Divinitas' has been suggested.

X   2   'se se' must be either a clerical error for 'esse,' which however is not wanted, or a late Latin equivalent for 'illum.' See Part i. fol. 13v. note 1.

 "   3, 4   See [13] stanza xxii. where similar doctrinal phrases occur in an undoubtedly Irish composition.

[13]

Introductory note.   There are many copies existing both in MS. and in print of this celebrated Hymn composed by St. Sechnall (Secundinus) in praise of St. Patrick. We subjoin a list of the earlier MS. texts, and of the more important printed editions :

LIST OF MANUSCRIPTS.

	Name of MS.	Date A.D.	Present Place.
I	Antiphonarium Benchorense [B]	680–91	Ambrosian Library, Milan.
II	Liber Hymnorum [L.H.]	XIth.	Trinity College, Dublin.
III	Liber Hymnorum [L.H.*]	XIth or XIIth cent.	Franciscan Convent, Merchant's Quay, Dublin.
IV	Lebar Brecc.	XIIIth or XIVth cent.	Royal Irish Academy, Dublin.

LIST OF PRINTED EDITIONS.

	Name of Editor.	MS. Authority.	Title of Book.	Place and Date.
a	Colgan.	Not stated.	*Trias Thaumaturga* (p. 211).	Lovanii, 1647.
b	Sir James Ware.	III.	*S. Patricii Opuscula.*	Londini, 1656.
c	Muratori.	I.	*Anecdota Bibliothecae Ambrosianae* (Tom. iv. pp. 127–159.) *Opera Omnia* (reprinted in P.L. Tom. lxxii.)	Patavii, 1713. Arezzo, 1770.
d	Gallandius.	Reprint of b.	*Bibliotheca Patrum* (Tom. x. p. 183.)	Venetiis, 1765–81.
e	Dr. J. H. Todd.	II.	*Leabhar imuinn [Liber Hymnorum] or the Book of Hymns of the Ancient Church of Ireland*, in 2 vols. (Irish Archæological and Celtic Society.)	Dublin, 1855, 1869.
f	H. A. Daniel.	Reprint of c.	*Thesaurus Hymnologicus* (Tom. iv. p. 91.).	Lipsiae, 1855.
g	Haddan and Stubbs.	Reprint of e.	*Councils and Ecclesiastical Documents*, etc. (vol. ii. part ii. p. 324.)	Oxford, 1869.
h	Whitley Stokes.	III.	*Tripartite Life of St. Patrick* (p. 386.)	London, 1887.

To which must be added the present edition of the Antiphonary of Bangor, under the auspices of the Henry Bradshaw Society, in two parts, London, 1893 and 1895. Some further publications of this Hymn in honour of St. Patrick are mentioned in U. Chevalier's *Repertorium Hymnologicum*, Louvain, 1889, fasc. i. pp. 91–2.

Very little is known about St. Sechnall or S. Secundinus, the composer of this Hymn. The Irish annals simply record his death. The following is the notice of that event in the Annals of Ulster, A.D. 447. "Quies Secundini sancti lxxv° anno etatis sue." (Edit. W. H. Hennessey, Dublin, 1887, vol. i. p. 12.) He is enumerated in Tirechan's Collections among the Bishops ordained by St. Patrick in Ireland, but no further details about him are given (*Book of Armagh*, fol. 9v.; W.S. p. 304.) In the notes by Muirchu Maccumachtheni he is not even mentioned.

In the 'Liber Angueli' (or Book of the Angel) an early ninth century forgery to promote the primatial claims of Armagh and the papal claims of Rome, inserted between the Additions to Tirechan's Collections and St. Patrick's Confession in the *Book of Armagh*, Secundinus is mentioned along with Auxilius, Patricius, and Benignus, as ordering that appeals should lie in case of disputes, first to the Archiepiscopal See of St. Patrick [Armagh] and secondly to the See of St. Peter at Rome. (*Ibid.* fol. 21v.; W.S. p. 356.)

In later Irish literature e.g. the Preface to this Hymn in L.H.* (printed with a translation W.S. pp. 382–5) and in the Preface to it in the *Lebar Brecc* (printed with a translation in L.H. pp. 26–34) which are too lengthy to reproduce here, several other traditions are recorded about St. Sechnall, e.g. we are told that the Hymn was written in Domhnach Sechnaill (now Dunshaughlin in Meath) by the St. Sechnall from whom that place received its name. The occasion of its composition was the reconciliation of the two saints after their estrangement owing to a depreciatory remark made by St. Sechnall about the teaching of St. Patrick. Sechnall was the Irish and Secundinus the Roman name of the author, who was the son of Restitutus ua Baird, a Lombard of Leatha, and Darerca, a sister of St. Patrick. These statements involve ethnographical and geographical points of difficulty and obscurity, which are discussed at length by Dr. Todd (*Ibid.* pp. 35–40) but into which we refrain from entering here.

H

The Hymn does not add to our knowledge of facts in the history of the life of St. Patrick, but it tells a good deal about his moral and spiritual character.

Stanza   I The goodness of his life makes St. Patrick comparable to the Angels and Apostles.

,,   II In everything he keeps God's Commandments.

,,   III Constant in the love of God, and immovable in the faith, he received his Apostleship directly from God, so that the [Irish] Church is founded on him, as the Church [Universal] was founded on St. Peter.

,,   IV The Lord chose him to be a fisherman in Gentile waters.

,,   V He trades with the Gospel talents, and exacts usury from the Irish clans, and as a reward for his labours will one day possess the joys of the heavenly kingdom.

,,   VI As a faithful minister and messenger of God, he exhibits the form and action of an Apostle, practising what he preaches.

,,   VII God sent him, as He sent St. Paul, to lead the Gentiles to God.

,,   VIII And like St. Paul he bears the marks of the Lord Jesus on his body (stigmata Christi.)

,,   IX He feeds believers with celestial food and Gospel words.

,,   X He keeps his own flesh chaste, as the temple of the Holy Ghost, offering it as a living sacrifice, well pleasing to God. . .

,,   XIII He preaches the Name of the Lord with boldness to the Gentiles, offering to them the laver of salvation, praying daily for their sins, and offering worthy sacrifices to God.

,,   XIV He despises the glory of the world, counting it but as refuse compared to the Table of the Lord. Unmoved by the world's thunders he rejoices to suffer adversity for Christ.

,,   XV He is the good and faithful shepherd of the Gospel sheep, chosen by God to watch over His people, and to feed them with holy doctrine.

,,   XVII Clad in the wedding garment, as the king's messenger, he invites believers

to the marriage feast, drawing the heavenly wine in heavenly vessels and giving God's people drink from a spiritual chalice.

Stanza   XXI Christ has chosen him to be His vicar upon earth, to redeem innumerable men from the captivity of Satan.

,,   XXII He sings Hymns, the Apocalypse, and the Psalms, explaining them for the edification of God's people, teaching the doctrine of the Three Persons and the one Substance.

,,   XXIII He prays to God, without ceasing, day and night ; and hereafter, when he shall receive the reward of his great labours, he shall reign with the Apostles, a saint over Israel.

We have translated or paraphrased so much of this hymn because the universal acceptance of its genuineness, as a fifth century composition, is to a large extent based on internal evidence supplied by its style, substance or matter, and grammar. As to matter there is a total absence of the miraculous and legendary element which is found in all biographies of St. Patrick from the seventh century onwards, nor is there any reference to St. Patrick's visit to Rome, or to his Roman mission, or to his deference to Roman authority, of which we first find a trace in the seventh century, and of which the *Book of Armagh*, and, still more, later authorities are so full. As to style, in addition to a ruggedness of metre, there is a simplicity of style and diction which it is easier to observe than to describe, and which is redolent of antiquity. As to grammar, it is to be noticed that it speaks of St. Patrick throughout in the present tense, implying that it was written in that Saint's life-time, except indeed in the last verse, when his death is referred to, and then the present is exchanged for the future, and we get ' percepturus ' and ' regnabit.'

It should be noted that in this Hymn we find certain statements about St. Patrick in their original and credible form, which afterwards developed into exaggerated and improbable or impossible legends, e.g. in the last stanza but one we are told that St. Patrick chaunted Hymns with the Apocalypse and Psalms to God, a perfectly possible feat, which before the close of the seventh century had grown into the almost impossible statement that St. Patrick repeated all the Psalms and the Apocalypse of St. John, together with Hymns and Canticles, daily, and that he crossed himself 100 times in every hour of both day and night.

" Omnes Psalmos et apocalipsin Iohannis et omnia

kantica spiritalia scripturarum cotidie decantans, siue manens, aut in itinere pergens, tropeo etiam crucis in omni hora diei noctisque centies se signans, et ad omnes cruces quascumque vidisset orationis gratia de curru discendens declinabat." (Notes by Muirchu Maccu-Machtheni in the *Book of Armagh*, fol. 7. W.S. p. 293.)

In the last line of the last stanza, it is stated that hereafter St. Patrick will reign with the Apostles over Israel. This simple statement grew into the legend that at the last day St. Patrick will act as the Judge of the Irish race. Tirechan's Collections in the *Book of Armagh* speak of his 'Conductio omnium Sanctorum Hiberniae in die judicii.' (Fol. 15v.)

An old Gaelic life of St. Patrick, preserved in the *Lebar Brecc*, asserts "that though great is St. Patrick's honour still among men, it will be yet greater at the meeting of Doom, when he will be, like every chief Apostle, passing judgment on the men of Ireland to whom he preached." (Fol. 29v.)

It was said to be one of the three requests granted to St. Patrick before his death "ut Hybernenses omnes in die judicii a te judicenter" (*Vit. S. Patricii*, inter Bedae *Opp*. Basil. ii. p. 333. See also W.S. pp. 258, 260.)

There is evidence that this Hymn was known and amous at a very early date. The second of four petitions granted through an angel to St. Patrick before his death was :

"ut quicumque ymnum qui te de compossitus est, in die exitus de corpore cantauerit, tu iudicabis poenitentiam eius de suis peccatis." (Notes by Maccu-Machtheni in the *Book of Armagh*, fol. 8r. W.S. p. 296.)

The third among four ways of honouring St. Patrick's memory in all Irish monasteries and churches in the seventh century was, "Ymnum eius per totum tempus cantare." (Tirechan's Collections in the *Book of Armagh*, fol. 16r. W.S. p. 333.)

This is generally accepted as referring to the Hymn of St. Secundinus, because the vernacular Hymn, composed by St. Patrick himself, is referred to in the following line :

"Canticum eius scotticum semper canere." (*Ibid.*) Muirchu Maccu-Machtheni probably had the fourth stanza of St. Sechnall's Hymn in his mind when he wrote the words, which describe an angel's prophecy to St. Patrick, "dicens ei adesse tempus ut ueniret et aeuangelico rete nationes feras et barbaras, ad quas docendas misserat illum Deus, ut piscaret." (*Book of Armagh*, fol. 2r. W.S. p. 272.)

Lengthy Irish prefaces to this Hymn have been preserved in the *Lebar Brecc*, and in L.H.* They have

both been printed with translations (L.H. pp. 26-34 W.S. pp. 382-5) and we forbear from reproducing them here.

Metre. Each stanza in this Hymn consists of eight lines, which are trochaic dimeter acatalectic, and trochaic dimeter catalectic alternately.

It is an alphabetical Hymn consisting of twenty-three stanzas. Each stanza begins with one of the twenty-three letters of the Latin alphabet in succession.

This was a favourite device among Irish as well as other early Hymn writers. Sometimes each stanza commenced, as here, sometimes each line commenced with each letter of the alphabet in succession. Other examples in the Antiphonary of Bangor will be found in the Hymn of St. Comgall [14] the Hymn of St. Camelac [15] and the memorial Poem of the Abbots of Bangor [129.] In L.H. there are examples in the Hymn of St. Brigid, of which, however, only the last three stanzas (x, y, z) are preserved (p. 57) and in the Hymn of St. Columba (p. 205.) The well known Hymn of Sedulius, 'A solis ortus cardine,' is an alphabetical Hymn ; so is the less known Hymn 'Alma fulget in coelesti,' both of which occur in MS. Reg. A. xx. (see Index.) There can be little doubt that this alphabetical arrangement of verses or lines is in imitation of the Scriptural precedent afforded by Pss. xxiv. xxxi i. cxviii. Lamentations i. ii. iii. iv.

Title. The 'magister' in the MS. title is obviously a clerical error for 'magistri.' The title in L.H. is 'Incipit ymmus sancti patricii episcopi scotorum.' 'Magister' is a title given to more than one Irish saint e.g. to St. Finnian of Clonard by Adamnan (*Vit. S. Columba*, Lib. iii. cap. 4, where see Bishop Reeves' note) and to St. Patrick himself in the Kalendar of Oengus, if we may identify (though Oengus does not) Sen Patrick with St. Patrick of Armagh.

> 'senpatraic cing catha
> coemaite arsrotha'

e.g. 'old Patrick, champion of battle,
> lovable tutor of our sage.'

(August 24, Edit. W. Stokes, Dublin, 1880, pp. cxxv. cxxxiii.)

Stanza.	Line.	
I	1	'Audite.' According to the last paragraph in the Preface in the *Lebar Brecc* (p. 238b, lines 7, 8) this Hymn was written 'similitudine Moysi dicentis, Audite celi quae loquor (Deut. xxxii, 1) et Dauid dicentis, Audite haec omnes gentes (Ps. xlviii, 2.)' There seems to have been a special tendency among Irish Hymn-

Stanza. Line.

writers to begin their Hymns with
the word 'Audite.' For other specimens in the present MS. see the
Hymns of St. Comgall [14] and of St.
Camelac [15.] The verse now at the
end of the Hymn of St. Brigid, but
which the Irish Preface thereto states
to have been its first verse, commences thus :

Audite Virginis laudes sancta
quoque merita (L.H. pp. 57–8).

Two Hymns in praise of the Irish
Virgin St. Monenna preserved in
Cott. MS. Cleop. A ii. begin with the
same word e.g.

'Audite fratres facta' etc.

'Audite sancta studia virginum,'etc.

(J. Julian, *Dict. of Hymnology*, pp.
547, 551.)

An alphabetical Hymn in praise of
St. Peter has been printed by Mone
from an Irish MS. formerly at
Reichenau, now at Karlsruhe, which
he assigns to the eighth century. It
commences with the line :

'Audite fratres fama Petri.'

(*Lateinische Hymnen des Mittelalters*,
Freiburg, 1855, Tom. iii. p. 68.)

It may be added that the lamentation
of Sefla, Jephthah's daughter, begins

'Audite montes threnum meum'
(*Apocrypha Anecdota*, edit. M. R.
James, Cambridge, 1893, p. 182.)

I   5   'bonum ob actum,' for a summary of
the good actions and good characteristics ascribed to St. Patrick throughout this Hymn see introductory note.

„   8   There may be a reference here to St.
Paul's claim to be not a whit behind
the very chiefest Apostles (2 Cor. xi.
5.)

II   8   There is probably a reference in this
line to St. Matt. v. 16, where the Old
Latin reads 'magnificent' instead of
the Vulgate 'glorificent.'

III   4   'Petrum,' which is the original reading
of B. is also the reading of L.H.,
whereas Petrus is found in L.H.*
The former seems to be the prefer-
able reading as far as grammar and
sense are concerned.

Stanza. Line.

The comparison of St. Patrick to St.
Peter was a favourite one in the early
Irish Church. A table is prefixed
to the *Martyrology of Tallaght* in
which thirty-two Irish saints are told
off against the same number of saints
of the New Testament, or of Western
Christendom. In this list 'Patricius'
is equated with Petrus Apostolus.
(L.H. p. 69.) The same equation is
made in a similar list preserved in the
Book of Leinster. (Facsimile Edition,
Dublin, 1880, p. [370] 3rd col. line
5.)

III   7   'Adversum' must be taken as a sub-
stantive, equivalent to 'adversitatem.'
The reading in both L.H. and L.H.*
is 'adversus.'

This stanza is based on St. Matth. xvi.
18.

IV   1–8 There is a reference in this stanza to St.
Matth. iv. 19. The acquaintance of
Muirchu Maccu-Machtheni with this
verse has been already referred to in
the introductory note.

V   1–8 This stanza is based on St. Matth. xxv.
14–30. The construction of the last
four lines is difficult. We may bear
in mind that according to the Preface
to this Hymn in L.H.* "there are
three places therein, in which 'are
'three words without meaning, inserted for the sake of the rhythm.'"

VI   8   The first word of this line is torn : it
may be 'fructu' or 'factu.'

VII   5–8 There is a reference here to Gal. i. 12,
16. St. Patrick is called, in the *Tripartite Life*, "Lestar togai frifuacra
firinni amal Pol nabstal" i.e. a choice
vessel for proclaiming righteousness,
like Paul the Apostle. (W.S. pp.
256–7.) In the *Book of Obits* it is
said, "Sicut Paulus apostolus gentium
apellatur, sic Sanctus Patricius Scotorum apostolus nuncupatur." (Dublin, 1844, p. 96.)

VIII   5, 6 There is a reference here to Gal. vi. 17,
where St. Paul says : 'Ego enim
stigmata Domini Jesu in corpore
meo porto,' 'cujusque' must be bad
Latin for 'Quique,' the reference

Stanza. Line.

being to St. Patrick, whereas the 'cujus' in line 7 refers to Christ. See [94] line 8.

IX   1–8   This stanza is based on Exod. xvi. 15, and St. Matth. xv. 33–8.

     3, 4   Either the 'Quam' in line 3 must be altered to 'Qui' or the 'que' in line 4 must be rejected as superfluous.

X   7, 8   These two lines are based on Rom. xii. 1.

XI   8   This stanza is based on St. Matth. v. 14, 15.

XII   1–8   Compare the sentiment expressed here with the epitaph on St. Gregory the Great preserved by Bede, *Hist. Eccles.* Lib. ii. cap. i.

       Implebatque actu quicquid sermone docebat,

       Esset ut exemplum mystica verba loquens.

     6   'Formamque' may be regarded as a mistake for 'formaque' the ablative case being required.

XIII   1–8   This stanza may be interpreted as enumerating four chief means of grace ; Preaching, Baptism, Prayer, and the Eucharist.

"   8   The 'que' here is misplaced being in sense connected with 'pro quibus' in line 7.

"   5, 6   With regard to the frequency of prayer St. Patrick himself tells us in his Confession : "postquam in Hiberione deueneram cotidie atque pecora pascebam, et frequens in die orabam, ... ut in die una usque ad centum orationes et in nocte prope similiter. (H. and S. vol. iii. pt. ii, p. 300.) See stanza xxiii; see also [14] stanza xxii. and [15] stanza iv.

"   7, 8   The 'ut' and the 'que' in the last two lines, though required by the metre, are not wanted by the sense. See note to stanza v.

We suppose that 'hostias' refers to the Eucharistic Sacrifice in view of the reference to the 'Mensa Domini,' 'The Lord's Table,' in the next stanza.

XIV   1–8   This stanza is to be compared with Phil. iii. 7, 8. In L.H. there is an Irish

gloss over this line which translates or glosses it thus "in comparison of which he also estimates all things as chaff.' This makes Dr. Todd suggest that 'mensa' ought to be taken in the sense of 'mensura' and as 'mensa' is an impossible contraction for 'mensura,' he proposes to read the line thus, 'cuncta ad cujus mensuram.' 'Mensura' occurs in full in [60] line 2. We prefer to think that the writer of the gloss was mistaken ; and to interpret 'mensa' of 'the Lord's Table.' The word was not unknown in Irish in that connection. In the *Lebar Brecc* we find the words: 'do méis Dé .i. don altoir noib,' which are 'off the table of God, that is, the holy altar' [Fol. 126.] As quoted by E. M. O'Curry. (*Lectures on the MS. materials of ancient Irish history*, Dublin, 1878, p. 377.)

XIV   4   quiscilia MS. ciscilia L.H.

XV   1–8   Throughout this stanza there seems to be a reminiscence of such passages as St. John x. 14 ; xv. 13 ; xxi. 15. Variations from the MS. text have been introduced into the latter part of this verse.

XVI   6   'vestibus.' The 'vestes,' like the 'annona,' are of course metaphorical, and may probably be explained by reference to such passages as St. Matth. xxii. 11 ; Rev. xvi. 15.

XVII   1–4   The imagery here is drawn from the parable of the marriage of the king's son in St. Matth. xxii. 1–14.

"   5, 6   An Irish gloss in L.H.* interprets 'vinum' of 'the wine of the doctrine of the Gospel,' but we are inclined to see here, as well as in the last two lines of this stanza, a reference to the Eucharistic chalice.

"   7, 8   See note [2] stanza xiii. line 4.

"   8   'spiritale poculum.' Compare the expression 'spirituale sacrificium' for the Eucharist in the *Stowe Missal,* and in a 'Postcommunio' for St. Patrick's Day in the Corpus and Rosslyn Irish Missals. (W. pp. 237, 271.) The phrase 'spirituale

Stanza.   Line.

poculum' occurs in the following passage in a Mozarabic Preface for *ii. Domin. post Oct. Epiphan.* " Nam licet verum corpus edatur, et sanguis manifestissimus hauriatur, nullus tamen horror incutitur, cum salus animarum in spirituali cibo et poculo ministratur. (P.L. Tom. lxxxv. col. 249.)

XVIII   7, 8   These two lines refer to a popular but erroneous interpretation of the name ' Israel' as meaning ' Vir aut mens videns Deum.' (P.L. Tom. xxiii, col. 788.) This interpretation is given in the work *De interpretatione nominum Hebraeorum,*' attributed to St. Jerome, who elsewhere, however, gives the true meaning of the word ' princeps cum Deo.' (*Quaest Hebraeae in Genesim* cap. xxxii. vv. 27, 28. P.L. Tom. xxxiii. col. 988.) Claudius of Turin said : " Israel Dei, id est, eos qui vere ad visionem Dei praeparantur.' (*Enarratio in Epistolam D. Pauli ad Galatas* in cap. vi. P.L. Tom. civ. col. 910.)

The expression ' Israel Dei ' in Gal. vi. 16, is glossed in the eighth or ninth century Irish MS. of St. Paul's Epistles at Würzburg ".i. sanctos videntes Deum et comalnatar toil dé," " The saints who see God and who fulfil God's will.' (W. Stokes, *The Old-Irish Glosses at Würzburg and Carlsruhe.* Hertford, 1887, pp. 120, 301.)

In the Benediction at the close of the Liturgy of St. Clement the phrase occurs 'ο Θεὸν Ἰσραήλ τοῦ ἀληθινῶν ὁρῶντον.' (Hamm. p. 23.)

XIX   7   This line is corrupt. The reading in L.H. is ' sed coeleste salluintur.' Mr. Whitley Stokes prints ' sed celesti sallientur' from L.H.* (W.S. p. 388), but the right reading would seem to be ' sed coelesti saliantur.' The reference is to St. Matt. v. 13.

XX   1-8   The whole of this stanza seems to be suggested by St. Matt. xiii. 1-9.

   7   The ' que' is again superfluous. ' Quorumque' stands for ' Et eorum.'

XXI   2   ' vicarium.' It is noteworthy that the title ' vicar of Christ' is here given

to St. Patrick. Compare the corresponding verse in the Hymn of St. Comgall [14.]

XXI   7   ' zaboli' see part 1. Introd. p. xxv. note. ' zabuli ' L.H. ' stabuli ' L.H.*

XXII   1   ' cum apocalypsi.' The following have been suggested as possible reasons why the Apocalypse may have had an especial attraction for St. Patrick and other Celtic saints. Its Johannine authorship, the Celtic Church, through the Gallican, claiming a special connection with St. John ; the prominence therein of the number 'seven,' which is also prominent in Celtic ecclesiology and literature. (T. Olden, *Epistles and Hymns of St. Patrick,* London, 1894, pp. 38–9.)

St. Patrick is said to have built seven churches at the river Fochaine (W.S. p. 154), and in Cianacht (*Ibid.* p. 160), and in Hui Tuirtri (*Ibid.* p. 168.)

In an Irish Homily on St. Patrick, preserved in the *Lebar Brec,* the devils are recorded to have been expelled from Ireland by St. Patrick for seven days, seven months, and seven years. (*Ibid.* p. 476.)

„   2   salmosque MS. ψalmosque L.H. *

XXIII   4   For St. Patrick's habits of prayer see stanza xiii. lines 5, 6.

„   For the inference as to the date of the composition of this Hymn based upon the two future tenses ' percepturus ' and ' regnabit ' see introductory note.

Anthems. In lieu of the two anthems which have been added to the Hymn in B. the following sets of three Anthems are found in the two copies of the Irish *Book of Hymns.*

in L.H.

1. In memoria eterna erit iustus,
   Ab auditione mala non timebit.
2. Patricii laudes semper dicamus,
   Ut nos cum illo defendat Deus.
3. Hibernenses omnes clamant ad te pueri,
   Veni sancte patricii saluos nos facere.

in L.H.*

1. Patricii laudes semper dicamus,
   Ut nos cum illo defendat deus.
2. Hibernenses omnes clamant ad te pueri,
   Veni sancte patricii saluos nos facere.

3. Patricius sanctus episcopus
   Oret pro nobis omnibus,
   Et misereatur protenus
   Peccata quae commisimus.

The anthem L.H. 1 is taken from Ps. cxi. 7.

The anthem L.H. 3 is based upon the following story in the *Tripartite Life of St. Patrick* :

"Quotiescumque enim somni quietem capere cupiebat, videbatur sibi ante oculos continuo prospicere Hibernorum insulam, ita quod perciperet sermonem et clamorem puerorum in sylua Fochladensi dicentium : 'Veni sancte puer Patrici, et inter nos ambula '" (W.S. p. 25.)

An extravagant version of the same story is told in the Notes on St. Fiacc's Hymn (*Ibid.* p. 421.)

[14]

'Hymnus Sancti Comgilli Abbatis nostri.' This is an alphabetical Hymn of twenty-three stanzas, to which an introductory stanza has been prefixed. Each stanza consists of eight lines, except the second stanza, which consists of ten lines. The metre is iambic dimeter acatalectic. Every line in almost every stanza either begins, or ends, or both begins and ends with the same letter. It was impossible to carry out this principle in its completeness throughout a long Hymn, but it has been carried out to an extent which leaves it still a very remarkable *tour de force*.

Stanza.	Introd.			
I	All lines begin with			'a'
II	Two ,,	,,	,,	'b'
III	Two ,,	,,	,,	'c'
IV	All ,,	,,	,,	'd'
V	Three,,	,,	,,	'e'
VI	Two ,,	,,	,,	'f'
VII	Two ,,	,,	,,	'g'
VIII	Three,,	,,	,,	'h'
IX	Three,,	,,	,,	'i'
X	Three,,	,,	,,	'k'
XI	Two ,,	,,	,,	'l'
XII				
XIII				
XIV	Every other line begins with 'o'			
XV				
XVI	,,	,,	,,	,, 'q'
XVII	Two lines begin with			'r'
XVIII	Two ,,	,,	,,	's'
XIX				
XX	Three ,,	,,	,,	'u'
XXI	Two ,,	,,	,,	'x'
XXII				
XXIII				
Refrain.				

Stanza.	Introd.				
I	All · lines end with			'e' (ae)
II	,, ,,	,,	,,	'a'
III	,, ,,	,,	,,	'm'
IV	,, ,,	,,	,,	'm'
V	, ,,	,,	,,	's'
VI	,, ,,	,,	,,	'o'
VII	,, ,,	,,	,,	'e'
VIII	,, ,,	,,	,,	's'
IX	,, ,,	,,	,,	's'
X	,, ,,	,,	,,	's'
XI	,, ,,	,,	,,	'm'
XII	,, ,,	,,	,,	'e'
XIII	,, ,,	,,	,,	'm'
XIV	,, ,,	,,	,,	's'
XV	,, ,,	,,	,,	'm'
XVI	,, ,,	,,	,,	'e' (i)
XVII	,, ,,	,,	,,	'a'
XVIII	,, ,,	,,	,,	'm'
XIX	Four lines end with 's,' four with 'a'			
XX	All lines end with			'm'
XXI	,, ,,	,,	,,	'a'
XXII	,, ,,	,,	,,	'm'
XXIII	,, ,,	,,	,,	'o'
XXIV	,, ,,	,,	,,	'e'
Refrain	,, ,,	,,	,,	'a'

It may be noticed that in the Anglo-Saxon *Troparly of Ethelred* all the lines or many of the lines in the majority of the Proses are made to end with the letter 'a,' but there does not appear to be any attempt to regulate the letters with which the lines commence. (Surtees Society Publications, vol. lx. pp. 285–318.) See also a Sequence for 'Fer. iv. post Pentecosten' in the *York Missal* (*Ibid.* vol. lix. p. 156.) For other Irish specimens of such arrangement see the 'Versiculi familiae Benchuir' [95] and the poem 'in memoriam abbatum nostrorum' [129] further on in this Bangor book.

St. Comgall. In addition to the facts mentioned about this Saint in Part I. p. ix. it is worthy of mention that he is invoked in the following places :

(a) Among the 'Sancti Monachi' in a ninth century 'Libellus precum' published in Mart. (Tom. iii. Lib. iv. cap. xxxiv. p. 238.) This is a Fleury MS. exhibiting traces of Celtic influence, and probably therefore coming originally from Brittany. A list of the Celtic Saints invoked in it will be found in a note in the appendix to this volume. See p. 96.

(b) Among the 'Sancti Abbates,' after St. Benedict in the Culdee Litany, connected with Dunkeld in Scotland, and printed in H. and S. vol. ii. Pt. i. p. 278.

(e) Among the 'Sancti Confessores,' next before St. Antony, in the Litany for 'Fer. iv. in xl.' in the *Aberdeen Breviary.* (London, 1854. Pars hyemalis,. fol. lxxxi.)

Stanza   Line.

Introductory stanza. This stanza seems to have been composed for and pre-fixed to the following Hymn in order to attach that Hymn to St. Comgall. The Hymn itself is general in its phraseology. It contains no bio-graphical details about St. Comgall, and no such special description of his character that it might not be applied with equal propriety to al-most any saint, unless stanza xviii is an exception, *q.v.*

Refrain   2   This verb, as similar verbs in stanza xx. line 2, &c., is in the past tense, and there is no indication, as there was in the last stanza of [13] that the Hymn was written in the life time of the saint whom it commem-orates.

I   1   For Hymns beginning with the word 'Audite' see note to [13] stanza i. line 1.

"   "   'pantes ta erga.' For a list of Greek words introduced into the Latin text of this Service-book see Part I. Introd. p. xix. § 14. See also [10] note to stanza xiii. line 1.

"   3   The MS. form 'anthleta' is the usual Irish form of athleta (see W. p. 260. note 60a.) 'Anthletae' are invoked in the Lorica of Gildas, line 22. (*Book of Nunnaminster*, ed. by W. de G. Birch, London, 1889. p. 91.) The Greek form is 'αθλητὴν (Ep. S. Ignatii *ad Polycarpum* cap. ii) or ἀθλοφόρος, *Lit. of St. James* (C. A. Swainson, *Greek Liturgies*, London, 1884, pp. 234-5.)

IV   6   'Stefanus' (MS.) is presumably to be taken as a proper name, 'the holy Stephen of God.'

"   "   'agius.' See note to [10] stanza xiii. line 1.

V   6   'Carus' MS. but the sense evidently requires 'carum.' The scribe may have been misled by the 'pignus' in line 7.

Stanza.   Line.

'Carus' is a specially Ephesine epithet and occurs frequently in the Old-Gallican Liturgy. (W. p. 258 n. 43.) The 'Deo cari' are mentioned by Tertullian (*De Poenitentia* cap. ix) and by Pseudo-Dionysius. (*De Coelesti Hierarchia* cap. vii. § 7.) The word 'carus' only occurs twice in the Vulgate, viz. : in Thren. i. 2 ; 2 Macc. xiv. 24. It never occurs in the Roman Breviary or Missal, except where Thren. i. 2, is read as in 'Lect. i. in Coena Domini.' It occurs several times in the Bangor Antiphonary. See Index. It is interesting to find St. John the Divine entitled 'Domini carus' in a trope of Gallican origin in an English Service Book. (W.T. p. 9.)

IX   1-8   This description of St. Comgall as learned in the Scriptures, and care-ful in the administration of the Sacraments, recalls the similar de-scription of St. Patrick in [13] stanzas xvii, xviii, &c.

"   8   'carus.' See note to stanza v. line 6.

XII   1   'apprendit,' a shortened form of 'appre-hendit' which would make the line too long by a syllable. 'bradium' is probably a mistake for 'brabium,' a late Latin form of the Greek 'βραβίον.'

XIII   1-4   Compare the enumeration of 'martyres, confessores, virgines, anchoritae, monachi, episcopi, abbates catholici' in a Collect in the *Stowe Missal* (W. p. 244.)

"   5   'synodum' gen. plur.

XIV   1, 2   There seems to be a reference here to St. Matt. xvi. 18.

XV   1-8   The reference throughout this verse is to Jer. i. 10. This makes us con-clude that 'eremiae' in line 7 stands for the name of the prophet, and not for 'eremitae.'

XVII   5   This line occurs again in stanza xix line 4.

"   7   'gratiam' MS. to preserve the uniform ending of the lines of this verse in 'm.'

Stanza.	Line.	
XVIII	1-8	This stanza may preserve some personal recollection of the habits or of the deathbed of St. Comgall.
,,	7, 8	Acts x. 1, 2.
XIX	3	'Caram Deo' see stanza v. line 6.
,,	4	See stanza xvii. line 5.
,,	7	The metre requires two more syllables; some such word as 'pergens' has been left out. We have not found any authority for the MS. form 'domuens.' Is it an amalgamation of 'domans' and 'pergens'? Possibly we should put the comma after 'insaniam,' and treat 'domuens' as a corruption of 'domum habens.'
XX	4	This line is the fourth line of the refrain of this Hymn, as given in full after the introductory verse.
XXI	1	The MS. form of Christus is retained as essential to the alphabetical sequence of the verses.
,,	3	This is equivalent to styling St. Comgall the Vice-gerent of Christ, in the same way that St. Patrick was called the Vicar of Christ. See [13] stanza xxi. line 2.
XXII	1, 2	'ymnum immolabat.' Compare the expressions 'immolatione per psalterium' in [93] 'psalterium immolate' in [100]. There is Vulgate authority for such a use of 'immolare' in Ps. xlix. 14. It helps to explain the term 'Immolatio' which, as well as 'Contestatio,' is frequently found as a title instead of 'Praefatio' in the Old-Gallican Liturgy.
,,	3, 4	'orans.' Compare the habit of continuous prayer attributed to St. Patrick in [13] stanza xxiii. See also [15] lines 13, 14.
,,	5	See note to refrain, line 2. Does 'sub numero' here mean 'in rhythm'? or is there a reference to the 'numerus signatorum' in Apoc. vii. 4?
Refrain.	4	There is an 's' on the margin, with a mark of abbreviation over it, after the last line of the refrain, to which it is difficult to assign any meaning.

The anthem or collect after the refrain may be intended to be a rudely rhyming anthem, as in the case of the anthems at the end of [13].

[15]

'Hymnus Sancti Camelaci.' This is an alphabetical Hymn of twenty-four lines, each line beginning with a separate letter of the alphabet. The twenty-fourth line is accounted for by the insertion of an extra line beginning with 'p,' and not in regular alphabetical order, between the line beginning with 'x' and the line beginning with 'y.' The 'z' of the last line is not at its commencement but is buried in the word 'elizaro.'

There are eight or seven syllables in the lines, which are trochaic dimeter acatalectic and trochaic dimeter catalectic alternately.

Very little is known about the saint who is commemorated in this Hymn. His name, Camulacus, occurs in the list of Bishops ordained by St. Patrick in Tirechan's Collections in the *Book of Armagh* (Fol. 9 b. W.S. p. 304.) In the same document the following incident is narrated in connection with him. It is said of St. Patrick: 'Et uenit per flumen Ethne in duas Tethbias et ordinauit Melum episcopum, et aecclessiam Bili fundauit, et ordinauit Gosactum, filium Milcon Maccu Booin, quem nutriuit in seruitute septem annorum, et mittens Camulacum Commiensium in Campum Cuini, et digito illi indicauit locum de cacumine Graneret, id est, aecclessiam Raithin.' (*Book of Armagh*, Foll. 10 b, 11 a. W.S. pp. 310, 311.) For the identification of the persons and places named in this passage except 'Camulacum Commiensium,' see notes in the *Analecta Bollandiana*, Tom. ii. p. 44. But no one has hitherto offered any explanation of the epithet 'Commiensium' or 'Cumiensis' as the word stands in the Antiphonary of Bangor. The nationality of Camulacus or Camelacus is uncertain. This name 'Caomlach' or 'Caomhelach' means 'the gentle' or 'the kindly one,' and has an original Irish ring about it, but then is it the Irish equivalent for Camulacus, or is Camulacus, or Camelacus, the Latinized form of Caomlach? St. Camelac is not commemorated in the *Martyrologies of Oengus*, or *Tallaght*, or *Gorman*, but in the *Martyrology of Donegal* there is this entry.

Nov. 3, 'Caomlach o' Raithin' [Caemhlach of Raithin, now Rahen, in the barony of Ballycowan, King's county.]

If the word 'Commiensium' is formed from his Irish tribe or native place, there is a place in the northern part of co. Kilkenny, called 'The Three Commons,' which may have some connection with it. (*Annals of the Four Masters*, A.D. 870. 2nd Edit. Dublin, 1856, vol. i, p. 516, note l.)

If St. Camelac was a foreigner who accompanied St. Patrick into Ireland, the Commienses might be the inhabitants of some district in Gaul.

I

The lines of this Hymn run on continuously in the MS., but the sense seems to suggest a division into stanzas of four lines each.

Stanza.	Line.	
I	1	For Irish Hymns beginning with 'Audite' see note to [13] stanza i. line 1.
"	3	'Cumiensis.' See note to title.
II	3	The metre requires 'gratiasque.'
IV	1, 2	Compare the habits of continual prayer attributed to St. Patrick in [13] stanza xxiii, and to St. Cumgall in [14] stanza xxii.
	2	The perfect tense used from this point onward (for we have ventured to alter 'regnabit' into 'regnavit' in the twenty-third line, treating it as an instance of the confusion between 'b' and 'u') prove that this Hymn was composed after the death of St. Camelac.
VI	3	ymparadiso MS. The 'y' is introduced here as the first letter, in order to preserve the alphabetical sequence of the lines.
"	4	'elizaro' MS. The form 'Eleazarus' for 'Lazarus' occurs in the *Codex Usserianus alter*, an early Irish Biblical MS. (T. K. Abbott, *Evangeliorum Versio Antehieronymiana*, Dublin, 1884. Pars posterior, pp. 571, 573.) We have previously called attention to the fact that the 'z' with which the last line ought to begin is buried in this word.

[16]

One would have expected a marginal cross to have been placed before this Collect, to denote the commencement of a series of Collects for the Day and Night Hours, or, if not here, then before [17] where a set of such Collects commences, no. [16] being perhaps, an additional Collect thrown in to fill up space, when the scribe found that the Hymn of St. Camelac did not occupy the whole of fol. 17v. For the number and arrangement of such Hours at Bangor see Introd. § 3.

'Secunda' as the equivalent of 'Prima,' the usual title of the first of the Day-Hours is a very ancient title, but has now gone out of use. It is found in the *Missale Gallicanum* (p. 179), also in C. C. C. C. MS.

272, a ninth century *Rheims Psalter*, where the following collect occurs among *Orationes ad secundam :*

'Domine Deus omnipotens, qui nos ad hanc oram secundam per nocturnas caligines incolomes peruenire fecisti, conserua nos hodie per omnium orarum spatia et momenta temporis, et in tua gratia nos semper fac permanere.'

The office of Prime was not an original part of the scheme of the Divine Office, but was introduced, first at Bethlehem at the end of the fourth century, to fill the gap between Mattins and Terce (Migne P.L. Tom. l. col. 1135, note.)

There may have been room on the last part of this leaf for the usual concluding formula 'Qui regnas.'

[17]

For 'secunda' see note to [16.]

This is the first of a complete series of rhyming collects for the Day and Night Hours. Metrical devotions, except in the form of Hymns, are very rare. Their form here suggests that these collects may have been intended for choral recitation as a kind of 'responsoria' at the end of their respective Hours, but we can adduce nothing in support, much less in proof of such a suggestion. It is made by Dr. O. Seebass, *Columba von Luxeuil's Klosterregel*, Dresden, 1883, p. 27.

For something analogous to these metrical prayers at Bangor, we may refer to an ancient Gallican Mass written throughout in hexameter lines (*Missale Richenovense*, Missa viii. p. 21) to the metrical Litanies for Rogation-tide published from tenth century MSS. by Gerbert (*Monumenta Vet. Liturg. Aleman.* St. Blaise, 1779, pars. ii. pp. 87–91) to a set of 'Benedictiones nocturnales ante Lectiones' written in rude hexameters in the *Office Book of the Abbot of Evesham* (edited by H. A. Wilson for the Henry Bradshaw Society in 1893, coll. 55–7) to the numerous metrical Tropes in W. T.; to the metrical 'Communiones' which occur sparsely in the Sarum, York, and Hereford Missals (J. Julian, *Dict. of Hymnology*, London, 1892, *sub voc.* 'Communio,' where see also 'Offertorium,' 'Trope.')

It is to be noticed that the dotted ornamentation of capital letters which has prevailed hitherto is discontinued throughout this set of Collects.

Line 1. 'Te.' See Introd. § 5 (g.)

[18]

The grammar would appear to require 'regnat' but it has not been thought worth while to alter the text.

[19]

'Ad sextam.' 'In cruce positus.' We have here a very early, if not the earliest Service Book authority for assignation of the various Night and Day Hours to commemorate and correspond to the incidents of our Lord's Passion and Death.

'Dominus noster Jesus Christus . . . . . extitit matutinalibus a Judaeis captus,

prima	coram Pontio Pilato judice ductus,
tertia	illusus, corona spinea coronatus,
sexta	cruci ab ipsis Judaeis perfidis conclav. atus,
nona	in cruce pendens mortuus,
vespertina	de ipsa cruce depositus,
completoria	traditus sepulturae.

Sicque circa ejus flagellationes, passionem, et ipsius sanctissimi corporis mysterium erat tota expedita dies ipsa.' (*Constitt. Dni. Johannis de Sancto Paulo Archiepiscopi Dublinensis de jejunio passionis* A.D. 1351. Wilkins' *Concilia*, London, 1737, Tom. iii. p. 19.) See the 'Orationes de Passione Domini, respondentes septem Horis Canonicis (*Brev. Roman.* ex Ducali Campidonensi Typographeo, 1705, pars Aestiv. p. 125.)

According to John Cassian the sixth hour, as an Hour of Prayer, commemorated (1) our Lord's ascent of the cross ; (2) the vision of St. Peter recorded in Acts x. 9 ; " Hora autem sexta immaculata hostia Dominus noster atque Salvator oblatus est Patri, crucemque pro totius mundi salute conscendens, humani generis peccata delevit . . . Eadem quoque Petro hora in excessu mentis vocatio gentium omnium per submissionem vasis evangelici delati coelitus, &c." (*De Institutis Coenobiorum*, Lib. iii. cap. 3.)

[20]

'Ad nonam.' Instead of commemorating the death of Christ upon the cross at the ninth hour (see note to [19]) this Collect refers to the visit of the angel to Cornelius at that hour.

Cassian mentions three events as commemorated by the selection of the ninth Hour as an Hour of Prayer (1) Our Lord's descent into hell ; (2) the vision of Cornelius recorded in Acts x. 3 ; (3) the visit of SS. Peter and John to the temple recorded in Acts iii. 1. " Hora vero nona inferna penetrans, inextricabiles tartari tenebras coruscatione sui splendoris extinxit, &c. . . . Eadem quoque hora Cornelius centurio in precibus solita devotione persistens, commemorationem orationum et eleemosynarum suarum ante Dominum factam, angelo sibi colloquente, cognoscit . . . Petrus autem et Ioannes ascendebant in templum, ad horam

orationis nonam." (*De Institutis Coenobiorum*, Lib. iii. cap. 3.)

[21]

'Ad vesper.' MS. 'Ad vesperas' M. but 'Ad vespertinam' is suggested by the first word of the Collect, and this form of the title is written in full on fol. 18v. [31.] There is no reference here to the taking down of our Lord's body from the cross. See note to [19.] Vespers are not here followed by Compline, as the Hour of our Lord's burial, nor does there appear to be either here or elsewhere in the MS. any reference to that service. But see note to [22.]

[22]

'Collectio ad initium noctis.' This Hour of Prayer is thus named in the Rule of St. Columbanus, which does not mention vespers, but passes on from the mention of the 'Horae diurnae,' to the mention of this service 'ad initium noctis,' or 'First nocturn :' " Per divinas terni Psalmi horas, pro operum interpositione, statuti sunt a senioribus nostoris . . . Ad initium vero noctis duodecim Psalmi, ad mediumque noctis duodecim similiter psalluntur, ad matutinum vero his deni bisque bini per tempora brevium, ut dictum est, noctium &c." (*Regula S. Columbani*, cap. vii. Holst. Pars. ii. p. 94.) Menard interpreted this phrase, as found in the ' Regula S. Columbani ' to be equivalent to Compline 'Ad initium noctis' 'quod respondet Completorio.' (Menardi, *Notae in S. Benedicti Anianensis Concordiam Regularum*. P.L. Tom. ciii. col. 884. See Mart. Tom. iv. p. 37.) But there is no support for this conjecture, and no proof that such an office as Compline was known to the monks of Bangor, or recognized in the monastic order of St. Columbanus. Compline had, however, been recognized, and Psalms had been assigned to it, in the Rules of St. Isidore of Seville, ob. 636, cap. 7, St. Aurelian of Arles (545-53, cap. 35) and in the Rule of St. Benedict, who died in 543 (Capp. 17, 18.) There is no known reference to Compline before his time.

Collects 'ad initium noctis' occur again in [32] [33] where see notes.

[23]

Line 2. 'nocte orantes media.' This line settles the fact that this second Nocturn or night-hour was at midnight. See also [37.]

[24]

'Ad matutinam.' This is the last of the night-hours, and includes, though it does not consist exclusively of, Lauds.

Line 2. The line 'te ter sanctum laudantibus' is

suggestive of the fifth verse of 'Te Deum laudamus' or of the Trisagion.

Line 4. The line 'sacris hymnorum cantibus' is suggestive of Lauds.

[25]

Line 1. 'Gallorum cantibus.' This expression bears two meanings. It sometimes means midnight, and sometimes early morning about 3 a.m.

The first of the three Christmas Masses was entitled 'Missa in Gallicantu' (Sarum) or 'Missa ad pullorum cantum' (*Vetus Missale Romanum*, Romae, Ed. sec. 1756 p. 17.) This Mass was almost universally celebrated at midnight, or near midnight, for which 'gallicantus' is evidently the equivalent. But in a long passage (Lib. iv. cap. xii. § 19. p. 35) Martene has shown that there was a 'primus gallorum cantus' and a 'secundus gallorum cantus,' and that the expression 'gallicantus' refers sometimes to one sometimes to the other, that is to say, either to midnight or to 3 a.m. We subjoin a passage in which 'pullorum cantus' evidently bears the second meaning: "In officio nocturno uno tempore psalluntur ante pullorum cantum in hyeme nocturni, dicente propheta 'media nocte surgebam ad confitendum tibi' . . . Pullorum cantus declinantis est terminus noctis qui mox diem parit." (*Regula Magistri* cap. 33. Holst. Pars ii. p. 230.)

'Gallorum cantus' evidently means 3 a.m. in the Bangor MS.

Line 3. The MS. reading 'ob' in the third line makes neither sense nor grammar, and we have substituted 'ut' as probably the true reading. There is nothing in the context to account for the scribe writing 'ob.'

[26]

The language of this prayer clearly points to daybreak, or about 3 a.m., as the hour of mattins or 'hora matutina.'

[27]

'Ad secundam.' A new set of day and night hour Collects begins here. Its commencement is marked by a marginal cross. The dotted ornamentation of the capital letters which had been omitted throughout the previous set is now resumed. For the title 'secunda' see note to [16.] Note the phrase 'in hac hora prima diei,' in line 2.

[28]

'Ad horam tertiam.' Instead of one of the scenes in the Passion (see note to [19]), the descent of the Holy Ghost on the Apostles on the Feast of

Pentecost, as recorded in Acts ii. 13, is commemorated in this Collect. Thus Cassian says: 'Hora namque tertia repromissus olim per prophetas Spiritus Sanctus super Apostolos in orationum officio constitutos descendisse primitus comprobatur.' (*De Institutis Coenobiorum*, Lib. iii. cap. 3.)

[29]

See note to [19.]

[30]

Line 3. 'divina miracula.' This expression may refer to the earthquake, and the graves opened, and the veil of the Temple rent at the death of Christ. See note to [20.]

[31]

This collect contains a reference to Ps. cxl. 2. This Psalm is sung daily at Vespers in the Greek and Armenian offices, and was perhaps sung daily at the same service at an early date in the West. It is now sung at Friday Vespers in the Roman, and at Thursday Vespers in the Benedictine Breviary. See Apost. Constitt. lib. ii. cap. 59.

[32]

See note to [22.]

[33]

The language of this Collect 'ad initium noctis,' implies a time coinciding with the close of day and the fall of night, a time which might be earlier but could hardly be later than 9 p.m. See note to [22.]

[34]

'Ad pacem celebrandam.' The devotions accompanying the bestowal of the Pax here are two anthems taken from Ps. cv. 6, and from Ps. cxviii. 165, each anthem being followed by a collect.

The first anthem 'Injuste egimus' &c. which also occurs in Judith vii. 19, but which is evidently there, as here, a quotation from Ps. cv. 6, is part of the Psalmellus at Mass on Sexagesima Sunday in the Ambrosian Rite. (*Antiphonarium Ambrosianum Vetus*, p. 8, appendix to *Missale Ambrosianum Vetus*, edit. Ceriani, no place or date.) It also occurs among the Suffrages at the end of the Litany in the *Sarum Breviary*. (Cambridge reprint, 1879. Fasc. II. col. 253.)

The second anthem occurs as a Communio in the *Stowe Missal* (W. p. 242.)

From the language of the second Collect, which embodies a reference to Ps. xc. 5 ('ut non timeamus a timore nocturno') we may infer that Ps. xc. was used at the service at which the Pax was given, entitled 'ad initium noctis,' and that the Pax here is part of that

Service, and is connected with the Divine Office, and not with the Liturgy.

The Pax is not found in connection with any of the Day or Night Hours in any Western Breviary, whether secular or monastic, at the present day. A Benediction at the end of Compline is an ancient custom which has survived. That in the Benedictine Breviary runs thus : ' *Benedictio*. Benedicat et custodiat nos omnipotens et misericors Dominus, Pater, et Filius, et Spiritus Sanctus. Amen.'

This is also given in the Roman Breviary, and in the Sarum Breviary, in the latter case ending with ' Dominus.'

But to find something in Western Breviaries resembling the Pax we have to go back as far as the Breviary of the Humiliati, published in 1548. There after the Collect ' Visita quaesumus &c.' comes this rubric : *Hinc praepositus vel hebdomadarius det benedictionem omnibus in choro stantibus, capite inclinato, dicendo.* ' Pax, et benedictio Dei Patris omnipotentis, et Filii, et Spiritus Sancti descendat super vos, et maneat semper vobiscum. Ŗ. Amen.' *Mox incipiatur Salutatio ad Virginem.* Salve regina misericordiae, &c. (From a paper by Dr. J. Wickham Legg in the *Transactions of the St. Paul's Ecclesiological Society*, vol. ii. part v. London, 1890, p. 281.) It may be said that the presence of the word ' Pax ' in the above salutation does not necessarily involve the formal bestowal of the Pax. This is true, but its presence is almost certainly a survival from, and a reminiscence of, a time when the ceremonial of the Pax was in existence. An examination of the ancient Celtic surviving formulae of benediction commencing with the word ' Pax,' shows them to be connected with the actual bestowal of the Kiss of Peace. *Book of Dimma* (W. p. 170); *St. Gall MS.* 1394 (W. p. 177); *Stowe Missal* (W. p. 242.) There may be an allusion to the now obsolete Pax at Compline in the following passage in the *Mitrale* of Sicardus : ' Hae tres horae (i.e. Laudes Matutinae, Vesperae, Completorium) pertinent ad octavam, scilicet Domini resurrectionem, qui mane surrexit, in vespere se discipulis manifestavit, in Completorio discipulis ait ' Pax vobis.' (Lib. iv. cap. ix. P.L. Tom. ccxiii. col. 135.)

It appears that the Pax was once given in the Chapter House, after Prime, on Christmas Day at Laon, and therefore perhaps also elsewhere. " Decanus dicit versum, ' Puer natus est nobis ' alii respondent, ' et Filius datus est nobis.' Postea decanus dat osculum pacis his qui sunt juxta eum, prius a dextris, postea a sinistris, et osculantur se in osculo pacis ex utraque parte usque ad ultimos. (A 13th century *Ordinarium Laudunense* quoted in Mart. Tom. iii. p. 37.)

In the Divine Office of the East Syrian Church, the Kiss of Peace is given both at the commencement and close of the evening service; at the commencement, after the ' Gloria in Excelsis ' and before the ' Pater Noster '; at the close, before the Nicene Creed ; also in the same position at the commencement of the night service ; also after the Pater Noster in the morning service. (A. J. Maclean, *East Syrian Daily Offices*, London, 1894, pp. xiii. xiv. xvi. 1, 22, 68, 82, 84, 85, 171, &c.)

The presence of the Pax here in the Bangor MS. may therefore be regarded as a link with Eastern usage, and also as a mark of great antiquity, · because all the above instances must be looked upon as survivals or as echoes of what was probably the universal custom of the first Christians never to meet together for purposes of worship without the salutation of the kiss of peace.

Tertullian alludes to it in a passage which is interesting as showing that as early as his time the custom began to be omitted on certain occasions, an omission to which he refers with disapproval except with reference to one day, Good Friday : "Alia jam consuetudo invaluit ; jejunantes, habita oratione cum fratribus, subtrahunt osculum pacis, quod est signaculum orationis . . . . Quae oratio cum divortio sancti osculi integra? Quem Domino officium facientem impedit pax ? " &c. (*De Oratione*, cap. xiv. Edit. Paris, 1842. Tom. i. p. 253.)

Origen asserts : ' Mos ecclesiae traditus est, ut post orationes osculo se invicem suscipiant fratres.' (*Comment. in Epist. ad Rom.* Lib. x. n. 33. Migne, *Patrol. Graeca*, Tom. xiv. col. 1282.)

There is a reference to the Pax in cap. xiv. of the ' Regula Coenobialis ' of St. Columbanus, where among various offences and penalties the following offence and penalty are named : ' Si[quis] post pacem sonaverit, quinquaginta [verbera]. (P. Fleming, *Collectanea Sacra*, Lovanii, 1667, p. 24.) The text and context make it probable that the Pax of the Divine Office, and not the Liturgical Pax, is referred to in this passage.

The Pax, Credo, and Pater Noster [34] [35] and [36] have been elsewhere quoted as connected with the Mass and not with the Divine Office (W. pp. 102, 189.) In the Mozarabic Liturgy the Constantinopolitan Creed immediately precedes the Lord's Prayer in accordance with the direction of Canon ii. of the iii. Council of Toledo ' ut priusquam dominica dicatur oratio [symbolum fidei] voce clara a populo decantetur.' (Mansi, *Concilia*, Tom. ix. col. 993.)

But the Pax is given at a much earlier point in that Liturgy, and in view of that fact. and also of the wording of the second Bangor Pax Collect, the theory of liturgical usage is now abandoned, and the Pax [34], Creed [35], and Lord's Prayer [36] are believed to belong to the Divine Office, and to be an appendage to the Service 'ad initium noctis.'

The writer of an article in the *Church Quarterly Review* (Jan. 1894, vol. xxxvii. p. 347) maintains the correctness of the liturgical theory. It is *primâ facie* in favour of that theory that the second Bangor Pax anthem 'Pax multa diligentibus, &c.' should be found in the *Stowe Missal* (W. p. 242), but that fact must be regarded as a coincidence. The bulk of proof lies on the other side.

[35]

'Incipit Symbolum.' For the position of this Creed in the Divine Office at Bangor, see note to [34].

This Creed is to a large extent unique, many of its readings not being found elsewhere.

The *Ordo Romanus vii.* published by Mabillon, and which is not necessarily a Roman *Ordo*, contains the first words of a baptismal Creed which may have resembled the Bangor Creed. It began Πιστεύω εἰς ἕνα κ. τ. λ. and was afterwards repeated in Latin ' Credo in unum Deum, Patrem omnipotentem, visibilium,' &c. (*Museum Italicum*, Paris, 1689, Tom. ii. p. 81.)

The triple and emphatic repetition of the word ' Credo ' introducing the statement of belief in each separate person of the Holy Trinity is a remarkable feature in the Bangor Creed.

Credo in Deum Patrem.
Credo et in Jesum Christum.
Credo et in Spiritum Sanctum.

Two more Credos are added toward the end.

Credo vitam post mortem.
Haec omnia credo in Deum. Amen.

The separate 'Credo' for each Person in the Holy Trinity is found in the Baptismal Creed in the *Sacramentarium Gallicanum*. The two further additions of ' Credo ' at the close find no parallel either there or, so far as we know, elsewhere.

As the creed in the *Sacramentarium Gallicanum* is not easily accessible, and as it contains further points of similarity to the Bangor Creed, we print it at length, marking the points of similarity by the use of italic letters. (Mabillon *ut supra*, Tom. i. p. 312.)

Credo in Deum Patrem omnipotentem, creatorem coeli et terrae.

Credo in Jesum Christum, Filium ejus unigenitum sempiternum : *conceptum* de Spiritu Sancto, *natum* ex Maria Virgine, *passum* sub Pontio Pilato, crucifixum, mortuum, et sepultum. Descendit ad inferna ; tertia die resurrexit a mortuis ; ascendit ad coelos, *sedit* ad dexteram Dei Patris omnipotentis, inde venturus judicare vivos et mortuos.

Credo in Spiritum Sanctum, sanctam ecclesiam catholicam, sanctorum communionem, remissionem peccatorum, carnis resurrectionem, vitam aeternam. Amen.

Line		
„	2	' invisibilem,' peculiar to B. If idolatry still existed in some parts of Ireland, we should understand the reason for the addition of the epithet.
„	„	' Creaturarum . . . conditorem,' peculiar to B.
„	4	' Credo,' so in *Sacram. Gallican.*
„	5	' unicum,' peculiar to B.
„	„	' Deum omnipotentem,' *ditto.*
„	6	' conceptum,' so in *Sacram. Gallican.*
„	„	' natum,' *ditto.*
„	7	' passum,' *ditto.*
„	8	' qui . . . inferos,' peculiar to B.
„	10	in coelis, *ditto.* ' In coelos ' occurs among the ' Interrogationes de fide ' in the *Sacram. Gallican.* p. 269, ' ad coelos ' in the *Missale Gallicanum Vetus*, p. 162.
„	10	sedit, so in *Sacram. Gallican.* and in the *Missale Gallicanum Vetus* (p. 163).
„	„	' que,' peculiar to B.
„	11	' exinde,' peculiar to B.
„	„	omission of ' est.' So in *Sacram. Gallican.*
„	13, 14	' Deum omnipotentem ' peculiar to B.
„	14, 15	' habentem . . . Filio,' peculiar to B.
„	15	' et Filio.' The three points placed in the MS. after and above ' Filio ' are probably equivalent to ' dele,' and, if so, denote on the part of the scribe dislike to, or unfamiliarity with, the addition of the words ' et Filio.' Three points so placed are frequently found in the *Book of Armagh*, and always as equivalent to ' dele.' They are also placed once with the same meaning over a repeated ' Madiani ' in the *Stowe Missal* (W. p. 240.)
„	„	' esse,' peculiar to B.
„	16, 17	The position of the clause ' abremissa[m] peccatorum' before ' sanctorum communionem' is peculiar to B. The word ' abremissa ' is, so far as we know, only found elsewhere in a passage from a fifth century Gallican writer, of British or Breton origin, i.e. Faustus of Riez, who mentions among the articles in the Gallican Creed of his date, " in Spiritum sanctum.

sanctam ecclesiam, sanctorum communionem, abremissa peccatorum, carnis resurrectionem, vitam aeternem." (*De Spiritu Sancto*, Lib. i. § 2, edit. Engelbrecht, Vindob, 1891, p. 104.)

The simpler word 'remissa' is found in African authors, e.g. 'Diximus de remissa peccatorum' (Tertullian, *adv. Marcionem*, Lib. iv. cap. xviii.) 'baptizare et remissam peccatorum dare.' (Cyprian, *Ep*. lxxiii. and in several other passages in the same Epistle.)

Line 18–20 'Credo vitam. . . . Amen,' peculiar to B. The meaning of ' in Deum' here is thus explained by Faustus of Riez ' credamus in deum, id est, ut haec a deo disposita, et in deo constare fateamur' (*ut supra*, p. 104). The distinctive mark of this Creed, as it differs from other known Creeds, is its emphatic insistence upon the deity of each of the Persons in the Holy Trinity.

It may be of interest to print two more early forms of the Creed. The first [I] is from MS. Reg. 2, A xx. fol. 12*r*. an eighth century MS. of which a full description will be found in the Appendix; the second [II] is a Gallican Creed contained in a letter of St. Cyprian Bishop of Toulon, addressed to Maximus, Bishop of Geneva, c. 524–33, ex Cod. Colon. 212 (olim D. 2326) saec vii. fol. 113*r*.

[I] has not been printed before. [II] has been recently printed for the first time by W. Gundlach among the *Epistolae Aevi Merowingici*, in the *Monumenta Germaniae*, Tom. iii. pp. 434–6.

I.	II.
Credo indeum patrem omnipotentem.	Credo in deum patrem omnipotentem.
et in ihesum christum filium eius unicum dominum nostrum.	credo et in ihesum christum filium eius unigenitum dominum nostrum.
qui natus est de spiritu sancto et maria uirgine.	qui conceptus de spiritu sancto, natus ex maria uirgine.
qui sub pontio pilato crucifixus est et sepultus.	passus sub pontio pilato crucifixus et sepultus.
tertia die resurrexit amortuis.	tertia die resurrexit a mortuis.
ascendit in coelos.	ascendit in coelos.
sedit ad dexteram dei patris.	sedet ad dexteram patris.
unde uenturus est iudicare uiuos ac mortuos.	inde uenturus iudicaturus uiuos ac mortuos.
et inspiritum sanctum. sanctam ecclesiam catholicam. remisionem peccatorum. carnis resurrectionem. Amen.	*Omitted by Cyprian as unconnected with the purport of his letter.*

[36]

For the use and intention of the 'Pater Noster' here see note to [34] *ad finem*.

For the various readings in the text see Introd. § vii.

Line 6. 'Demittimus' MS. The words 'peccata demittas' occur [64] line 5; but the word is probably a clerical error for ' dimitti·nus.'

Lines 6, 7. ' ne patiaris nos induci.' This is the reading of other Irish MSS. viz. the *Book of Dimma*, the *Book of Mulling*, the *Gospels of Mac Regol* and the *Book of Armagh*, where the clause is written in Greek letters, ' ετ μη πατιαρις νώς. ινδυει. ικτεμπτατιωΝεμ.'

On the other hand the ordinary Vulgate text is found in the *Book of Durrow* and the *Book of Kells*, while *Codex Usserianus* i. and ii. are both defective, so that their readings in St. Mat. vi. 13, cannot be ascertained.

[37]

Line 1. 'Per horam mediae noctis.' The hour of this Nocturn is hereby identified with midnight. See [23].

[38]

' Illuminator caliginum.' This expression points to dawn of day or about 3 a.m. See note to [25]. 'Tu.' See Introd. § 5 (g).

[39]

See notes to [25] [38] [59].

[40]

The anthem is taken from Ps. lxxviii. 8.

[40*]

We now come to a long list of 'preces' or intercessions to be used at the Day Hours. They consist, with exceptions which will be noticed, of an anthem followed by a Collect. The order and number of them deserve notice.

In the *Regula S. Columbani*, cap. vii. the order of intercessions for use ' per diurnas horas' (not 'ad matutinam et ad vesperam ') is thus described : " Cum versiculorum augmento intervenientium pro peccatis primum nostris, deinde pro omni populo Christiano, deinde pro sacerdotibus, et reliquis Deo consecratis sacrae plebis gradibus, postremo pro eleemosynas facientibus, postea pro pace regum, novissime pro inimicis, ne illis Deus statuat in peccatum quod persequuntur nos, et detrahunt nobis, quia nesciunt quod faciunt." (Holst. Part. ii. p. 94.)

Let us place the order of these intercessions in the Rule of St. Columbanus side by side with the order for intercessions in B.

Regula S. Columbani (cap. vii.).	Antiphonarium Benchorense (foll. 20v.–22r.).
1. Pro peccatis nostris.	1. [Pro peccatis nostris.]
2. Pro omni populo Christiano.	2. Pro baptizatis.
3. Pro sacerdotibus et reliquis. Deo consecratis sacrae plebis gradibus.	3. [Pro sacerdotibus.]
4. Pro eleemosynas facientibus.	4. Pro abbate.
5. Pro pace regum.	5. [Pro fratribus.]
6. Pro inimicis.	6. Pro fraternitate.
	7. Pro pace populorum et regum.
	8. Pro blasphemantibus.
	9. Pro impiis.
	10. Pro iter facientibus.
	11. [Pro gratias agentibus.]
	12. Pro elemosi[nas facientibus.] or Pro eleemosynariis.
	13. Pro infirmis.
	14. [Pro captivis.]
	15. [Pro tribulantibus.]
	16. [Pro poenitentibus.]

In the above lists the first three titles correspond; No. 4 = No. 12; No. 5 = No. 7; No. 6 = No. 8. All the subjects for intercession enumerated in the Rule of St. Columbanus are found in the Antiphonary of Bangor with ten additions. The normal structure of these intercessions or 'Preces' or 'Orationes' is an anthem or Versicle followed by a short Collect, but No. 4 consists of three anthems without a Collect, and in the Nos. 14 and 16, two anthems are prefixed to the Collect.

The anthem in [40*] is from Ps. lxix. 2. It is used at the commencement of the Hours in the Roman, Benedictine, &c. Breviaries. The title is accidentally omitted.

Compare with the Bangor 'Preces' the following Preces taken from C. C. C. MS. 272. o. 5. It is a Rheims Psalter, which can be proved from internal evidence to have been written somewhat earlier than A.D. 882.

ORATIONES MAIORES AD MATUTINAM UEL AD UESPERAS.

Oremus pro omni gradu ecclesiae.
　Sacerdotes tui induantur.
[Oremus] pro pastoribus nostris.
　Beatus qui intellegit super aegenum
[Oremus] pro rege nostro.
　Domine saluum fac regem et exaudi nos.
[Oremus] pro liberis eius.
　Saluos fac seruos tuos deus meus sperantes in te.
[Oremus] pro abbate nostro.
　Deus conseruet eum et uiuificet eum.
[Oremus] pro cuncto populo catholico.
　Saluum fac populum tuum
[Oremus] pro fratribus et sororibus nostris.
　Propter fratres meos, propter domum.

[Oremus] pro pace.
　Fiat pax in uirtute tua et habundantia.
[Oremus] pro iter agentibus.
　O domine saluos nos fac o domine prosperare
[Oremus] pro nauigantibus.
　Exaudi nos deus salutaris noster spes.
[Oremus] pro persequentibus et calumniantibus nobis.
　Domine ihesu christe ne statuas illis hoc peccatum quia nesciunt quid faciunt.
[Oremus] pro discordantibus.
　Pax dei quę exsuperat omnem sensum custodiat corda illorum in pace.
[Oremus] pro penitentibus.
　Conuertere domine usquequo et deprecabilis.
[Oremus] pro omnibus elemosinas facientibus.
　Dispersit dedit.
[Oremus] pro infirmis.
　Et clamauerunt ad dominum cum tribularentur.
[Oremus] pro fidelibus defunctis.
　Requiem aeternam dona eis domine et lux perpetua luceat eis.
　Requiescant in pace. Amen.
Oremus pro peccatis et negligentiis nostris.
　Domine ne memineris.
　Adiuua nos deus salutaris noster propter gloriam nominis tui.
　O domine libera nos et propitius esto peccatis propter nomen tuum.
　Adiutorium nostrum in nomine domini.
[Oremus] pro fratribus nostris absentibus.
　Saluos fac seruos tuos deus meus.
　Mitte eis auxilium de sancto et de sion tuere eos.
　Domine exaudi orationem meam.

The absence of any intercession 'pro fidelibus defunctis' among the Bangor preces is remarkable. See note to [61] ad finem.

[41]

The anthem is from Ps. xxvii. 9. It occurs among the 'Preces' at Lauds and Vespers in the Roman Breviary, and in the opening Versicles of the Anglican Mattins and Evensong. It is also found among the suffrages at the end of the Litany in the Sarum Breviary, (Cambridge, 1879, Fasc. 11. col. 254) in answer to the bidding '[Oremus] pro cuncto populo Christiano,' a phrase which is equivalent to 'pro baptizatis.' It occurs without a preceding bidding among some 'Capitula per omnes Horas' printed by Martene (2) from a most ancient Breviary 'Monasterii Cassinensis'; (b) an ancient MS. Collectaneum of the Monastery S. Mariae

[et] S. Petri supra Divam ; (c) a MS. Breviary S. Germani a Pratis. (Mart. Lib. cap. i. iii. § xv. Tom. iv. p. 14.)

[41*]

The missing title ' Pro sacerdotibus ' has been supplied from Cap. vii. of the *Regula S. Columbani*. See note to [40*].

The anthem is taken from Ps. cxxxi. 8, 9. ' Induentur justitia ' may be a genuine various reading or a clerical error for ' induantur justitiam ' (Vulgate). See Introd. § 7. The latter verse is found among the suffrages at the end of the Litany in the *Sarum Breviary*. (Cambridge, 1879. Fasc. ii. col. 253.) There it occurs in response to the bidding ' Oremus pro omni gradu Ecclesiae.' The ' qui ' at the end of this anthem seems to be misplaced ; it must belong to the following collect.

[42]

This section consists of three anthems without a collect.
The first anthem is from Ps. xl. 3.
The second „ „ Ps. cxx. 7.
The third „ „ Ps. cxx. 8.
All three anthems are repeated in [118] on Fol. 34v. p. 32, under the title of ' Oratio pro abbate nostro.'

[43]

The title has been accidentally omitted in the MS. text. The anthem is from Ps. xvi. 8.

[44]

The anthem is from Ps. xi. 8.

[45]

The anthem is from Ps. xxviii. 1 L.

[46]

The anthem is from Ps. cxxxvii. 8.
The Collect is based upon Acts vii. 59. The same passage is referred to in the extract from the Rule of St. Columbanus quoted in the note to [40*], and establishes the identity of this intercession with the intercession, ' pro inimicis ' therein named.

[47]

The anthem is from Ps. v. 11.

[48]

The anthem is from Ps. cxvii. 25.

[49]

The title has been accidentally omitted in the MS. text.
The anthem is from Ps. cxliv. 10.

[50]

' Pro elee[mosynariis] ' or ' Pro elee[mosynas facientibus].' The title is only partly written in the MS. text. The scribe may have intended to write ' Pro eleemosynariis,' but it is equally probable that he intended to write the title as it stands in cap. vii. of the *Regula S. Columbani*, as quoted in the note to [40*]. It is to be noticed that the words ' eleemosynas facientibus ' occur in the Collect.

The anthem is from Ps. cxi. 9.

[51]

The anthem is from Ps. cvi. 6. See Part i. Fol. 21v., note 1.

[51*]

There is no title here in the MS. text and therefore we have conjecturally supplied one. The language of the anthem and Collect is somewhat vague, and the restoration of the title must remain somewhat uncertain, but the word ' redime ' in the first anthem seems to suggest some such title as ' Pro Captivis.' The title ' Pro afflictis et captivis ' is found in the 'Capitula per omnes horas' printed by Mart. (Lib. i. cap. iii. § 15, Tom. iv. p. 14.)

The first anthem is from Ps. xliii. 26.
The second „ „ Ps. cxxiii. 8.

[52]

This is the first of a considerable number of commemorations of Martyrs which occur in the Antiphonary of Bangor, about which see Introd. § 6.
It comes in rather awkwardly at this point before the last of the ' Preces ' or intercessions.
Line 2. The double stop placed in the MS. after ' martirii ' is evidently a mistake.

[53]

[Pro tribulantibus.] There is no title here in the MS. text. In part i. in a note on Fol. 20v. the title ' Pro tribulantibus ' was suggested. ' Tribulantibus ' is a mediaeval Latin equivalent to ' tribulatis.' See Du Cange, *Glossarium, sub voc.* A ' Missa pro tribulantibus, &c.' occurs in the eighth century *Codex Rhenaugiensis* of the *Gelasian Sacramentary*. (M. Gerbertus, *Monumenta Veteris Liturgiae Alemannicae*, Typis San Blasianis, 1777, vol. i. p. 273.) Similar titles are frequently found

K

among the 'Suffragia Communia' or 'Preces' or 'Capitula' of Breviaries, and among the 'orationes ad diversa' in Missals of various dates, e.g.:

Orationes in Tribulatione (including ten Masses). (*Gelasian Sacramentary*, col. 706.)

Missa in tribulatione. (*Leofric Missal*, Oxford, 1883, p. 175.)

Missa pro quacunque tribulatione. (*Ibid.* p. 14. *York Missal*, Surtees Soc. 1874, vol. ii. p. 172.)

Missa pro tribulatione. (*Hereford Missal*, Leeds, 1874, p. 445.)

Missa pro tribulatione cordis. (*Sarum Missal*, Burntisland, 1861, col. 797*.)

Missa pro tentatis et tribulatis. (*Roman Missal*, p. lxxxv.)

Missa de tribulationibus. (*Mozarabic Missal*, col. 997.)

The first anthem is from Ps. xxvii. 1.
The second   „   „   Ps. xlv. 8.

[54]

'Collectio.' We take the 'collectis' of the MS. to be a mistake for 'Collectio.' There is nothing to support the conjecture that it might be equivalent to 'ad collationes,' meaning a Collect to be used after 'collationes' or lections from the lives of the Fathers. The Collect seems to be a general supplication for pity addressed to the Second Person in the Holy Trinity. As such it is as appendage to, if not a part of [53] or an appendage to all the preceding Preces.

[55]

See Introd. § 6.

[56]

The title has been accidentally omitted from the MS. text.

The anthem is from Ps. l. 3.

The word 'Poenitentes,' if we are right in supplying it for the title, must probably be considered as used in a general sense ; but it may be used in the technical sense in which it occurs in the various Ordines for the ejection of Penitents on Ash Wednesday, e.g. in the *Sarum Missal*. (Burntisland, 1861, col. 135. See also the 'Missa pro Poenitentibus,' col. 794*.)

[57]

The long series of 'Preces' or 'Capitula' for use at the Day Hours being now completed, the scribe proceeds to write down some more Collects for use at the night-hours. A marginal cross denotes the change of subject.

The Collect, No. [57], is based upon St. Mat. xxv. 6. Some such verb as 'da' is wanting in the middle of it. The phrase 'media nocte' fixes the time of this service to be midnight.

[58]

The phrase 'de luce' points to daybreak or about 3 a.m. We have transposed the last 'et' and 'ut' in this Collect.

[59]

This is an adaptation from various texts in Holy Scripture, e.g. Ps. cxlv. 5 ; Is. xxxiii. 2. See [39.]
'Tu.' See Introd. § 5 (g).

[60]

This Collect is partly adapted from Pss. cxii. 5, 6 ; cxliii. 1.

[61]

See Introd. § 6. This Collect occurs with verbal variations in the *Stowe Missal* as part of a 'Missa Apostolorum et Martyrum et Sanctorum et Sanctarum Virginum.' It there merges into a Praefatio leading up to the 'Sanctus' (W. p. 245).

Line 9. After the word 'augmentum' the prayer in the *Stowe Missal* proceeds thus :—

'Orent pro nobis sancti martires et pro defunctis nostris, et pro pecoribus, et pro omnibus terrae nostrae fructibus, et pro omnibus in hoc loco commorantibus,' &c.

It is to be remarked that the Bangor Collect stops short at the passage which introduces intercession for the departed, among many other things. See note to [40*] *ad finem*.

[62]

'Collectio post Canticum.' This is the first Collect in the first of several series of Collects for use after certain Canticles, Hymns, &c. See Introd. § 3.

The Canticum in each set [62] [68] [71] [76] [81] [88] [91] [94] is the Canticle 'Cantemus Domino' [5] and not the Canticle 'Audite Coeli' [1]. This is proved by the language of the Collects themselves.

We think that the faint remains of a cross may be detected beneath the upper stroke of the capital D.

Line 4. 'diluio' MS. The single 'u' frequently stands for the double 'u' in Irish MSS. and less frequently *vice versâ*. It may be worth noting that the word 'dilui,' so spelt, occurs in the first few lines of the *Stowe Missal* (W. p. 226.)

Lines 6, 7. 'Salvator mundi.' For the origin and significance of this title, which occurs here and frequently afterwards, see Introd. § 5 (a).

[63]

'Collectio post benedictionem puerorum.' The word 'trium,' which usually forms part of this title, has been omitted by the rubricator as in [6], perhaps intentionally for want of space. The Canticle is sometimes mentioned under its opening word 'Benedicite.' See [77.]

Line 5. 'Salvator mundi.' See Introd. § 5 (a.)

[64]

'Collectio post tres psalmos.' The three Psalms referred to in this title are proved by internal evidence supplied by the language of the Collects which follow this title, here and elsewhere, to be the three Psalms universally associated with ancient Mattins, now generally called Lauds, viz : Pss. cxlviii.–cl.

'In fine.' The words 'in fine' at the bottom of the first column of fol. 23v. though detached, seem to belong to the title of this Collect, if so, they are either an amplification of the words 'post tres psalmos' and mean that the Collect is to be used at the end of the 'three Psalms' (cxlviii.–cl.); or else they represent the words 'In finem' which occur frequently in the Vulgate [in LXX. 'Εις τὸ τέλος'] in the title at the commencement of a Psalm. See Psalms iv. v. vi. &c. But the words are not prefixed in the Vulgate to any Psalm after cxxxix.

Line 1. There is a prayer commencing with the same first five words as this Collect in S. It occurs there after Ps. cl. on f. 99v. and is prefixed to the 'Canticum Moysi,' 'Audite coeli,' &c. It runs thus :

'Te dominum de coelis laudamus,
Teque omnium regem regum rogamus ;
Tibi uni et trino in quem speramus
Cum excelsis angelis imnum cantamus,
Per dominum nostrum, et rl.'

'Te.' See Introd. § 5. (h)

Line 5. 'peccata dimittas.' For this verb see the Pater Noster [36] line 6.

„ „ Salvator mundi.' See Introd. § 5(a.)

[65]

'Collectio post Evangelium.' In the Benedictine rite a Collect follows the Gospel Lection at the end of the last Nocturn, which helps to explain the title 'collectio post Evangelium' which occurs here, and several times later on in the Bangor MS. From the position of this Collect in each series of Collectiones, it is evident that at Bangor the Gospel did not occupy the Benedictine position at the end of Nocturns, but that it came after Pss. 148-150 in Mattins. Three lections, including a Gospel, are provided on Sundays in Lent, 'ad Matutinum' in the Mozarabic *Liber Comicus.* (Maredsous, 1893, p. 66 etc.)

[66]

The language of this Collect leads to the conclusion that it was meant to be used after [12] 'Hymnus ad matutinam in. Dominica.'

[67]

See Introd. § 6. The realistic character of the language here used makes it impossible to believe that any metaphorical kind of martyrdom is referred to. See Introd. § 6. The Collect, no doubt, is an importation from the Continent. It has the ring about it of a Gallican or Mozarabic Preface, but we have not been able hitherto to trace it to any such source.

[68]

The cross prefixed to this Collect, of which a very small fragment remains, the rest of it having been cut off or worn away, indicates the commencement of a new series of Collects.

Line 8. 'Salvator mundi.' See Introd. § 5 (a.)

[69]

See [63.]

Line 2. for 'et' the MS. reading is 'ad.'
„ 3. 'quartus assistis.' This phrase occurs again in [72] q.v.
„ 9. 'Salvator mundi.' See Introd. § 5a.

[70]

The title 'Post laudate Dominum de coelis' is equivalent to the title 'Post tres Psalmos' in [64], the four words 'Laudate Dominum de coelis' being the first four words of Ps. cxlviii.

Line 1. for 'canunt' the MS. reading is 'canite.'

[71]

See [62.] The cross prefixed to the title indicates the commencement of a fresh set of Collects.

Line 5. 'Salvator mundi.' See Introd. § 5 (a.)

[72]

See [63.]

Line 3. The words 'quartus assistis' have already occurred in [69]. Compare the Ambrosian

K 2

Collect belonging to 'Benedicite' at Sunday Lauds 'Deus, qui tribus pueris in camino ignis positis quartus adesse dignatus es,' &c.

[73]

See [70.]

Line 11. 'vigilia sollemnitatis.' Compare the expression 'vigilia matutina' in [66]. 'sollemnitas Domini' is a term for a Feast of our Lord. 'sollemnitas,' though it is a word of wide signification, is possibly used in the same sense here. All Sundays are Feasts of our Lord. 'Vigilia sollemnitatis' would then be Saturday, and this Collect would be for use on that day. The expression 'Vigiliarum sollemnitas' is used by Cassian of the prolonged Saturday night service. (De Instit. Lib. iii. cap. ix.)

„   6. 'Salvator mundi.' See Introd. § 5 (a.)

[74]

See note to [65.]

Line 1. 'resurrectionis initium.' The language of this Collect seems to be specially appropriate to Easter Day or Easter-tide.

„   3. 'Dominus,' perhaps 'Domini' converted into 'Dominus' in MS.

[75]

'Post Hymmum.' See note to [66.] The same Hymn [12] may be referred to, but the language of this Collect is too vague to substantiate any connecting link.

[76]

The cross prefixed to this title denotes the commencement of a new series of Collects.

[77]

See note to [63.]

[78]

See note to [70.]
Line 1. 'Te.' See Introd. § 5 (g.)

[79]

See note to [65.]

Line 1. 'Resurgentem' &c. The language of this Collect points to Easter Day or Easter-tide.

[80]

Line 1. 'Resurrectionem' &c. The language of this Collect points to Easter Day or Easter-tide, but does not suggest a connection

with any Hymn in the Bangor Antiphonary.

[81]

['Post Canticum.'] This title has been accidentally omitted from the MS. text, but the cross prefixed to the marginal space which the title should occupy indicates the commencement of a new series of Collects. See note to [62.]

[82]

'Post Hymnum trium puerorum.' 'Benedictio' [63] and 'Benedicite' [89] are more usually found connected with the title of this Canticle than Hymnus.

Line 1. 'Te. See Introd. § 5 (g.)

[83]

See note to [70.]
This rhyming Collect is also found in S. It occurs there on fol. 35v. after Ps. l, and prefixed to the 'Benedictio trium puerorum.'

Line 3. gloriae MS. gloria S.
Line 5. [saeculorum.] This missing word is supplied from S.

„   „   S. adds Amen.

[84]

See note to [65.]
This Collect occurs as an anthem to the 'Hymnus S. Hilarii in laudem Christi' in L.H. p. 161. It is No. [2] in the Bangor Antiphonary.

Line 2. after 'tria' add 'Domine' L.H
„   3. after 'oblata' add 'Deo' L.H.
„   4. for 'Qui tecum vivit' read 'per te Christe Jesu Salvator' L.H.

[85]

See note to [65.]
Line 1. 'diluculo'. . . 'resurgente.' The language of this Collect points to daybreak, and would be specially appropriate to Easter Day or Easter-tide.

[86]

The Hymn referred to in this title is probably [12.] The opening words of the Collect, 'Lux orta est in luce,' recal the words 'Lumen de lumine,' which are the opening words of stanza iii. of that Hymn. We may also note the expression 'Filius divinae lucis' in stanza viii. The title 'Unigenitus' which is used in this Collect is found in stanzas iv. vii. and ix.

[87]

See Introd. § 6.

[88]

See note to [62.] The cross prefixed to this title indicates the commencement of a fresh series of Collects.

[89]

See note to [63.]

Line 3. 'angelum magni consilii.' This may be Jesus Christ, who is called in the Preface of the *Clementine Liturgy*, ' Λόγου, Θεόν, σοφίαν ζῶσαν, πρωτότοκον πάσης κτίσεως, ἄγγελον τῆς μεγάλης βουλῆς σου' . . . (Hamm. p. 12.)

He has been referred to already as such in [3] stanza xxix.

' Adversus eum
 Initur consilium
 Qui magni dictus
 Consilii est nuntius.'

The title is connected with Is. xi. 2. It is found in the opening Antiphona in 'Vigilia Nativ. Domini' in the Liber Antiphonarum S. Gregorii magni, P.L. Tom. lxxviii. col. 646, and in the Introit 'ad iii. Missam in die Nativitatis Domini' in the Roman Missal. According to a popular medieval explanation of the very obscure passage in the Roman Canon,

' Supplices te rogamus, omnipotens Deus, jube haec perferri per manus sancti Angeli tui in sublime altare tuum,' &c.

The 'Angelus' therein named is to be interpreted of Jesus Christ. (Honorius, *Gemma animae*, Lib. i. cap. 106. Bonaventura, *Expositio Missa*, cap. 4. Edit. i. Romae, 1588-96, Tom. vii. p. 84, &c.) The passage is too difficult, and too remotely connected with the text of [89] to be discussed further here.

[90]

See note to [70.]

This is a favourite prayer in Irish Psalters. It occurs in MS. Vitell. F. xi. (ninth or tenth century) and in S. There it follows Ps. c. and precedes the 'Canticum Annae matris Samuelis' (fol. 69v.) It also occurs on fol. 133r. of MS. Palatin. 65, an eleventh century Irish Psalter in the Vatican Library.

The following is the full text in S.

' Deus, quem exercitus canet angelorum,
 Quemque aecclesiae laudet sanctorum,
 Quem spiritus ymniinizat universorum,
 Miserere, obscere, omnium nostrorum tuorum,
 Qui regnas in saecula saeculorum. Amen.'

[91]

See note to [62.]

The cross prefixed to this title denotes the commencement of a fresh series of Collects. There is a marked change of handwriting here, and the new scribe commences a set of much longer and very remarkable Collects, which in length, structure, and language bear little or no resemblance to Petrine Collects and probably are of Gallican origin.

Lines 13, 14. 'Salvator mundi.' See Introd. § 5 (n.)

[92]

See notes to [63] and [91.]

Line 1. 'Tris' MS. The confusion between 'i' and 'e' is very common. The form 'tris' for 'tres' occurs again in [91] 2. 4. 10. 12; also in line 6 of the 'Altus prosator' of St. Columba in L.H. p. 205.

[93]

See notes to [70] and [91.]

Line 18. 'Salvator mundi.' See Introd. § 5 (n.)

[94]

See notes to [62] and [91.]

The cross prefixed on the margin denotes the commencement of a fresh series of Collects, but only the first of the series was ever written down. Its text is so corrupt that it appears as if the scribe must have copied a Collect which he did not understand. Can he have been translating from a Greek original which was unintelligible to him? If so, probably some Greek word or some Graecism would have survived, but such is not the case. It has been thought better to print it as it stands in the MS instead of attempting to mend it.

Line 1. 'Cinchrim.' See note to [3] stanza xii. line 2. The presence of this form of the name of Pharaoh points to the prayer being of Irish origin. So does the ungrammatical use of 'cujus' in line 8, with which we may compare the use of 'cujus' in line 5 of stanza viii. of the undoubtedly Irish Hymn of St. Patrick [13.]

[95]

'Versiculi familiae Benchuir.' The third and last division of the Antiphonary of Bangor begins here. It is in the main a collection of anthems or antiphonae, and so far justifies the title of 'Antiphonarium' which Muratori gave to the whole MS. But in addition to anthems, this third part contains a great deal of miscellaneous material. It begins and ends with a hymn, or rather with a commemorative or historical poem. With the first of these two hymns [95] we are concerned here. It is difficult to regard it as part of the Divine Office, unless we may conjecture it to have been connected with the reading of the Rule, or, a portion of the Rule, after mattins or at any other time.

It is a panegyric of the monastic Rule of Bangor, of the monastic family of Bangor, and of the monastery of Bangor generally, but the panegyric is couched in too general language to yield historical information on any of these subjects. With regard to the Rule, it may be mentioned that there exists an unpublished Irish MS. Rule of St. Comgall at Brussels. (Bibliothèque Royale, vol. xvii. No. 5100-4 p. 31.) It is a transcript from an ancient Irish MS. copied by the Franciscan Michael O'Clery in the earlier part of the seventeenth century. The metrical defects seem to show that O'Clery, who was a careful copyist, had a defective MS. to copy from. This makes the Rule difficult, and in parts impossible to translate, and we do not attempt to present our readers with a copy of it. It has been described by M'Eugene O'Curry as 'a poem of 36 quatrains, containing 144 lines, addressed alike to abbots, to monks, and to devout Christians in general.' (*Lectures on the MS. Materials of Ancient Irish History*, Dublin, 1878, p. 374.) Dr. Reeves has also described it, together with other Irish Rules at Brussels, as totally insufficient to convey any definite idea of the peculiarities of the Orders to which they profess respectively to belong. (*Adamnan's Life of St. Columba*, Dublin, 1857, p. 337.)

It is worthy of remark that the laudatory language applied in the poem in the Antiphonary of Bangor to the monastery and Rule of Bangor is to a large extent identical with, or similar to, the laudatory language applied in later Latin Breviaries to the Blessed Virgin Mary. The following parallel table will illustrate this point:

Antiphonarium Benchorense.	Breviarium Romanum.
Nuptiis quoque parata regi domino sponsa. Stanza III.	Maria Virgo assumpta est ad aethereum thalamum. ℣ ad Sextam in Assumptione B.M.V.
Arca Cherubin tecta. Stanza VI.	Hodie sacra et animata arca Dei viventis. Lectio iv. in ii. Noct. Ibid.
	Cujus supernus Artifex. Ventris sub arca clausus est. Hymnus ad Matutinum. In festis B.M.V. per annum.
Christo regina apta. Stanza VII.	Gloriosa Regina mundi. Ad. Magn. Antiph. Officium B.M. in Sabbato.
	Astitit regina a dextris tuis. Ps. xliv 10 in ii Noct. In festis B.M.V. per annum.
Solis luce amicta. "	Quae est ista, quae processit sicut sol? ℟ post Lect. v. In festis B.M.V. per annum.

Antiphonarium Benchorense.	Breviarium Romanum.
	Amictam sole mulierem. Mense Octobri, Lect. iii. Officium B.M. in Sabbato.
Vere regalis aula. Stanza VIII.	Tu Regis alti janua. Et aula lucis fulgida. Hymnus ad laudes. In festis B.M.V. per annum.
Virgo valde fecunda. Stanza IX.	Post partum virgo inviolata permansisti. In iii. Noct. Antiph. In Assumptione B.M.V.
Haec et mater intacta. "	Beata Mater et intacta Virgo. Ad Magnificat. Antiph. Officium Parvum B.M. Extra Adventum. Ad Vesperas.

The inference which we would draw from this table of comparison, which might probably be extended, is this: that expressions and similitudes which in later times became appropriated exclusively to describe the B.V.M. had no such appropriation in the seventh century in the Irish Church, but were capable of being applied, as in the Hymn before us, to other objects, such as the monastery of Bangor, which is called the Virgin Bride of Christ, and the prolific Mother of many Saints.

The Hymn is in ten stanzas of four lines each. The lines consisting of seven syllables, are iambic dimeter catalectic in structure. Every line throughout the Hymn ends with the letter 'a.'

See note to [14.]

A translation of this Hymn by Bishop Reeves is given in the *Ulster Journal of Archæology*, vol. i. p. 175.

Stanza. Line.

I. 1 'Benchuir.' So far as form goes this word may be either the Vocative or the Genitive case.

The first line may be translated either 'O Bangor, thy rule is excellent,' or 'The rule of Bangor is excellent.'

II 1 'Munther.' This is one of the few Irish words introduced into the text of this MS. It means 'monastic family.' With regard to its form Mons. d'Arbois de Jubainville remarks: "Munther" "famille" avec un *th* au lieu d'un *t*, comme on le trouve déjà observé dans la *Grammatica Celtica* 2ᵉ édition, p. 943, contredit la régle 64 de la Kurzgefasste irische Grammatik que nous devons à M. Windisch. p. 67, 68. (*Revue Celtique*, Paris, Janvier, 1894, p. 136.) For a similar introduction

Stanza. Line.

of a solitary Irish word into a Latin text compare the use of the Irish preposition "hi" in Adamnan's *Life of St. Columba*, Lib. iii. cap. 3. *ad finem*.

III   4   See introductory note, 'nuptis' MS. as required by the metre.

IV   1, 2   Adapted from St. Mat. xvi. 18, 'delicis' MS. as required by the metre.

,,   3, 4   Adapted from Ps. lxxix. 9.

V   1-4   Adapted from St. Mat. v. 14.

VI
 VII   }   See introductory note.
 VIII

VIII   2   'Waris' MS. as required by the metre.

,,   3   'Caula' in the sense either of 'τέμενοϲ' or 'ovile.'

IX   See introductory note.

X   See Part I, p. vii. note 4.

After stanza x the first line only of stanza i. is written. This is not an indication that the first stanza is to be

repeated at the conclusion of the Hymn, but in accordance with an ancient custom in Irish hymnological writing, it is to show that the end of the Hymn has been reached, and that the words which follow afterwards have no connection with it. Other examples may be seen in L.H. pp. 23, 80, 257.

[96]

'Collectio super hominem qui habet diabolum.' It is difficult to see why this, or any form of Exorcism should have been included in this Service-book. This Collect is found, more suitably placed, at the commencement of the 'Ordo Baptismi' in the *Stowe Missal* (W. p. 207); among the Orationes 'super Daemoniacum' in a tenth century Vienna Codex, published by M. Gerbert (*Monumenta Veteris Liturgiae Alemannicae*, Typis San-Blasianis, 1779, pars. ii. p. 132), and among the Orationes 'super energumine baptizato' in the *Leofric Missal*. (Oxford, 1883, p. 235.)

There is some variation of text among these versions as may be seen by the following parallel table. See also Part I. Fol. 30, note 2.

I.	II.	III.	IV.
Antiphonary of Bangor. VII. Cent.	Stowe Missal. IX. Cent.	Leofric Missal. X. Cent.	Vienna Codex. X. Cent.
1. Domine sancte Pater omnipotens aeterne Deus.	1. Domine sancte Pater omnipotens aeterne Deus.	1. Domine sancte Pater omnipotens aeterne Deus.	1. Domine sancte Pater omnipotens aeterne Deus.
2. *deest.*	2.	2. per impositionem scripturae hujus.	2. *deest.*
3. *deest.*	3. *deest.*	3. et gustum aquae.	3. *deest.*
4. expelle diabolum et gentilitatem.	4. expelle diabolum et gentilitatem.	4. expelle diabolum.	4. expelle diabolum.
5. ab homine isto.	5. ab homine isto.	5. ab homine isto.	5. de homine isto N.
6. de capite.	6. de capite.	6. de capite.	6. de capite.
7. de capillis.	7. de capillis.	7. de capillis.	7. de capillis.
8. de cerebro.	9. de vertice.	8. de vertice.	8. de vertice.
9. de vertice.	8. de cerebro.	9. de cerebro.	9. de vertice.
10. de fronte.	10. de fronte.	10. de fronte.	10. de fronte.
11. de oculis.	11. de oculis.	11. de oculis.	11. de oculis.
12. de auribus.	12. de auribus.	12. de auribus.	15. de ore.
13. de naribus.	13. de naribus.	13. de naribus.	12. de auribus.
14. de labiis.	14. *deest.*	14. *deest.*	14. *deest.*
15. de ore.	15. de ore.	15. de ore.	13. de naribus.
16. de lingua.	16. de lingua.	16. de lingua.	16. de lingua.
17. de sublingua.	17. de sublingua.	17. de sublingua.	17. de sublingua.
18. de faucibus.	19. de guttore.	18. *deest.*	18. *deest.*
19. de guttore.	18. de faucibus.	19. de guttore.	19. de guttore.
deest.	*deest.*	*deest.*	de gula.
20. de collo.	20. de collo.	20. de collo.	20. de collo.
deest.	de pectore.	*deest.*	*deest.*
21. de corde.	21. de corde.	*deest.*	*deest.*
22. de corpore toto.	22. de corpore tota.	22. de corpore toto.	22. de corpore toto.
23. de omnibus compaginibus membrorum suorum.			
24. intus et deforis.	24. intus de foris.	*deest.*	*deest.*
deest.	de manibus.	*deest.*	*deest.*
deest.	de pedibus.	*deest.*	*deest.*
deest.	de omnibus membris.	de omnibus membris.	de omnibus membris tuis.
	23. de compagnibus membrorum suorum.	23. de compaginibus membrorum suorum.	23. de compaginibus membrorum tuorum.
		24. intus et foris.	24. intus de foris.
25. de ossibus.	25. *deest.*	25. de ossibus.	25. de ossibus.
26. de venis.	26. *deest.*	26. de venis.	26. de venis.

I. Antiphonary of Bangor. VII. Cent.		II. Stowe Missal. IX. Cent.		III. Leofric Missal. X. Cent.		IV. Vienna Codex. X. Cent.	
27.	de nervis.	27.	deest.	27.	de nervis.	27.	de nervis.
28.	de sanguine.	28.	deest.	28.	de sanguine.		deest.
29.	de sensu.	29.	deest.	29.	de sensu.		deest.
30.	de cogitationibus.	30.	et de cogitationibus.	30.	de cogitationibus.		deest.
31.	de verbis.	31.	de verbis.		deest.		deest.
32.	de omnibus operibus suis.	32.	de operibus.	32.	deest.	32.	de omnibus operibus malis.
33.	de virtute.	33.	deest.	33.	deest.	33.	de virtute.
34.	de omni conversatione ejus.	34.	et omnibus conversationibus.	34.	de omni conversatione.	34.	de omni conversatione.
35.	hic et in futuro.	35.	hic et futuro.	35.	deest.	35.	et in futuro.
36.	sed operetur in te virtus Christi.	36.	deest.	36.	et operetur in te virtus Christi.	36.	operetur in te virtus Christi.
37.	in eo qui propassus est.	37.	deest.	37.	in eo qui pro te passus est.	37.	deest.
38.	ut vitam aeternam mereamur.	38.	deest.	38.	ut vitam aeternam mereamur.... aris.	38.	deest.
39.	Per Dominum nostrum Jesum Christum.	39.	Per te Jesu Christe.	39.	Per.	39.	deest.
40.	Filium suum.	40.	Qui reg[nas.]	40.		40.	Qui viv[it.]

Far longer and more curious enumerations of the parts of the human body are found in the *Lorica* of Gildas (frequently printed e.g. W. Stokes, *Irish Glosses*, Dublin, 1860, p. 133; F. J. Mone, *Lateinische Hymnen*, Freiburg, 1853, Tom. i. 367, &c.), and in a form of confession in the Franco-Celtic Fleury MS. (cent. viii) printed by Mart. (Lib. iv. cap. xxxiv. Tom. iii. p. 243.)

Line 2. 'gentilitatem.' This word points to a date when the candidate for baptism was generally a convert from heathenism. It will be seen by the parallel tables that it occurs in the two older Irish forms of the Exorcism, while it is omitted from the two somewhat later continental versions. Though used by Leofric at Exeter, this part of the Missal which bears his name was brought over to England by him from Burgundy.

[97]

See Introd. § 6, and note to [52.]

This Collect, probably intended for use at Mattins, is carelessly written, and casually placed here, with no connexion with what precedes or follows it.

The cross which we have printed at the commencement of the Collect is written on the top right hand corner of Fol. 31r.

[98]

For 'secunda' see note to [16.]

This is a casual insertion in its present position. From the title we learn that Ps. lxxxix. the 'Oratio Moysi' was used at Bangor at Prime on Christmas Day. It is not specially appropriate to that Festival, but we know from [105]-[107] that it was also used on Sundays, and from [108] that it was used on weekdays as well.

It was therefore used daily at Prime, as it is in the Eastern Church at the present day. We should perhaps have been inclined to guess that its use was at Mattins had it not been for the distinct statement in this title that it was used at Prime. In Western Breviaries, Roman, Benedictine, &c. it is said at Thursday Lauds, but its original position was, probably everywhere, as at Bangor, at Prime.

Line 1. The words of this anthem are appropriate and peculiar to Christmas Day. The fixture of Christmas Day on December 25, and of St. John the Baptist's Day on June 24, is connected with St. John iii. 30, and with the natural phenomena referred to in this anthem.

Line 8. 'transferentur' MS.

[99]

Here follow eight anthems arranged for use in connection with the Canticles 'Cantemus Domino' and 'Benedicite omnia opera.'

[1. *Super Cantemus.*] Source unknown.
[2. *Super Benedicite.*] Source unknown.
[3. *Super Cantemus.*] Source unknown.
[4. *Super Benedicite.*] Compare No. 12.
[5. *Super Cantemus.*] This is from Exod. xv. 11, and has already appeared as part of [5] on p. 8.
[6. *Super Benedicite.*] This is substantially the first half of the last verse which is appended to 'Benedicite' in B. and elsewhere, and forms part of it, viz. 'Benedicamus Patrem, et Filium, et Spiritum Sanctum,' &c.
[7. *Super Cantemus.*] 'polum' is an evident MS. error for 'populum.' This rhyming anthem has not been found elsewhere.

[8. *Super Benedicite.*] It will be noticed that, though its lines can hardly be said to rhyme, there is a triple assonance in the construction of this anthem, as there is in several of the preceding ones. These anthems are continued after [100.]

[100]

'Super laudate Dominum de coelis.' There is only one anthem to which this heading applies. It breaks into the course of a long series of twenty anthems connected with 'Cantemus Domino' and 'Benedicite omnia opera.' It is a cento from Pss. clxviii. 1; lxxx. 3; cl. 3. See also Ps. cxlix. 3.

[99]

The title 'Antiphonae super Cantemus Domino et super Benedicite,' has not been repeated in the MS. text. It applies to the twelve following anthems, six of which belong to 'Cantemus Domino' and six to 'Benedicite omnia opera,' arranged alternately. They form therefore a continuation of [99.]

[9. *Super Cantemus.*] We should have expected the last word in this anthem to be 'Cantemus' rather than 'Cantate'; for 'Cantemus' is the opening word of Moses' song in Exod. xvi. 1, and of the refrain as sung by Miriam. (*Ibid.* 21.)

[10. *Super Benedicite.*] This is intended to be a roughly rhyming stanza of three lines.

[11. *Super Cantemus.*] 'populum.' See [99] 7.

[12. *Super Benedicite.*] This anthem resembles [99] 4.

[13. *Super Cantemus.*] Exod. xv. 18.

[14. *Super Benedicite.*] Dan. iii. 87.

[15. *Super Cantemus.*] Exod. xv. 3. Also in Judith xvi. 3; but evidently there as here a quotation from Exod. xv. 3.

[16. *Super Benedicite.*] Dan. iii. 57 (part.)

[17. *Super Cantemus.*] Exod. xv. 1. There appears to be a cross prefixed on the margin to this anthem, but it is indistinct, and perhaps not *prima manu.*

[18. *Super Benedicite.*] Dan. iii. 57 (part.)

[19. *Super Cantemus.*] Exod. xiv. 29 (part.)

[20. *Super Benedicite.*] This anthem has already occurred in the same connection in [99] 6, where see note.

[101]

See Introd. § 6. This anthem is perhaps to be regarded as a stanza of five lines, of which the first two and the last three lines rhyme together; but correct grammar requires the accusative instead of the ablative case in the fifth and sixth lines. See Introd. § 5 (*k.*)

[102]

See Introd. § 6. This anthem is from Apoc. vii. 14.

[103]

See Introd. § 6. This is perhaps a rhyming anthem of two lines, with 'Christe' added at the conclusion.

[104]

See Introd. § 6. Also a rhyming anthem of two lines.

[105]

This anthem is from Ps. lxxxix. 13. We learned from the title of [98] that this Psalm was used at Bangor on Christmas Day, and we here learn that it was used there on Sundays as well. See note to [98.]

[106]

This anthem is from Ps. lxxxix. 16.

[107]

This anthem is from Ps. lxxxix. 14 (part.)

[108]

This anthem is from Ps. lxxxix. 17 (part.)

From the title we learn that Ps. lxxxix. was used daily at Bangor, having already learned that it was used on Christmas Day [98], and on Sundays [105], and at Prime [98].

[109]

'Ad commonicare,' MS. *i.e.* 'Ad communionem.' The cross prefixed here on the margin denotes the introduction of a new subject.

This is the first of a series of seven Eucharistic anthems. This one corresponds to the 'Communio' of the Mozarabic Liturgy which is sung by the choir after the reception of Communion has taken place. See PL. Tom. lxxxv. col. 120. It is known as the 'Transitorium' in the Ambrosian Rite.

This first anthem is identical with a 'Transitorium' which occurs in the *Antiphonarium Ambrosianum Vetus* published by Dr. Ceriani (no place or date) p. 21. It there runs as follows : 'Corpus Christi accepimus, et sanguinem ejus potavimus, ab omni malo non timebimus, quia Dominus nobiscum est.'

The latter part of it is adapted from Ps. xxii. 4.

Line 1. 'accipimus' MS.

[110]

'Item alia.' Ps. xxxiii. 9. This anthem is sung during the fraction in the Greek Liturgy of St. James. (Hamm. p. 51.) The whole of this Psalm was ordered to be sung during the Communion of the people

L

in the Apostolic Constitutions (Lib. viii. c. 13. al. 20.) St. Cyril speaks of this verse being sung in his time (A.D. 348–86) at Jerusalem: Μετὰ ταῦτα ἀκούετε τοῦ ψάλλοντος μετὰ μέλους θείου προτρεπομένου ὑμᾶς εἰς τὴν κοινωνίαν τῶν ἁγίων μυστηρίων, καὶ λέγοντος Γεύσασθε καὶ ἴδετε ὅτι χρηστὸς ὁ Κύριος κ. τ. λ. (Κατήχησις μυσταγωγική). St. Ambrose alludes to it as sung at Milan in the same century: "Unde et ecclesia videns tantam gratiam hortatur filios suos, hortatur proximos, ut ad sacramenta concurrant dicens 'Edite proximi mei, et bibite, et inebriamini fratres mei.' (Cant. v. 1.) Quid edamus, quid bibamus, alibi tibi per prophetam Spiritus sanctus expressit dicens, Gustate et videte quoniam suavis est Dominus: beatus vir qui sperat in eo." (*De Mysteriis*, cap. ix.) These words form the Milanese 'Transitorium' for Easter Monday for use in 'Ecclesia aestiva' (*Antiphonarium Ambrosianum Vetus*, edited by Dr. Ceriani, no place or date, p. 15.) It is the ordinary 'Antiphona ad accedentes' in the Mozarabic Liturgy except from the first Sunday in Lent to the Vigil of Pentecost. (Hamm. p. 349.) It does not form part of the Roman Liturgy now, though it may have done so in St. Jerome's days, who said: "Quotidie coelesti pane saturati dicimus, Gustate et videte quam suavis est Dominus" (*Comment. in Isaiam*, ii. cap. v. § 20 : P.L. Tom. xxiv. col. 86); but, as this Commentary was written in Palestine, St. Jerome may be referring to the Liturgy of St. James.

For a somewhat similar Old-Gallican 'Antiphona cum plepst communicet,' the use of which is stated still to survive at Lyons, see W.T. pp. xxvi. 19.

[111]

'Item alia.' Ps. cxviii. 171. This anthem is found as a 'Communio' in the Celtic Liturgical fragment at *St. Gall. MS.* 1394 (W. p. 178) and in the *Stowe Missal.* (W. p. 243.)

[112]

'Alia.' This anthem, founded on a formula of administration, occurs also in the *St. Gall. MS.* 1394 (W. p. 178) and in the *Stowe Missal* (W. p. 243.) Compare the formula in the eleventh century Irish *Drummond Missal*, which seems to imply simultaneous communion in both kinds: "Corpus et sanguis Domini nostri Jesu Christi mihi indigno maneat ad salutem, et proficiat ad remedium in vitam aeternam. Amen." (Burntisland, Edit. G. H. Forbes, 1882, p. 23.)

A similar formula is found in the Syriac Liturgy of St. James. "*Mox Eucharistiam distribuit Sacerdotibus, Diaconis, deinde Laicis, dicens:*

'Corpus et sanguis Domini nostri Jesu Christi datur

tibi in veniam delictorum, et remissionem peccatorum in utroque saeculo.'" (Hamm. p. 80.)

The Gallican origin of this anthem is established by its being found, with the variation of a single word in the *Vita S. Burgundofarae*, abbess of Faremoûtier, where she introduced the Rule of St. Columbanus, dying there in 655. "Hoc sacrum corpus Domini et Salvatoris sanguinem sumite vobis in vitam aeternam." (Mabillon, *Annal. O.S.B.* Paris, 1669, Tom. ii. p. 443.)

Mabillon's marginal note to this passage is 'nota communionem sub utraque specie.'

[113]

'Item alia.' Ps. cxviii. 103. This anthem is not known to occur elsewhere.

[114]

'Item alia.' St. John vi. 59. This anthem also occurs in *St. Gall. MS.* 1394 (W. p. 177), and in the *Stowe Missal* (W. p. 243.) The first part occurs as part of the formula of the administration of the Host in the Ethiopic Liturgy. (Hamm. p. 262.) The whole occurs in the 'Antiphona ad accedentes' in the Mozarabic Liturgy for the third and fifth Sundays in Lent. (P.L. Tom. lxxxv. coll. 343, 347.)

[115]

'Item alia.' This anthem is found frequently in Celtic Liturgical documents, e.g. in the *Book of Deer* (W. p. 165); the *Book of Dimma* (W. p. 171); the *Book of Mulling* (W. p. 173); the *Stowe Missal* (W. p. 225.) In all these four cases it is part of an 'Ordo ad communicandum infirmum.' It is a characteristically, and so far as we know an exclusively, Ephesine formula. It opens the 'Prefatio' or bidding to the Postcommunion thanksgivings on all Sundays and Holy Days in the Mozarabic Liturgy:

"*Item orationes quae sequuntur dicuntur per totum annum tam diebus Dominicis quam in Festis post Eucharistiam:*

"Refecti Christi corpore et sanguine pariter quia sanctificati Deo Patri omnipotenti gratias referamus, ut nos in eadem refectione et sanctificatione habentes, hic et in futuro saeculo gloriam percipiamus. Ry. Amen." (P.L. Tom. lxxxv. col. 567.)

One similarly worded 'Consummatio Missae' is found in a 'Missa Dominicalis' of the Old-Gallican Liturgy.

"Refecti corpore (MS. corporis) et sanguine (MS. sanguinis) Domini nostri Jesu Christi, in aeternum restituti. hilares Domini misericordiam deprecemur. Per." (*Missale Gothicum*, No. lxxv. p. 143.)

Such similar prayers as are to be found 'ad

complendum' in the Gregorian Sacramentary always commence with 'Refecti cibo' or 'Refecti pane' or 'Refecti participatione' or 'Refecti vitalibus alimentis.'

[116]

The cross prefixed upon the margin to this title denotes the commencement of a fresh subject. Following close upon the Eucharistic Anthems we should perhaps have inferred that 'Gloria in Excelsis' was here intended for Eucharistic use, if by any mischance the rubricator had omitted to insert the title which tells us that it is for Mattins and Vespers (morning and evening) use. This or similar to this was its original position and use in both Eastern and Western Christendom. In Pseudo-Athanasius *de Virginitate*, which may be as old as the fourth century, it is directed to be said 'sub diluculum' at daybreak. In the *Codex Alexandrinus* (fifth century) it is entitled 'Ὕμνον ἑωθινόν.' In the Apostolic Constitutions the time and mode of its use are not stated, but it is placed immediately before another Canticle, which is always associated with evensong, viz.: 'Nunc Dimittis' (Lib. vii. capp. 47, 48.) We may, therefore, conclude that it was for use 'ad vespertinam.' And now in this early Irish Service book it is directed to be used in the Divine Office both 'ad vesperum et ad matutinam.'

This corresponds to its position and use in the Divine Office of the Greek Church at the present day.

There it is said daily after the three Psalms (148–150) in the Ὄρθρος, corresponding to Western Lauds, a longer recitation of it (δοξολογία μεγαλή) being used on Feast-days, and a shorter one (δοξολογία μικρά) being used in Lent and at other times of fasting. It is also sung daily at Compline, in its shorter forms, both at the Ἀποδείπνον μικρόν, and at the Ἀποδείπνον μέγα. (*Horologion*, pp. 69, 71, 167, 178.)

It is both curious and interesting to find that the Irish use of the seventh century and the Greek use of the present day are alike in directing that this Hymn shall be recited in the morning and in the evening in the Divine Office.

As to authorship the Bangor MS. is silent.

Line 9. 'et omnes dicimus amen.' This curious addition to the text of this Hymn is also found in three other early Irish versions of it, viz. those in L.H. L.H.* and in the *Stowe Missal* (W. pp. 197, 227) It has the appearance of a rubric gone astray, but there is no proof that this is the true origin of it.

The same words are also inserted in the Armenian Office for Vespers, in the text of the well known Eastern 'ἐπιλύχνιον εὐχαριστία' commencing 'Φως ἱλαρὸν ἁγίας δόξης.' Immediately after the words 'And the Holy Spirit, God' is added 'jev amenekeàn assemk. amén,' *i.e.*, 'and we all say, Amen.' (*Jamagarkhootiun*. Ed. Hajast. Vienna, 1879, p. 235.)

The twelve anthems which are here appended to 'Gloria in Excelsis' are in six cases taken from Holy Scripture, and in six cases from elsewhere.

Anthem.

(1.) Ps. cxliv. 2.

(2.) A translation of the second anthem after this Hymn in the *Codex Alexandrinus*, p. 59a, col. 1, No. 28.

(3.) Dan. iii. 26. 'Amen' is omitted in L.H.* but with this exception the readings in L.H. and L.H.* are identical. The opening words of this anthem have been detached in the MS. and added to the preceding anthem to which they do not belong.

(4.) Ps. cxxii. 3.

(5.) Ps. v. 2, 3.

(6.) Ps. v. 4.

(7.) Ps. lxxxvii. 4.

(8.) Not from Holy Scripture. It occurs in L.H.*

(9.) *do.*

(10.) *do.*

(11.) *do.* 'uniuersa' MS.

(12.) 'Gloria et honor' &c. This is the Mozarabic form of Gloria Patri. It may be seen on almost any page of the *Mozarabic Breviary*. An early mention of it occurs in Canon 13 of the fourth Council of Toledo (A.D. 633) which combating the opinion of those who at that time objected to the use of all Hymns of human composition, ran thus : " Respuant ergo et illum hymnum ab hominibus compositum, quem quotidie publico privatoque officio in fine omnium Psalmorum dicimus, ' Gloria et honor Patri, et Filio, et Spiritui Sancto, in secula seculorum. Amen.' " Canon 15 of the same Council explains the origin and orders the use of this Mozarabic formula instead of the form 'Gloria Patri' &c., which some people were seeking to introduce.

The exact words of the second part of the ' Gloria,' as found in the Bangor MS. omitting ' sicut erat in principio' are given by Walafrid Strabo as the Greek form (*De Rebus Ecclesiasticis*, cap. 25.)

SIX PARALLEL TEXTS OF 'GLORIA IN

ONE GREEK, ONE AMBROSIAN,

I.	II.	III.
Codex Alexandrinus in British Museum Fol. 569, rt col. Fifth Century.	*Ambrosian MS. Antiphonary* in British Museum, Add. MS. 34,209. Foll. 133v. 134r. Eleventh Century.[1]	*Antiphonary of Bangor.* Irish. Ambrosian Library, Milan. Fol. 33r. Seventh Century.
1. Δόξα ἐν ὑψίστοις θεῷ.	1. Gloria in excelsis deo.	1. Gloria in excelsis Deo.
2. καὶ ἐπὶ γῆς εἰρήνη ἐν ἀνθρώποις εὐδοκεία.	2. et in terra pax hominibus bone uoluntatis.	2. et in terra pax hominibus bonae uoluntatis.
3. αἰνοῦμέν σε.	3. laudamus te.	3. laudamus te.
4. εὐλογοῦμέν σε.	4. hymnum dicimus tibi.	4. benedicimus te.
5. προσκυνοῦμέν σε.	5. benedicimus te.	5. adoramus te.
6. δεξαλογοῦμέν σε.	6. glorificamus adoramus te.	6. glorificamus te. magnificamus te.
7. εὐχαριστοῦμέν σοι.	7. gratias tibi agimus.	7. gratias agimus tibi.
8. διὰ τὴν μεγαλήν σου δόξαν.	8. propter magnam gloriam tuam.	8. propter magnam misericordiam tuam.
9. κύριε βασιλεῦ.	9. domine rex.	9. domine rex.
10. ἐπουράνιε.	10. cęlestis.	10. coelestis.
11. θεὶ πατὴρ παντοκράτωρ.	11. deus pater omnipotens.	11. deus pater omnipotens.
12. κύριε υἱε μονογενῆ.	12.	12. Domine filii unigenite.
13. ᾽ιησοῦ χριστέ.	13. ihesu christe.	13. ihesu christe.
14. καὶ ἅγιον πνεῦμα.	14. sanctę spiritus.	14. sancte spiritus dei. et omnes dicimus. Amen.
15. κύριε ὁ θεὸς.	15. domine deus.	15. Domine.
16. ὁ ἀμνὸς τοῦ θεοῦ.	16. filius patris. ii.	16. filii dei patris.
17. ὁ υἱὸς τοῦ πατρὸς.	17. agnus dei.	17. agne dei.
18. ὁ αἴρων τὰς ἁμαρτίας τοῦ κόσμου.	18. qui tollis peccata mundi.	18. qui tollis peccata mundi.
19. ἐλέησον ἡμᾶς.	19. suscipe deprecationem nostram.	19. miserere nobis.
20. ὁ αἴρων τὰς ἁμαρτίας τοῦ κόσμου.	20.	20.
21. ἐλέησον ἡμᾶς.	21.	21.
22. πρόσδεξαι τὴν δέησιν ἡμῶν. ὁ καθήμενος ἐν δεξίᾳ τοῦ πατρός ἐλέησον ἡμᾶς.	22. qui sedes ad dexteram patris. miserere nobis ii. miserere nobis, subueni nobis, dirige nos, conserua nos, munda nos, pacifica nos, iii. libera nos ab inimicis a temptationibus, ab hereticis, ab arianis, a sismaticis, a barbaris.	22. suscipe orationem nostram qui sedes ad dexteram dei patris miserere nobis.
23. ὅτι σὺ εἶ μόνος ἅγιος.	23. quia tu solus sanctus.	23. Quoniam tu solus sanctus.
24. σὺ εἶ μόνος κύριος.	24. tu solus [altissimus.	24. tu solus dominus. tu solus gloriosus.
25. ἰησοῦς χρίστος.	25. ihesu christe.	25.
26. εἰς δόξαν θεὸν πατρός. ἀμήν.	26. in gloria dei patris.]² cum sancto spiritu. in secula seculorum. Amen.	26. cum spiritu sancto. in gloria dei patris. Amen.

EXCELSIS' WITH APPENDED ANTHEMS, VIZ. :

AND FOUR IRISH TEXTS.

IV.	V.	VI.
Stowe Missal.	*Book of Hymns.*	*Lebar Brecc.*
Irish. Royal Irish Academy, Dublin.	Irish. Trin. Coll., Dublin.	Irish. Royal Irish Academy, Dublin.
Fol. 14v.	Fol. 9, pp. 178–81.	p. [136], 2nd col.
Ninth Century.	Eleventh Century.	Fourteenth Century.
1. Gloria in excelsis deo.	1. Gloria in excelsis deo.	1. Gloria in excelsis deo.
2. et in terra pax	2. et in terra pax	2. et in terra pax
hominibus bonae uoluntatis.	hominibus bonae uoluntatis.	ominibus bone uoluntatis tue.
3. laudamus te.	3. Laudamus te.	3. laudamus te.
4. benedicimus te.	4. benedicimus te.	4. benedicimus te.
5. adoramus te.	5. adoramus te.	5. adoramus te.
6. glorificamus te.	6. glorificamus te.	6. glorificamus te.
magnificamus te.	magnificamus te.	
7. gratias agimus tibi.	7. Gratias agimus tibi.	7. gratias agimus tibi.
8. pro magnam misseric ordiam tuam.	8. propter magnam misericordiam tuam.	8. propter magnam gloriam tuam.
9. domine rex.	9. domine rex.	9. domine deus rex.
10. coelestis.	10. celestis.	10. celestis.
11. deus pater omnipotens.	11. deus pater omnipotens.	11. deus pater omnipotens.
12. domine filii dei unigeniti.	12. Domine fili [filii L.H.*] unigenite.	12. domine fili unigenite.
13. ihesu christe.	13. ihesu christe.	13. ihesu christe.
14. sancte spiritu dei.	14. sancte spiritus dei.	14.
et omnes dicimus. Amen.	et omnes dicimus. Amen.	
15. domine.	15. Domine.	15.
16. filii dei patris.	16. fili [filii L.H.*] dei patris.	16.
17. agne dei.	17. agne dei.	17.
18. qui tollis peccatum mundi.	18. qui tollis peccata mundi.	18. qui tollis peccata mundi.
19. misserere nobis.	19. miserere nobis.	19. miserere nobis.
20.	20.	20.
21.	21.	21.
22. suscipe orationes nostras qui sedis ad dexteram dei patris misserere nobis.	22. Suscipe orationem nostram qui sedes ad dexteram [dei L.H.*] patris miserere nobis domine.	22. qui tollis peccata mundi suscipe deprecationem nostram qui sodes ad dexterem patris miserere nobis. ,
23. quoniam tu solus sanctus.	23. Quoniam tu solus sanctus.	23. quoniam tu solus sanctus.
24. tu¹ solus dominus.¹	24. tu solus dominus.	24. tu solus dominus.
tu solus gloriosus.	tu solus gloriosus.	tu solus altisimus.
25.	25.	25. ihesu christe.
26. cum spiritu sancto.	26. cum spiritu sancto.	26. cum patre spiritu sancto.
in gloria dei patris.	in gloria dei patris. Amen.	in gloria dei patris. Amen.
Amen.		

⌐¹ Written twice, by accident.

SIX PARALLEL TEXTS OF 'GLORIA IN

ONE GREEK, ONE AMBROSIAN,

I.	II.	III.
Codex Alexandrinus in British Museum. Fol. 569, rt col. Fifth Century.	*Ambrosian MS. Antiphonary* in British Museum, Add. MS. 34,209, Foll. 133v. 134r. Eleventh Century.	*Antiphonary of Bangor.* Irish. Ambrosian Library, Milan. Fol. 33r. Seventh Century.

I.

καθ' ἑκάστην ἡμέραν εὐλογή
σω σε.
καὶ αἰνέσω τὸ ὄνομά σου
εἰς τὸν αἰῶνα
καὶ εἰς τὸν αἰῶνα τοῦ αἰῶνος
[*Ps.* 144. 2.]

καταξίωσον κύριε καὶ τὴν ἡμέ
ραν ταύτην
ἀναμαρτήτους φυλαχθῆναι ἡμᾶς.

εὐλογητὸς εἶ κύριε ὁ θεὸς τῶν πατέρων
ἡμῶν.
καὶ αἰνετὸν καὶ δεδοξασμένον
τὸ ὄνομά σου εἰς τοὺς αἰῶνας.   ἀμήν.
[*Song of the 3 Children,* 28–9.]
εὐλογητὸς εἶ κύριε δίδαξόν με
τὰ δικαιώματά σου.   [*Ps.* 118. 12.]
εὐλογητὸς εἶ κύριε δίδαξόν με
τὰ δικαιώματά σου.   [*Ps.* 118. 12.]
εὐλογητὸς εἶ κύριε δίδαξόν με
τὰ δικαιώματά σου.   [*Ps.* 118. 12.]

κύριε καταφυγὴ ἐγενήθης ἡμῖν.
ἐν γενεᾷ καὶ γενεᾷ.   [*Ps.* 89. 1.]

ἐγὼ εἶπα κύριε ἐλέησόν με.
ἴασαι τὴν ψυχήν μου ὅτι ἥμαρ
τόν σοι.   [*Ps.* 40. 4.]
κύριε πρὸς σε κατέφυγα.
δίδαξόν με τὸν ποιεῖν τὸ θέλη
μά σου ὅτι σὺ εἶ ὁ θεός μου.[1]
[*Ps.* 142. 9–10.]
ὅτι παρὰ σοὶ πηγὴ ζωῆς.
ἐν τῷ φωτί σου ὀψόμεθα φῶς.
[*Ps.* 35. 9.]
παράτεινον τὸ ἔλαιός σου τοῖς
γινώσκουσίν σε.[2]   [*Ps.* 35. 10.]

II.

Per singulos dies benedicimus te, et laudamus nomen tuum in eternum et in seculum seculi.
[*Ps.* 144. 2]

Dignare domine die isto sine peccatis nos custodire.

Benedictus es domine doce me iustitias tuas.   [*Ps.* 118. 12.]

Vide humilitatem meam et laborem meum et dimitte omnia peccata mea.   [*Ps.* 24. 18.]
Eructabunt labia mea hymnum hymnum† deo nostro.
[*Ps.* 118. 171.]

Viuet anima mea et laudabit te et iuditia tua adiuuabunt me.
[*Ps.* 118 175.]
Errauit sicut ouis que perierat require seruum tuum quia mandata tua non sum oblitus. iii.
[*Ps.* 118. 176.]
Cito anticipet nos misericordia tua domine quia pauperes facti sumus nimis adiuua nos deus salutaris noster. ii.   [*Ps.* 78. 8, 9.]
Benedictus es domine deus patrum nostrorum et laudabilis et gloriosus in secula seculorum. ii. Amen.   [*Dan.* 3. 52.]

III.

Cotidie benedicimus te et laudamus nomen tuum in aeternum et in saeculum saeculi.   Amen.
[*Ps.* 144. 2.]

Dignare domine die ista sine peccato nos custodire.

Benedictus es domine deus patrum nostrorum et laudabile et gloriosum nomen tuum in saecula. Amen.   [*Dan.* 3. 26.]

Miserere nobis domine miserere nobis.   [*Ps.* 122. 3.]

Verba mea auribus percipe domine intellige clamorem meum. Intende voci orationis meae rex meus et deus meus.
[*Ps.* 5. 2–3.]
Mane et exaudies uocem meam.
[*Ps.* 5. 4.]

Mane oratio mea praeueniet te domine.   [*Ps.* 87. 4.]

Diebus adque noctibus horis adque momentis miserere nobis domine.

Orationibus ac meretis sanctorum tuorum miserere.

Angelorum archangelorum patriarcharum prophetarum miserere nobis domine.
Apostolorum martirum et confessorum adque uniuersa gradus sanctorum miserere.
Gloria et honor patri et filio et spiritui sancto et nunc et semper et in saecula saeculorum.
Amen.

[1] Some of the letters in this anthem have suffered from alteration or erasure.
[2] All these anthems, with some additions, are found in the text of the δοξολογία μεγάλη or the δοξολογία μικρά, in the ἀκολουθία τῶν ὄρθρων in the Greek Horologion of to-day.   (pp. 69-72.)

EXCELSIS' WITH APPENDED ANTHEMS, VIZ. :

AND FOUR IRISH TEXTS.

IV.	*V.*	*VI.*
Stowe Missal. Irish. Royal Irish Academy, Dublin. Fol. 14*v.* Ninth Century.	*Book of Hymns.* Irish. Trin. Coll., Dublin. Fol. 9, pp. 178–81. Eleventh Century.	*Lebar Brecc.* Irish. Royal Irish Academy. p. [136], 2nd col. Fourteenth Century.

V.

In omni tempore benedicimus te et
laudamus nomen tuum in aeternum et in seculum seculi. Amen.
[*Ps.* 144. 2.]

Dignare domine nocte ista sine
peccato nos custodire.

Benedictus es domine deus patrum
nostrorum et laudabile et gloriosum nomen tuum in aeternum et
in seculum seculi. Amen.
[*Dan.* 3. 26.]
Domine deus salutis meae, in die
clamaui et nocte coram te.
[*Ps.* 87. 2.]
Intret oratio mea in conspectu tuo
inclina aurem tuam ad precem
meam domine.[1] [*Ps.* 87. 3.]

Scuto circumdabit te ueritas eius
non timebis a timore nocturno.
[*Ps.* 90. 5.]

IV. [desunt antiphonae.]

VI. [desunt antiphonae.]

[1] [The text of L.H.* follows that of L.H. to the end of Ps. 87. 3. The next anthem (Ps. 90. 5) is omitted and the following
are added :]

Noctibus ac diebus horis atque momentis miserere nobis domine.

Orationibus ac meritis sanctorum tuorum miserere nobis domine.

Angelorum et archangelorum patriarcharum profetarumque.

Apostolorum ac martyrum et confessorum atque uniuersi
gradus sanctoum tuorum miserere.

Et scribe nos in libro iuuentium ut per precem sanctorum
tuorum ueniam mereamur. miserere.

Praesta nobis domine ut hanc noctem sine peccato nos
transire possimus. miserere nobis domine.

Gloria et honor patri et filio et spiritui sancto. miserere.

Qui est ante saecula manet in aeternum miserere nobis
domine. miserere christe domine. miserere sancte domine.

Mirabilis deus in sanctis suis deus israhel ipse dabit
uirtutem et fortitudinem plebi suae benedictus deus. [Ps. 67. 38.]

In the *Ambrosian Breviary* A.D. 1508, after the anthem
(9) "Benedictus es . . . saeculorum " there follows a
rubric,

'*Sequitur.* Gloria et honor Deo Patri, et Filio, et
Spiritui Sancto.   Sicut erat in principio, nunc, et semper,
et per omnia saecula saeculorum.   Amen.'

This varying form of 'Gloria Patri' is also alluded to
by Beroldus in his twelfth century description of the
Ambrosian Mattins.

'*Deinde dicit* [*pontifex aut presbyter*] Gloria et honor
Deo.'   (Edit. Magistretti, Mediolani, 1894, p. 44.)

The short rubric in both these cases implies that this
formula was no longer, as in the Bangor Book, attached
to 'Gloria in Excelsis' as an anthem, but that it
followed it separately and independently.

The first of the twelve prayers of 'Ορθρον ends thus :
ὅτι πρέπει σοι πᾶσα δόξα, τιμὴ, καὶ προσκύνησις τῷ Πατρί, καὶ
τῷ Υἱῷ, καὶ τῷ Ἁγίῳ Πνεύματι, νῦν, καὶ ἀεὶ, καὶ εἰς τοὺς
αἰῶνας τῶν αἰώνων.   (*Euchologion*, pp. 24-5.)

After them comes the Συναπτὴ which concludes thus :
Τῆς παναγίας, ἀχράντου, ὑπερευλογημένης, ἐνδόξου Δεσποίνης ἡμῶν, Θεοτόκου καὶ ἀειπαρθένου Μαρίας, μετὰ
παντῶν τῶν Ἁγίων μνημονεύσαντες ἑαυτοὺς καὶ ἀλλήλους
καὶ πᾶσαν τὴν ζωὴν ἡμῶν Χριστῷ τῷ Θεῷ παραθώμεθα.

Ὁ Χορός.   Σοὶ Κύριε.

Ἐκφώνησις παρὰ τοῦ Ἱερέως.   ὅτι πρέπει σοι ut supra.
(*Euchologion*, pp. 16, 31.)

Σῶσον, ὁ Θεὸς, τὸν Λαόν σου, καὶ εὐλόγησον τὴν
κληρονομίαν σου· ἐπίσκεψαι τὸν κόσμον σου ἐν ἐλέει καὶ
οἰκτιρμοῖς· ὕψωσον κέρας Χριστιανῶν ὀρθοδόξων, καὶ κατά-
πεμψον ἐφ' ἡμᾶς τὰ ἐλέη σου τὰ πλούσια· πρεσβίαις τῆς
παναχράντου δεσποίνης ἡμῶν, Θεοτόκου καὶ ἀειπαρθένου
Μαρίας, δυνάμει τοῦ τιμίου καὶ ζωοποιοῦ Σταυροῦ·
προστασίαις τῶν τιμίων καὶ ἐπουρανίων Δυνάμεων ἀσωμάτων·
ἱκεσίαις τοῦ τιμίου ἐνδόξου Προφήτου, Προδρόμου, καὶ
Βαπτιστοῦ Ἰωάννου, τῶν ἁγίων, ἐνδόξων, καὶ πανευφήμων
Ἀποστόλων· τῶν ἐν ἁγίοις Πατέρων ἡμῶν, μεγάλων
ἱεραρχῶν καὶ Οἰκουμενικῶν Διδασκάλων, Βασιλείου τοῦ
Μεγάλου, Γρηγορίου τοῦ Θεολόγου, καὶ Ἰωάννου τοῦ
Χρυσοστόμου, τῶν ἐν ἁγίοις Πατρὸς ἡμῶν Νικολάου,
Ἀρχιεπισκόπου τῶν Μύρων τῆς Λυκίας τοῦ Θαυματουργοῦ·
τῶν ἁγίων ἐνδόξων καὶ καλλινίκων Μαρτύρων· τῶν Ὁσίων
καὶ Θεοφόρων Πατέρων ἡμῶν· τῶν ἁγίων καὶ δικαίων
Θεοπατόρων Ἰωακεὶμ καὶ Ἄννης· τοῦ Ἁγίου (τῆς Μονῆς)
καὶ πάντων σου τῶν Ἁγίων ἱκετεύομέν σε, πολυέλεε Κύριε,
ἐπάκουσον ἡμῶν τῶν ἁμαρτωλῶν, δεομένων σου, καὶ ἐλέησον
ἡμᾶς.

'ὁ Χορός.   Κύριε ἐλέησον (γ)'
                        (*Euchologion*, pp. 20, 31.)

The phrases which are identical with or resemble
anthems 4, 8, 9, 10, 11 in the Bangor Antiphonary have
been underlined.

We now come to a short series of 'preces,' occupying
fol. 34r.   Their titles seem to indicate that they were
intended for use at the lesser day hours, prime, terce,
sext, and none, 'ad horas diei oratio communis '; but as
the longer 'preces' previously given [40]-[56] were for
use, according to the Rule of St. Columbanus, 'per
diurnas horas.' perhaps these 'preces' [117]-[119] are a
short alternative set for occasional use.

Under the first title of 'oratio communis' there are
written three anthems and a Collect.

The first   anthem is from Ps. xxx. 2.
The second   ,,   ,,   ,,   Ps. xxxvii. 22, 23.
The third   ,,   ,,   ,,   Ps. lxix. 2.
      followed by the Collect 'Festina, Domine,' &c.

Although the word 'oratio' is used in this title, yet
there follow only three anthems without any Collect.

The first   anthem is from Ps. xl. 3.
The second   ,,   ,,   ,,   Ps. cxx. 7.
The third   ,,   ,,   ,,   Ps. cxx. 8.

The same three anthems have already been given in
[42] under the title 'Pro Abbate' (p. 22.)

'Common oroit dún.' i.e. 'Common Prayer of ours.'
This is the only vernacular title which occurs throughout the Bangor MS.   'dún' in modern Irish would be
'duin.'   The title is followed by :

   1. An anthem taken from Ps. xvi. 8.
   2. A short collect.
   3. The 'Pater Noster,' of which only the first two
      words are here given.   The full text has been
      given previously under the heading of 'Oratio
      divina' on Fol. 19 v. [36] p. 21.

Mons. d'Arbois de Jubainville thus remarks on the
rubric in [119].   "*Common oroit dún* littéralement
'*orate* common pour nous.'   On disait en Bretagne et en
Irlande *Orate* comme nous disons *Oremus*.   Dans *oroit*,
on peut remarquer, outre la prononciation bretonne de
l'*ā*, l'*i* interne représentant l'*e* final.   *Common* représente
la prononciation en irlandais du bas-latin, *commonis* pour
communis : ō =ū est très fréquent dans les manuscrits
irlandais.   *Dun* 'pour nous' est la forme irlandaise
du viii° et du ix° siècle dont la variante moderne 'duin '
apparait déjà dans le *Lebor na hUidre*." (*Revue Celtique*,
Paris, Janvier, 1894, p. 136.)

It is impossible to detect any order in the arrangement
of this and the following prayers.   The expressions 'de

luce vigilare' and 'excita de gravi somno' point to 3 a.m. or daybreak as the hour of the service 'ad matutinam.'

Line 3. 'et' for 'ut' MS.

 „ 4. 'ut' for 'et' MS.

[121]

This prayer seems to be a clumsy amalgamation of an Ephesine 'Prefatio' or 'bidding' with a prayer addressed to God.

For the scriptural events usually commemorated at none, see [20].

Line 4. 'et' for 'ut' MS.

[122]

For the title 'secunda' see note to [16.] The language of this collect—'qui diem clarificas et lumine luminas'—points to full daylight or about 6 a.m. as the hour of Prime.

Line 6. 'orietur' MS.

[123]

'Dominicorum' MS. 'Laudate pueri Dominum.' taken from Ps. cxii. 1, is the anthem prefixed to 'Te Deum laudamus' on p. 10, No. [7]. This is therefore a Collect to be used on Sunday after that Hymn. See note there to verse 26. The handwriting is notably different from all others which precede or follow it.

Line 1. 'Te.' Introd. § 5. (g.)

[124]

This is the only direct address to departed saints which occurs in the Bangor MS. It is rather a rhetorical appeal to the Martyrs to remember us than a direct prayer for their aid. The petition is 'mementote' not 'adjuvate.' See Introd. § 6.

[125]

See note to [123] which is a somewhat varied form of this Collect.

Line 1. 'Te.' See Introd. § 5 (g.)

 „ 9. It is to be noted that the words 'et filio' were not written at first by the scribe of [125] but were added afterwards, by way of an afterthought by the scribe of [126]. This is interesting as showing that the expression of the double procession of the Holy Spirit was now in process of establishing itself in the Irish Church. See the text of the Nicene Creed in the *Stowe Missal*, where the later scribe has added the 'filioque' to the original text in which it was wanting. (W. p. 232, and frontis-

piece.) See also the mark attached to 'et filio' in the Creed in this Antiphonary [35] line 15, where see note.

[126]

See note to [123]. This is another Collect for use after 'Te Deum laudamus.'

Line 1. 'Te.' See Introd. § 5 (g.)

[127]

The exact wording of this title is uncertain, as it has been partly obliterated. The Collect itself would be especially suitable to the lighting of the Paschal Candle on Easter Even, in consequence of the reference to the 'columna ignis' and the baffling thereby of Pharaoh and his army, but it would also be suitable for use at the daily 'lucernarium,' especially in Easter-tide. See note to [9.]

[128]

A large part of this Collect has been erased. It has already been written twice in [123] and [125]. See note to [123.]

The missing words within square brackets have been supplied from [123.]

[129]

'[In] memoriam abbatum nostrorum.' Either the opening word of this title has been accidentally omitted, or 'memoriam' is a mistake for 'memoria.'

For historical notes to this important hymn which sings the praises of the first fifteen abbots of Bangor, and which decides the date of the MS. as a whole, see Part i. Introd. pp. ix. x.

The Hymn consists of six stanzas. The first and sixth stanzas, which form an Introduction and Conclusion, contain eight lines apiece. The four intermediate stanzas contain six lines each. The lines of these four stanzas (except the last line of the fifth stanza) begin with the twenty-three letters of the Latin alphabet consecutively. Every line throughout all the verses ends with the letter 'a.' The two lines of the refrain, which is repeated after each of the first five verses, end with the letter 's.' The metre is iambic dimeter acatalectic. See note to title of [14]. A translation of this Hymn by Bishop Reeves is given in the *Ulster Journal of Archæology*, vol. i. p. 175.

Stanza.	Line.	
I	6	'tempra' MS. as required by the metre.
II	3	'carum' see note to [14] stanza v. l. 6.
„	4	'domnum.' This title is ordered to be given to the Abbot in chap. lxiii. of

M

Stanza. Line.

        the Rule of St. Benedict. 'Abbas autem, quia vices Christi creditur agere, Domnus et Abbas vocetur.'

V   1   'Colmanus.' In Part i. we followed Muratori and all previous editors of this Hymn in printing this name as 'Camanus.' The remnant of a letter preceding 'm' was taken to be part of the elongated upper stem of an 'a,' but a consideration of its square-headedness, and a consideration of the quotations from the *Annals of Tighernach* and the *Annals of Ulster* in Part i. p. x. together with the extremely diminutive form

Stanza. Line.

        frequently given to the letter 'o' as noticed in Part i. p. xxiii. make it practically certain that the name written here was 'Colmanus.'

V   3   'sedet.' For the inference drawn from the change here to the present tense, see Part i. p. x.

,,   5   'Zoen.' This Greek word has been introduced for the purpose of securing a 'z' for the opening letter of this line. For the use of Greek words see note to [10] stanza xiii. l. 1.

VI   8   The metre seems to require 'inter' for 'in.'

APPENDIX.

British Museum Harl. MS. 7653.

(Fol. 1 *r*.) estu mihi sanitas.[1] Cherubin estu mihi uirtus. Serabin estu mihi salus et arma. In nomine patris et filii et sp*iritus* sanc*t*i oro uos ac deprecor ut me in orationi-b*us* uestris habere dignemini. Ut pro me d*ei* famula oretis. Ut numqua*m*[2] in mundus sp*iritu*s siue aduersarius nocere me possit.

Dauid sanc*t*e te deprecor.[3]
Helias sanc*t*e te deprecor.
Moyses sanc*t*e te dep*r*ecor.
Sancte petre te deprecor.
Sancte paule te deprecor.
Sancte andrea te deprecor.
Sancte iacobe te deprecor.
Sancte thoma te deprecor.
Sancte iohannes te deprecor.
Sancte philippe te deprecor.
Sancte bartholomee te deprecor.

(Fol. 1 *v*.) Sanc*t*e iacobe te deprecor.

Sanc*t*e mathee te dep*r*ec*or*.
Sanc*t*e simon te deprecor.
Sanc*t*e taddee te dep*r*ecor.
Sanc*t*e iohanne bab*t*is*t*a† te deprecor
Sanc*t*e marce te deprecor.
Sanc*t*e luca te deprecor.
Sanc*t*a petronella[1]
Sanc*t*a agna.[2]
Sanc*t*a agatha.[3]
Sanc*t*a cecilia.[4]
Sanc*t*a eugenia.[5]
Sanc*t*a tecla.[6]
Sanc*t*a perpetua.[7]
Sanc*t*a benedicta.[8]
Sanc*t*a eufemia.[9]
Sanc*t*a constantina.[10]
Sanc*t*a iuliana.[11]
Sanc*t*a eulalia.[12]
Sanc*t*a lucia.[13]

---

[1] A later hand has written on the top margin above and a little to the right of this word ' legas claritas.'

[2] Over ' numqua*m* ' a later hand has written ' nærfə,' below it, to the right, these five letters ' a b c d d.' The former word shows us that the MS. was in England within two or three centuries after it was written, say, in the eleventh century at the latest.

[3] These deprecations ' Dauid,—anastasia,' are written continuously in the original MS. They have been printed out here in separate lines for the sake of clearness. Some of the following identifications of Virgins are necessarily uncertain, there being more than one saint of the same name. In some cases there is further uncertainty attaching to the date or place of the saint, or to the day of her commemoration.

[1] Legendary daughter of St. Peter, May 31.
[2] Martyr at Rome under Diocletian, Jan. 21.
[3] Martyr in Sicily, A.D. 251, Feb. 5.
[4] Martyr at Rome, 3rd cent. Nov. 22.
[5] Martyr at Rome, c. 260, Dec. 25.
[6] Martyr at Rome, 1st cent. Sep. 23.
[7] Martyr in Africa, c. 202, Mar. 7.
[8] Martyr in Gaul, c. 306, Oct. 8.
[9] Martyr at Chalcedon, 307, Sep. 16.
[10] or Constantia, d. of Constantine the Great, Virgin at Rome, 4th cent. Feb. 18.
[11] Martyr under Diocletian, Feb. 16.
[12] Martyr in Spain under Diocletian, Dec. 10.
[13] Martyr in Sicily under Diocletian, Dec. 13.

Sanc*t*a tarsilla.[1]
Sanc*t*a emiliana.[2]
Sanc*t*a iustina.[3]
Sanc*t*a cristina.[4]
Sanc*t*a scolastica.[5]
Sanc*t*a romula.[6]
Sanc*t*a musa.[7]
Sanc*t*a anastasia.[8]

Uos deprecor custodite anima*m* mea*m* et spiri*tu*m et cor et sensum et omnem mea*m* carnem.

(Fol. 2 *r*.) Angeli archangeli prophet*ę* apos*t*oli et beatissimi martyres nazareni coronati sine macula.

Et[9] sanc*t*us siluester et sanc*t*us laurentius in nomine sabahot.†

D*e*us abraha*m* et d*e*us isact et d*e*us iacob.
D*e*us angelorum.
D*e*us archangeloru*m*.
D*e*us patriarcharu*m*.
D*e*us prophetaru*m*.
D*e*us apostoloru*m*.
D*e*us martyru*m*.
D*e*us uirginu*m*.
D*e*us omnium sanc*t*oru*m*.
D*e*us patrum nostrorum miserere mei semper.[9]

Omnes inimici mei et aduersarii fugiant ante conspectum maiestatis tu*ę*. Et per istos angelos corruant sicut corruit goliat ante conspectum pueri tui dauid.

Uniuersos angelos deprecor (fol. 2 *v*.) expellite siquis in mundus[10] uel siquis obligatio uel siquis maleficia hominu*m* me nocere cupit. siquis hanc scriptura*m* secum habuerit non timebit a timore nocturno siue meridiano.

Uide ergo egipti ne' noceas seruos neque ancillas dei non[11] in esca non in potu no*n* in somno nec extra somno nec in aliquo dolore corporis ledere presumas.

Libera me do*m*ine libera me do*m*ine quia tibi est imperiu*m* et potestas p*er* dominu*m* ihesu*m* *christu*m cui gloria in secula seculorum :—

Me[12] cum esto sabaoth mane cum surrexero intende ad me et guberna omnes actost meos (fol. 3 *r*.) et[13] uerba mea et cogitationes meas.

Custodi pedes meos ne circu*m* eant domos[14] otiosi *sed* stant in oratione dei.

Custodi manus meas ne porrigantur sepe ad capienda munera.

Sed potius eleuantur in precib*us* do*m*ini mund*ę* et pur*ę* ut possim dicere. Eleuatio manu*um* mearu*m* sacrifiu*m*[15] uespertinu*m*.

Custodi os meu*m* ne loquar uana ne fabuler *ę*cularia ne detrahem proximo meo.

Custodi os meu*m* ne in uiter† alios ad uanum eloquiu*m* sed semp*er* prumptus ad laude*m* d*ei* tardus ad iracundiam.

Custodi aures meas ne audia*m* detractatione*m* nec mendaciu*m* nec uerbu*m* otiosum.

(Fol. 3 *v*.) Sed aperientur cotidie ad audi

---

[1] Aunt of St. Gregory the Great, 6th cent. Dec. 24.
[2] or Æmiliana, aunt of St. Gregory the Great, 6th cent. Dec. 24.
[3] Martyr, 1st cent. Oct. 7.
[4] Christina, martyr in Italy, 3rd cent. July 24.
[5] Scholastica, sister of St. Benedict, c. 543, Feb. 10.
[6] Virgin at Rome, 6th cent. July 23.
[7] Virgin at Rome, 6th cent. April 2.
[8] Martyr at Rome, c. 303, Oct. 28.
[9] —' These lines 'Et—semper' are written continuously in the MS.
[10] On the right margin after this line, in pale ink, partly erased, is written 'spiri*tus*' for insertion after 'inmundus.'

[11] Over the first letter of 'non' is a mark like ठ. It refers to this entry on the bottom margin 'no*n* in mare no*n* in flumine,' written in a contemporary hand, preceded by an 'h' crossed through its upper stem.
[12] This prayer is also contained in MS. Reg. 2 A. xx. fol. 22 *r*. where it is entitled 'oratio matutina.' It there begins at 'Mane cum surrexero,' and exhibits great variation of text (see page 96).
[13] The lines on fol. 3 *r*. printed here in paragraphs are written continuously in the MS.
[14] Over the second 'o' of 'domos' a small 'u' is written *prima manu*.
[15] Over the latter part of 'sacrifium,' 'ci' is written *prima manu*.

endum uerbum domini ut totum diem trans
eam in tua uoluntate.

Dona mihi domine timorem tuum cordis
conpunctionem mentis humilitatem conscientiam puram ut cęlum aspiciam terram
dispiciam peccata odiam iustitiam diligam.

Aufer a me domine sollicitudinem sęcu-
larem. gulę appetitum concupiscentiam fornicationis.

Custodi oculos meos ne uideant aliquem
ad concupiscendam per aliquid inlicitum. Nec
desiderem rem proximi. nec dilicias seculi.
Ut dicam cum propheta oculi mei semper ad
dominum. Et iterum ad te leuaui oculos
meos qui habitas in cęlo.

(Fol. 4 r.) Pater et filius et spiritus sanctus illa sancta trinitas esto mihi adiutrix.

Simul obsecro angelos archangelos uirtutes
potestates principatus dominationes thronos
chirubin et serabin ut intercedant pro me pec-
catri[1] apud iustum iudicem ut demittet omnia
peccata mea.

Michaelem sanctum gloriosum deprecor.

Rafael et uriel gabriel et raguel heremiel
et azael ut suscipiant animam meam in nou-
issimo die cum choro angelorum et perducent
eam ad amoenitatem paradisi.

Petrum rogo et paulum andream et iacobum iohannem et thomam bartholomeum et
matheum philippum et iacobum simonem et
tatheum (fol. 4 v.) ut adiubant mihi in die
iudicii ut lęta anima mea aspiciat purissimam
diuinitatem.

Rogo iohannem et clementem gregorium
et benedictum martinum et laurentem
stephanum et georgium ut adiubant mihi in
omni tempore.

Omnes sancti et martyres orate pro me.

INCIPIT ORATIO.

Spiritum[2] mihi domine tuę caritatis infunde
ut anima mea miserationum tuarum habundantia semper repleatur. Et qui mihi es
presidium ipsi sis premium.

Tuum est uere quod in te credo. Tuum
sit omne quod uiuam. Presta ut qui sine te
esse non possum secundum te uiuere ualeam.
(fol. 5 r.) Trahe me post te curremus. Quia
dixisti nemo uenit ad me nisi pater traxerit
eum. Trahe utcumque siue predicatione siue
conpunctione trahe ad culmen altum uirtutum. Considero non sufficere uires meas proprias nisi at te trahar. Trahe siue per
dolorem, siue per amorem. Trahe per amara
et dulcia per aduersa et pro spera per angusta et lata per mollia et dura. Scio quod
neque uolentis neque currentis sed miserentis
dei est. Trahe ut post uestigia mandatorum
tuorum curram. Ut dixisti uenite ad me
omnes. Trahe per quodcumque uolueris
tantum ut te habeam (fol. 5 v.) unicam atque
omnem spem hic et in futuro. Ut numquam
separer ab ingenti[3] amoris tui. Quia omne
quod desidero tu es neque habeo amplius
neque peto non solum super terram uerum
nec in cęlo excepto hoc ut semper tecum
sum in misericordia tua tantum gau debo et
gloriabor. Domine nihil terrenum desidero
et te solum deum integro affectu uiscerum
meorum concupisco :—

IN NOMINE DEI SUAMI.

Pater inmensę maiestatis per uenerandum
filium tuum uerum unigenitum te deprecamur
ut amoris tui ardor ageatur[4] in nobis. Sanctum quoque paracletum spiritum oramus ad-

---

[1] A small 'o' has been written over the latter part of
this word by an early correcting hand.

[2] This prayer with considerable variation of text, under
the heading of 'oratio sancta,' occurs on fol. 20 r. of
MS. Reg. 2 A. xx (see page 97).

[3] Here the word 'ardore' has been left out accidentally by the scribe.

[4] A small 'u' has been written, apparently
prima manu, over this word, between 'a' and
'g.'

iuuare nos. Te *dominu*m con- (fol. 6 *r.*)
fitemur. Te deum laudamus.[1] Te ęternu*m*
patre*m* omnis terra ueneratur. Tibi omnes
angeli tibi cęli et terra et uniuersę potestates.
Tibi cherubin et seraphin incessabili uoce
proclamant. Sanc*tu*s Sanc*tu*s Sanc*tu*s Dominus deus sabaoth pleni sunt cęli et terra
gloria tua osanna in excelsis. Te gloriosus
apostoloru*m* chorus te prophetaru*m* laudabilis numerus. Te martyru*m* candidatus
exercitus Te p*er* orbem terraru*m* sanc*t*a confitetur ęclesia patre*m* inmensę maiestatis
uenerandu*m* tuunι uerum unigenitu*m* filiu*m*.
Sanc*tu*m quoq*ue* paracletu*m* sp*iritu*m. Tu
rex glorię ch*riste*. Tu patri sempiternus es
filius. [fol. 6 *v.*] Tu ad liberandu*m* mundu*m*
suscipisti homine*m* non aborruisti uirginis
uteru*m*. Tu deuicta morte aculeo aperuisti
regna cęloru*m*. Tu ad dextera*m* sedis in gloria
patris ecce† uenturus. Te ergo quesumus
nobis tuis famulis subueni quos pretiosa sanguine redemisti ęterna*m* fac cum sanc*t*is in
gloria*m* intrare :—

D*eu*s altissime d*eu*s misericordię qui solus
sine peccato es. Tribue mihi peccatori fidu-
cia*m* in illa hora propter multas miserationes
tuas. Ut netunc apareat quę nunc uelata est
impietas mea cora*m* ex spectatorib*us* angelis
et archangelis patriarchis (fol. 7 *r.*) et pro-
phetis apostolis iustis et sanc*t*is. Sed salua
me pia gratia et miseratione tua induc me in
paradiso deliciaru*m* tuarum cu*m* omnib*us*
perfectis. Suscipe oratione*m* famulę tuę p*re*-

cibus omnium sanc*t*orum tuoru*m* qui tibi a
sęculo placuerunt. Quo*niam* tibi debetur
omnis adoratio et gloria per omnia sęc*u*la
seculor*um* :—

ORATIO.

I*N* pace ch*ris*ti dormia*m* ut nullu*m* malum uidea*m* a malis uisionib*us* in noctib*us* no-
centib*us*. Sed uisione*m* uideam diuina*m* ac
propheticam.

   Rogo[2] patrem et filium.
   Rogo sp*iritu*m sanc*tu*m.
   Rogo noua*m* ęclesiam.
   Rogo enoc et heliam.
(Fol. 7 *v.*) Rogo patriarchas [septem].[3]
   Rogo baptistam iohan*nem*.
   Rogo et b[onos][4] ange*los*.
   Rogo et omnes apostolos.
   Rogo prophetas p*er*fectos.
   [R]ogo[5] martyres electos.
   Rogo [sanctum] patricium.
   Rogo sa*n*c*tu*m [cirici]um.[6]
   Rogo mundi saluatorem.
   Rogo nostr*um* redemtore*m*.

ut anima*m* mea*m* saluare dignentur in exitu
de corpore. Te deprecor ut debea' ex intimo
cordis mei ne derelinquas in inferno anima*m*
mea*m* sed esse tecu*m* in cęlo in sempiterno
gaudio :—

ORATIO SA*N*C*T*I IOHAN*NIS*.[8]

Aperi mihi pulsanti ianua*m* uitę princeps
tenebrarum non occurrat mihi. No*n* noceat
mihi pes superbię. Et manus extranea*

---

[1] For this Irish version of 'Te Deum laudamus,' see
p. 93.

[2] These invocations are written continuously in the
MS.

[3] There is a space here in the MS. but the word
'septem' can be restored from the copy of this hymn
preserved in the *Lebar Brecc*, see p. 95.

[4] Only the first letter of 'bonos' is legible. The word
may be 'beatos.'

[5] Only part of this 'Rogo' is legible.

[6] The earlier part of this word is illegible, but the

name 'Ciricium' can be restored from the copy in the
Lebar Brecc (see p. 95).

[7] Presumably for 'debeo.'

[8] This title is written partly (viz. ORATIO) on the left
side of, partly (viz. SANCTI IOHANNIS) on the right side of,
and in the same line with, the last four syllables of the
previous prayer which are written exactly in the centre of
the page, viz. '·no gaudio.' For the prayer of St. John
see p. 95.

[9] Here the MS. breaks off abruptly at the bottom of
fol. 7 *v.*

Notes Upon Harl. MS. 7653.

This Manuscript is a fragment of seven leaves of vellum 8½ inches high by 8¾ inches broad, written in the eighth or ninth century in an Irish minuscule handwriting.

There is no pagination, or signature, or catchword.

The lines, eighteen on each page, are continuous throughout, except that the titles on foll. 4 *v.*, 5 *v.*, 7 *r.*, occupy the centres of otherwise blank spaces. If a word cannot be finished on the line on which it has been begun it is frequently finished at the extreme right of the line above or below it, being separated off by a slanting mark / from the rest of that line.

The only punctuation consists of the middle stop (·) and (:—) at the end of a section.

There are no illuminations. Separate prayers commence with capitals from half an inch to an inch high. These are filled with patches of red, yellow, or green paint. So are the interstices of the very slightly raised minuscule letters which commence fresh sentences. The titles on foll. 4 *v.*, 5 *v.*, 7, are written in red ink, now much corroded.

The MS. is in good preservation, and quite legible except on the first and last pages, which have suffered from the MS. having been formerly bound up with a modern English MS. with which it had no possible connexion. (Harl. MS. 7651 *olim* 5002.)

The Irish origin of the MS. is deduced from :

(*a*) The style of handwriting, and the formation of letters. Note a very small ' o ' on f. 3 *r.*, line 8.

(*b*) The coarse dark vellum used.

(*c*) The colours employed in embellishing the capital letters. The colours used in an English MS. of corresponding date have less body, and are of a lighter tint. (See Harl. MS. 2965.)

(*d*) The orthography of the writer, which exhibits the following peculiarities :

b for ph. as serabin f. 4 *r.*; b for v. as adiubant f. 4 *v.* (*bis*) ; f for ph. as rafael f. 4 *r.*; h prefixed as habundantia f. 4 *v.*; h omitted as aborruisti f. 6 *v.*; i for e as diliciarum, sedis, &c.; o for u as actos f. 2 *v.*; p omitted as apareat f. 6 *v.*; u for o as estu f. 1 *r.* (*ter*) apostulorum f. 2 *r.* prumptus f. 3 *r.*

None of these spellings is exclusively Irish. Every one of them, for example, is found in the Leofric Missal ; (p. xxxi.) but the last named substitution of u for o is, perhaps, more suggestive of the Irish than of other schools of spelling.

(*e*) The invocation of St. Patrick f. 7 *v.*

(*f*) The heading ' In nomine Dei summi' on f. 5 *v.* is specially Irish. It is found at the commencement of the Antiphonary of Bangor, where see note.

The MS. is part of a book of private devotions written by an Irish lady, probably a nun, as she describes herself as a "dei famula" on f. 1 *r.*, and uses the expression "famulę tuę" on f. 7 *r.* On f. 2 *v.* the devil is warned not to hurt the "seruos neque ancillas Dei." We also infer the sex of the writer from the invocation of twenty-one female saints in the Litany on f. 1, no male saints being therein invoked except those which are drawn from the pages of Holy Scripture.[1]

What else, it may be asked, can be inferred from the names of the saints which are invoked in this short MS. and from the order in which such invocations occur ? They point to a Celtic lady writing under Roman or Gregorian influence, at a time when the Roman Canon, in its Gregorian form, and perhaps Roman service books generally, had come to be in common use. This may seem to point to its having been written in England rather than Ireland, and the Anglo-Saxon gloss on f. 1 *r.* certainly indicates that the MS. was in England at a very early date, say about A.D. 1000, but the character of the vellum, and the character of the colouring, together with other indications already referred to, point to Ireland as the place of execution. And we have evidence from the Book of Armagh, written by Ferdomnach, a scribe of that city, that the Gregorian Canon was known in Ireland in A.D. 807.[2]

The invocation of Old Testament saints, *e.g.* of David, Elijah, and Moses in the Litany on f. 1 *r.* and of Enoch, Elijah, and the seven patriarchs in the hymn on f. 7 *v.* is a sign of antiquity, but nothing more. Such invocations are sometimes found in prayers or litanies later than the eleventh century. Commemorations in kalendars survived much later, and have survived in a single instance in the Roman kalendar of the present day.[3]

The Twelve Apostles are invoked next in the Litany, and also on f. 4 *r.* in Gregorian order, that is to say, in the order in which they are commemorated in the Gregorian Canon in its earliest MSS. and in the Roman Canon of the present day. Judas Iscariot is of course omitted, but his place is supplied not by St. Matthias, but by St. Paul, whose name stands second on the list next after that of St. Peter.

The following Irish list of the Apostles is taken from the Book of Hymns :

> Simon, madian, ismatha,
> partholon, tomas, tatha,
> petar, andreas, pilipp, pol,
> eoain, is da iacob.[4]

The following is the order in which they are commemorated in the Hymn of St. Cummain Fota : Petrus, Paulus, Andreas, Iacobus, Iohannes. Pilippus, Bartholomeus, Tomas. Matheus, Iacobus, Tatheus, Simon, Madianus, Marcus, Lucas, Patricius, Zefanus.[5]

Then follow in Harl. MS. 7653 the names of twenty-one virgins. They are chiefly of the age of the persecutions, and none of them seems to be later than the sixth century. Two of these virgins, Tarsilla and Emiliana, aunts of St. Gregory the Great, are very seldom invoked in

---

[1] The masculine form 'peccatori' occurs in the prayer immediately following *Te Deum* on f. 6 *v.* a few lines before 'famulę tuę,' which is probably due to the forgetfulness or inconsistency of the Irish lady who wrote the MS. The expression 'famula Dei' is equivalent to 'sanctimonialis' and occurs frequently in early Christian inscriptions in Gaul. (E. Le Blant, *Nouveau Recueil des Inscriptions Chrétiennes de la Gaule antérieures au viii* siècle. Nos. 5, 126, 143, 147, 225.)

[2] W. pp. 173-4.

[3] Kal. Aug. Commemoratio SS. Machabeorum Martyrum.

[4] Simon, [the Canaanite] Matthias, and Matthew, Bartholomew, Thomas, Thaddæus, Peter, Andrew, Philip Paul, John, and the two Jameses. *L. H.* f. 31 *v.*

[5] *Ibid.* p. 73. Madianus = Matthias, Zefanus = Stephanus.

Litanies or commemorated in kalendars, but they are found in the tenth century Breton Litany printed from a Rheims MS. by Mabillon[1] and reprinted by Haddan and Stubbs.[2] It is singular that the writer should not have added a single Irish virgin saint to the list nor is there any English saint in the list. It is perhaps still more singular that there should be no mention of the Blessed Virgin Mary either here or anywhere else in the MS.

The following Litany taken from MS. Reg. 2 A. xx. f. 26 r. written in England in the eighth century, is here printed for illustration and comparison with the Litany on fol. 1 of Harl. MS. 7653 (see p. 83.)

LAETANIA.

(col. a.) Christe audi nos.

Sancte michahel.	ora[3]	
Sancte gabrihel.	ora	
Sancte rapha[h]el.[4]	ora	
Sancte iohannes.	ora	
Sancta maria	ora	
Sancte petre.	ora	
Sancte paule.	ora	
Sancte andrea.	ora	
Sancte iacobe	ora	
Sancte iohannes.	ora	
Sancte philippe.	ora	
Sancte bartholome	ora	
Sancte thoma	ora	
Sancte mathe	ora	
Sancte iacobe	ora	
Sancte simon.	ora	
Sancte t[h]adde[4]	ora	
Sancte mathia	ora	

(col. b.)

Sancte barnaba	ora
Sancte marce	ora
Sancte luca	ora
Sancte stephane	ora
Sancte lini	ora
Sancte clete	ora
Sancte clemens	ora
Sancte xyste.	ora
Sancte corneli	ora
Sancte cypriane	ora
Sancte laurenti	ora
Sancte crysogone	ora
Sancte iohannes	ora
Sancte paule	ora
Sancte cosma	ora
Sancte damiane	ora

Sancte gerbasit	ora
Sancte protasi	ora
Sancte panchrati	ora

(f. 26 v. col. a.)

Sancte paule.	ora
Sancte antoni.	ora
Sancte sebastiane	ora
Sancte anastasi.	ora
Sancte policarpe.	ora
Sancte siluester	ora
Sancte leo.	ora
Sancte gregori.	ora
Sancte ambrosi.	ora
Sancte martine.	ora
Sancte augustine	ora
Sancte hieronyme.	ora
Sancte georgi.	ora
Sancte benedicte	ora
Sancta agnes.	ora
Sancta agathae	ora
Sancta iuliana.	ora
Sancta caecilia	ora

(col. b.)

Sancta anastasia.	ora
Sancta lucia.	ora
Sancta felicitas.	ora
Sancta perpetua.	ora
Sancta eugenia.	ora
Sancta eulalia.	ora
Sancta eufemia.	ora

Omnes sancti orate.
propitius esto parce.
propitius esto libera.
ab omni malo libera.
per crucem tuam libera.
peccatores te rogamus.
ut pacem dones te rogamus.

[1] Mabillon, *Analecta Vetera*, 1723, pp. 168-9.
[2] Haddan and Stubbs, *Councils, &c.*, vol. ii. part 1. p. 81.
[3] A mark of abbreviation over each 'ora' implies the remainder of the formula, 'ora pro nobis.'
[4] A small 'h' has been added over this word by an early correcting hand.

N

(col. b.) filius dei te tet rogamus.
agnus dei qui tollis
peccata mundi
miserere nobis.

christe audi nos.[1]
(fol. 27 r.) Summa trinitas una diuinitas auxiliare et miserere nobis.

On fol. 2 r. of Harl. MS. 7653 we find invoked by name St. Silvester and St. Laurence; Sylvester, the Roman bishop (ob. 335) of wide fame in consequence of his legendary connexion with the Emperor Constantine, and who heads the list of Confessors invoked in the Litany in the Roman Breviary; Laurence, the Roman deacon (ob. 258) whose fame was in all the churches, and who stands second to St. Stephen in the list of martyrs invoked in the same Litany.

In the line immediately preceding them it seemed at first sight as if the famous "Sancti Quatuor Coronati," were invoked under the title "beatissimi martyres Nazareni coronati sine macula," but a general view of the context, together with the omission of a specific number, leads to the conclusion that this invocation of martyrs is general.

On fol. 4 v. the following saints are invoked, and in the following order:

1. Iohannes: no doubt St. John the Baptist, who is generally ranked after the B. V. M. and the Archangels before the twelve Apostles.[2]
2. Clemens, Bishop of Rome, ob. c. 95–100, generally ranked fourth in the list of Martyrs.
3. Gregorius, Bishop of Rome, ob. 604, generally ranked high on the list of Confessors in position next to
4. Benedictus, ob. c. 542, of Nursia, founder of the Monastic Order of the Benedictines.
5. Martinus, ob. 397, Bishop of Tours. There are many traces of an early and special regard for St. Martin in the Celtic Church.
6. Laurentius, Deacon, Martyr of Rome, ob. 258.
   Martin and Laurence very early and widely obtained a recognized place in all Western Litanies and Kalendars.
7. Stephanus, possibly the protomartyr; possibly Stephen I. Bishop of Rome and Martyr, ob. Aug. 2, 257.
8. Georgius. This is the earliest known invocation of St. George in any Irish writing, but he is commemorated in the Kalendar of the Drummond Missal (Irish, 11th cent.) and invoked in two Litanies in the Corpus Missal (Irish, 12th cent. pp. 198, 212.) He is also invoked in the Litany on f. 26 v. of MS. Reg. 2 A. xx. printed on page 89.

These facts prove that the fame of St. George as a martyr spread at a very early date far and wide, and that he was specially invoked in these islands many centuries before he became chosen under special circumstances as the patron saint of England. The fame of St. George had been brought to Scotland in 698 by the Gallican Bishop Arculfus.[3]

---

[1] On the lower margin of fol. 26 v. a later hand has written: Reliquiae sanctorum tuorum domine intercedent pro me quorum iugiter . . . . exaudi psallentem et orantem te domine et conserua me in tua iustitia . . . .

[2] For illustration of this and the following remarks see any ancient or mediæval Litany, e.g. Leofric Missal, Oxford, 1883, Ed. F. E. Warren, p. 209. Irish Manuscript Missal, Lond. 1879, Ed. F. E. Warren, p. 198.

[3] See Adamnan, De locis Sanctis Lib. iii., cap. iv. P.L. Tom. lxxxviii. col. 810.

The following various deprecations in MS. Reg. 2 A. xx. f. 46 v. to 47 v. should be compared with those on f. 4 r. of Harl. MS. 7653.

(f. 46 v.) Te deprecor pater sancte ut digneris me saluare et non sinas interire in peccato et crimine.[1]

Chri*st*e cruci defixus per quam liberasti adiuua me ac defende magni factor *sec*uli.

Septiformis sp*iritus* lucis largitor spendidaet qui es fons luminis.

Trinitatis totius esto inluminator meae magnus animae.

Trinitas et unitas deitatis diuinitatis defendat me inmensitas magni regis et potestas.

Ordines angelorum archangelorum iustos cherubin *sanc*tam †pulso.

Intercessores thronos pincipatus† et seraphin potestates dominationes uos inuoco uirtutes.

Abel iustus et noe abraham atqu*e* isac iacob cum ioseph sacerdos melchisedech intercedant pro me.

Psalmista dauid citharesta d*ei* goliae interfector ouem de ore leonis ereptor figura chris*ti* eripientis totum de ore diaboli mundum roget pro me.

Uirga de radice iese exiens in cuius flore

(f. 47 r.) conquiescunt septiformis sp*iritus* dona id *est* sp*iritus* d*ei*. Sp*iritus* sapientiae et intellectus. Sp*iri*tus consilii et fortitudinis. Sp*iritus* scientiae et pietatis. Deprecetur pro me sp*iritus* timoris d*ei*.

Duodecim apostolos chris*ti* inuoco in adiutorium meum.

Clauicularium[2] simonem petrum.

Paulum mite*m*.

Andream uirilem.

Iacobum supplantatorem gratiam d*ei*.

Iohannem os lappadis.†

Philippum filium suspendentis aqus.†

Bartholomeum.

Thomam inuulnera chris*ti* credentem.

Abysum donatum mattheum.

Qui uocatur iudas iacobi uel libeus cuius nominis interpretatio corculus atqu*e*[3] ad abagarum regem missus.

Simonem cananeum.

Matthiam.

Marcum.

Lucam.

Stephanum.

Sanctum martinum.

Antonium heremitem.

Paulum.

Gregorium.

Hieronymum.

Augustinum.

Ambrosium.

Clementem.

Innocentium

Nazazenum gregoriam.[4]†

nic*e*ne ciuitatis episcoporum concilium.

Octo cum matre machabeorum.[5]

Kartaginiensem cyprianum.

*sanct*um essiodorum.[6]†

(f. 47 v.) Omnes *sancti* omnesqu*e* *sanct*ae omnes martyres atqu*e* cuncti confessores. septem caeli. et quattuor creaturae mundi. ignis. aer. aqua. terra.

Sol. luna. sidera fulgentia.

Omnis sp*iritus* qui laudat d*omi*n*um* deprecetur pro me omnipotentem d*eum*.

Cui honor est et imperium et potestas et gloria per infinita s*e*culorum s*e*cula. Amen.

In the Litany Hymn (Harl. MS. 7653, Fol. 7) on page 86, three saints are invoked by name.

1. St. John the Baptist, whose general place of honour in these lists has been already referred to (p. 90.)

2. St. Patrick. The occurrence here of this name of the patron Saint of Ireland clinches the proof, if clinching is needed, of the Irish character of this MS.

3. St. Cyriacus or Ciricius.[7] The selection of this Saint for invocation close to St.

---

[1] The paragraphs separated in the text as printed here are for the most part continuous in the original MS.

[2] A later hand has written in right margin : petr*us* clauicular*ius*.

[3] A later hand has written in the right margin : Abgar*us* Rex.

[4] St. Gregory of Nazianzus.

[5] Generally called the ' septem.'

[6] Isidorus Hispalensis (Bp. of Seville, 600–636.)

[7] The obliterated letters of the earlier part of this name have been restored by aid of the copy of this hymn on fol. 148 of the *Lebar Brecc*, 2nd col.

Patrick, is both curious and interesting.   His name frequently occurs in Celtic
names of places and dedications of churches, and under variously disguised
forms, Quiricius, Kirrig, Cyr, &c.   He was put to death as a boy, together with
his mother Julitta, in the Diocletian persecution, A.D. 303.   Gildas tells us that,
when the Diocletian persecution had passed away, British churches which had
been destroyed were re-built and re-dedicated in honour of the numerous
martyrs whom that persecution had produced.[1]   St. Cyriacus stands out
conspicuously among these martyrs.   The chapel at Tintagel, in Cornwall, the
churches at Cowley Bridge, in Devon, and at Capel Curig, in Wales, are examples
which may be adduced.   Others are given in the *Journal* of the Archæological
Association, vol. xxiii. p. 421.   He is commemorated in the Kalendar of the
Drummond Missal (Jun. 16) ; and in the Félire of Oengus (Jun. 16) where his
name appears as ' Giric.'

On fol. 4 *r*. the seven archangels are invoked by name in this order : Michael, Raphael,
Uriel, Gabriel, Raguel, Heremiel, Azael.   The first four names are common enough, being
found in various parts of the Bible, viz.

Michael.   Dan. x. 13, 21, xii. 1 ; Jude, 9 ; Rev. xii. 7.
Raphael.   Tobit, iii. 17, &c.
Uriel.   ii Esdras, iv. 1.
Gabriel.   Dan. viii. 16, ix. 21 ; Luc. I. 19, 26.

The other three archangels in Jewish tradition were usually named : Chamuel, Jophiel,
and Zadkiel.   The three names in the text are however found in Jewish apocryphal
literature.

Raguel.   Book of Enoch, xx. 4.
Heremiel (or Jeremiel.)   This name should be read in ii Esdras, iv. 36, where Uriel
      has taken its place in the A.V. by a mistake (Bensly's edition, Cambridge, 1875,
      p. 31.)
Azael (or Asael.)   Book of Enoch, vii. 9.

The devil is addressed as " Egiptius " on fol. 2 *v*.   The exorcised devil in the Book of
Tobit is represented as fleeing unto the utmost parts of Egypt where the angel bound him :
(Tobit viii. 3, A.V.) or, as the Vulgate has it, being bound by the angel in the desert of
Upper Egypt.

At the bottom of fol. 5 *v*. there commences one of the earliest extant texts of " Te
Deum laudamus."

It presents numerous variations of reading, some of which are unique, some remarkable
in character, some important in guiding us towards a decision as to the original text.   It is
also unique in ending at the close of verse 21, and omitting the eight last verses of the
Hymn as it is now generally known to us.   In addition to variations in which it agrees

---

[1] *Mon. Hist. Brit.* p. 9.   The British Church dedicated to God in the name of the 'Quatuor Coronati' at
Canterbury is an instance of this.   Bede, *Hist. Eccles.* ii. 7.

with the text in the Antiphonary of Bangor, the following exceptional readings will be noticed :

Verse 1. The inversion of the clauses.

     „   3. The addition of ' et terra.'

     „   6. The addition of ' osanna in excelsis.'

     „   9. The omission of ' laudat.'

     „ 15. ' patri ' for ' patris.'

     „ 16. ' aborruisti ' for ' horruisti.'

     „ 17. Omission of ' credentibus.'   In this verse 'devicta morte aculeo ' may be taken as a clerical error for ' devicto mortis aculeo.'

     „ 18. Omission of ' Dei.'

     „ 19. ' Ecce uenturus.'

     „ 20. Insertion of ' nobis.'

     „ 21. ' In gloriam intrare ' for ' in gloria numerari.'

     „ 22-29. Wanting.

Verses 5 and 6 are singularly suggestive of the Western Eucharistic Preface, and almost verbally identical with it in the shortened form which it has been made to assume in the vernacular Anglican Liturgy.

Appended in parallel columns follow three early Irish versions of " Te Deum laudamus " in juxtaposition with the *Textus receptus* of that Hymn at the present day.   Many points of interest about the original structure of "Te Deum" are raised or settled by these MSS. which have been recently handled by a writer who has specially devoted attention to this subject.[1]   The variations from the *Textus receptus* are printed in italics.

THREE OLD IRISH TEXTS OF "TE DEUM LAUDAMUS."

(Compared with ' Textus hodie receptus.')

I.	II.	III.	IV.
Textus hodie receptus. Roman Breviary, Tournay 1879, p. 13.	Antiphonary of Bangor. Milan, Ambrosian Library c 5, inf. I. 10, A.D. 680–691.	Harleian MS. 7653 [ff. 5 v. 6.] London, British Museum. VIII. or IX. Cent.	Book of Hymns, Trin. Coll. Dublin, E. 4, 2. (L.H. p. 196.) XI. Cent.
1. Te Deum laudamus : te Dominum confitemur.	1. *Laudate pueri dominum laudate nomen domini.* te deum laudamus te dominum confitemur : ·	1. Te dominum confitemur. te deum laudamus ·	1. *Laudate pueri dominum laudate nomen domini.* Te deum laudamus te dominum confitemur.
2. Te æternum Patrem omnis terra veneratur.	2. Te aeternum patrem omnis terra ueneratur ·	2. Te çternum patrem omnis terra ueneratur ·	2. Te æternum patrem omnis terra ueneratur.
3 Tibi omnes Angeli, tibi Cœli, et universæ potestates.	3. Tibi omnes angeli tibi coeli. et uniuersæ potestates. ,	3. Tibi omnes angeli tibi celi *et terra* et uniuersę potestates	3. Tibi omnes angeli tibi caeli et uniuersae potestates.
4. Tibi Cherubin et Seraphin incessabili voce proclamant :	4. Tibi hirubin et syraphin incessabili uoce proclamant	4. Tibi cherubin et seraphin incessabili uoce proclamant ·	4. Tibi hirupbin et zaraphin incessabili uoce proclamant *dicentes.*
5. Sanctus, Sanctus, Sanctus, Dominus Deus Sabaoth.	5. Sanctus sanctus sanctus dominus deus sabaoth. ,	5. Sanctus sanctus sanctus dominus deus sabaoth	5. Sanctus sanctus sanctus dominus deus sabaoth.
6. Pleni sunt cœli et terra majestatis gloriæ tuæ ·	6. Pleni sunt caeli et *uniuersa* terra *honore* gloriæ tuæ : ·	6. Pleni sunt celi et terra *gloria tua osanna in excelsis* ·	6. Pleni sunt celi et *uniuersa* terra honore gloriae tuae.
7. Te gloriosus Apostolorum chorus.	7. Te gloriosus apostolorum chorus ·	7. Te gloriosus apostolorum chorus	7. Te gloriosus apostolorum chorus.
8. Te Prophetarum laudabilis numerus,	8. Te prophetarum laudabilis numerus ·	8. Te prophetarum laudabilis numerus : ·	8. Te profetarum laudabilis numerus.
9. Te Martyrum candidatus laudat exercitus,	9. Te martyrum candidatus *laudat* exercitus ·	9. Te martyrum candidatus exercitus	9. Te martirum candidatus laudat exercitus.

---

[1] See the exhaustive article by our President, Dr. John Wordsworth, Bishop of Salisbury, on ' Te Deum ' in Julian's *Dictionary of Hymnology*, Lond. 1892, pp. 1119, 1547, and the authorities referred to therein.

Three Old Irish Texts of "Te Deum Laudamus"—*continued.*

I. *Textus hodie receptus.* Roman Breviary, *Tournay* 1879, p. 13.	*II.* *Antiphonary of Bangor.* Milan, Ambrosian Library c. 5, inf. f. 10, A.D. 680–691.	*III.* *Harleian MS.* 7653 [ff. 5 v. 6.] London, British Museum. *VIII. or IX. Cent.*	*IV.* *Book of Hymns,* Trin. Coll. Dublin, E. 4, 2. (L.H. p. 196.) *XI. Cent.*
10. Te per orbem terrarum sancta confitetur Ecclesia ·	10. Te per orbem terrarum sancta confitetur æcclesia : ·	10. Te per orbem terrarum sancta confitetur æclesia	10. Te per orbem terrarum sancta confitetur æcclesia.
11. Patrem immensæ majestatis,	11. Patrem immensæ maiestatis.	11. Patrem immensæ maiestatis	11. Patrem immensæ maiestatis *tua.*
12. Venerandum tuum verum et unicum Filium,	12. Venerandum tuum uerum *unigenitum* filium. ,	12. Venerandum tuum uerum *unigenitum* filium ·	12. Venerandum tuum uerum et *unigenitum* filium.
13. Sanctum quoque Paraclitum Spiritum ·	13. Sanctum quoque paraclitum spiritum ·	13. Sanctum quoque paracletum spiritum ·	13. Sanctum quoque paraclitum spiritum.
14. Tu Rex gloriæ, Christe ·	14. Tu rex gloriæ christe. ,	14. Tu rex gloriæ christe	14. Tu rex gloriæ christe.
15. Tu Patris sempiternus es Filius.	15. Tu patria sempiternus es filius ·	15. Tu *patri* sempiternus es filius.	15. Tu patris sempiternus es filius.
16. Tu, ad liberandum suscepturus hominem non horruisti Virginis uterum ·	16. Tu ad liberandum *mundum* suscepisti hominem : · non horruisti uirginis uterum ·	16. Tu ad liberandum *mundum* suscipisti hominem non ab *orruisti* uirginis uterum ·	16. Tu ad liberandum *mundum* suscepisti hominem non horruisti uirginis uterum.
17. Tu, devicto mortis aculeo, aperuisti credentibus regna cœlorum ·	17. Tu deuicto mortis aculeo aperuisti credentibus regna caelorum ·	17. Tu *deuicta morte* aculeo aperuisti regna cęlorum.	17. Tu deuicto mortis aculeo aperuisti credentibus regna caelorum.
18. Tu ad dexteram Dei sedes, in gloria Patris ·	18. Tu ad dexteram dei *sedens* in gloria patris ·	18. Tu ad dexteram sedis in gloria patris	18. Tu ad dexteram dei sedes in gloria patris.
19. Judex crederis esse venturus ·	19. Iudex crederis esse uenturus. ,	19. *Ecce uenturus* ·	19. Iudex crederis esse uenturus.
20. Te ergo, quaesumus, tuis famulis subveni : quos pretioso sanguine redemisti.	20. Te ergo quæsumus *nobis* tuis famulis subueni quos pretioso sanguine redimisti. . .	20. Te ergo quæsumus *nobis* tuis famulis subueni quos pretiosa sanguine redimisti ·	20. Te ergo quæssimus *nobis* tuis famulis subueni quos pretioso sanguine redemisti.
21. Æterna fac cum sanctis tuis in gloria numerari ·	21. *Aeternam* fac cum sanctis gloriæ *munerori*	21. *Eternam* fac cum sanctis *in gloriam intrare*—	21. Eternam fac cum sanctis tuis gloriæ munerari.
22. Salvum fac populum tuum, Domine, et benedic hæreditati tuæ.	22. Saluum fac populum tuum domine et benedic heredi·tati tuae.	22. *deest.*	22. Saluum fac populum tuum domine et benedic hereditati tuæ.
23. Et rege eos, et extolle illos usque in æternum.	23. Et rege eos et extolle illos usque in *sæculum* : .	23. *deest.*	23. Et rege eos et extolle illos usque in *seculum.*
24. Per singulos dies benedicimus te.	24. Per singulos dies beneuicimus te ·	24. *deest.*	24. Per singulos dies benedicimus te
25. Et laudamus nomen tuum in sæculum, et in sæculum sæculi ·	25. Et laudamus nomen tuum in *aeternum* et in saeculum saeculi *Amen*	25. *deest.*	25. Et laudamus nomen tuum in *aeternum* et in seculum seculi.
26. Dignare, Domine. die ista sine peccato nos custodire ·	26. *deest.*	26. *deest.*	26. *deest.*
27. Miserere nostri, Domine : miserere nostri.	27. *deest.*	27. *deest.*	27. *deest.*
28. Fiat misericordia tua, Domine, super nos, quemadmodum speravimus in te.	28. Fiat domine misericordia tua super nos quemadmodum sperauimus in te : ·	28. *deest.*	28. Fiat domine misericordia toa super nos quemadmodum sperauimus in te.
29. In te, Domine, speravi : non confundar in æternum.	29. *deest.*	29. *deest.*	29. *deest.*

The various readings in Coll. ii. iii. iv. are printed in italics, or called attention to in footnotes. Variations of spelling are not noticed.

Various readings occur in verses 1, 6, 9, 12, 16, 18, 21, 23, 25, 28.
Verses 26, 27, 29 are wanting.
15. Printed with the Ms. correction.
18. The same.
20. 'Sanguinem' is evidently a clerical error for 'sanguine,' and has not been printed in italics as a various reading.
21. Omission of 'tuis in'
22. For the groups of points after ' domine ' s·e facsim le
24, 25, 26, 27 are appended as 'antiphonæ' to Gloria in excelsis, f. 33v.
28. The second, third, and fourth words are transposed.

Various readings occur in verses 1, 3, 6, 9, 12, 15, 16, 17, 18, 19, 20, 21.
Verses 22–29 are wanting.
1. Inversion of clauses.
9. Omission of 'laudat.'
13. It is difficult to decide if 'paracletus' is a different word from 'paraclitus' in ii. and iv. or whether they only afford instances of confusion between 'i' and 'e.'
17. Omission of 'credentibus.'
18. Omission of 'dei.' Instead of ' sedes ' there is 'sedis.'
21. Omission of 'tuis.'

Various readings occur in verses 1, 4, 6, 12, 16, 20, 21, 23, 28.
Verses 26, 27, 29 are wanting.
Then follow these words in a different and more angular handwriting, but by the same scribe :
Te patrem adoramus eternum. Te sempiternum filium inuocamus. teque spiritum sanctum in una diuinitatis substantia manentem confitemur.
Tibi uni deo in trinitate debitas laudes et gratias referimus ut te incessabuli uoce laudare meremur per eterna serula.
This ascription of praise occurs thrice in the Antiphonary of Bangor. ff. 35 r., 35 v., 36 r. It is labelled for use 'Post laudate etc.' on ff. 35 r., 35 v. On f. 36 r. the title is wanting. 'Laudate pueri dominum' is equivalent to 'Te Deum laudamus,' to which hymn it is prefixed on f. 10r.
21. Omission of 'in.'
28. The second, third, and fourth words are transposed.
The text of 'Te Deum' in L.H.* is identical with the above except that it omits 'nobis' in verse 20.

A text of the Hymn 'Rogo patrem' in Harl. MS. 7653, fol. 7, is also preserved in the *Lebar Brecc*, a large folio vellum volume in the Royal Irish Academy, Dublin, containing a collection of pieces in Irish and Latin, compiled from ancient sources about the end of the fourteenth century. It was published in facsimile from the original MS. at Dublin, in 1876.

It is found on fol. 148 second column, in this form. Contractions and abbreviations are lengthened out.

Rogo patrem per filium, rogo spiritum sanctum, rogo patriarchas vii.[1] rogo omnes apostolos, rogo sanctos angelos, rogo iohannem bauptistam, rogo nouam eclesiam, rogo enoc et eliam, rogo prophetas perfectos, rogo martyres electos, rogo iustum patricium, rogo sanctum ciricium, rogo mundi saluatorem, rogo nostrum redemptorem, ut animam meam saluare digneris in exitu de corpore. Te debeo cordis mei ex intimo non relinquas in inferno animam meam pesimam, sed ut sit secumt in seculo sempiterno in gaudia, ut audiam angelorum uocem deum laudantium.[2]

By the aid of the two texts, both in parts corrupt, the Hymn may be tentatively reconstructed in the following form:

1. In pace Christi dormiam,
   Ut nullum malum videam
   A malis visionibus
   In noctibus nocentibus,
   Sed visionem videam
   Divinam ac propheticam.

2. Rogo Patrem et Filium,
   Rogo [et] Spiritum Sanctum,
   Rogo novam ecclesiam
   Rogo Henoch et Eliam
   Rogo Patriarchas septem
   Rogo Baptistam Iohannem.

3. Rogo et bonos Angelos
   Rogo omnes Apostolos
   Rogo Prophetas perfectos

   Rogo Martyres electos
   Rogo sanctum Patricium
   Rogo sanctum Ciricium.

4. Rogo mundi Salvatorem
   Rogo nostrum Redemptorem
   Ut animam meam salvare
   Dignentur in exitu de corpore.

5. Te deprecor, ut debeo,
   Cordis mei ex intimo
   Ne relinquas in inferno
   Animam meam pessimam.

6. Sed ut sit tecum in celo
   In sempiterno gaudio,
   Ut audiam angelorum
   Vocem Deum laudantium.

The 'Oratio Sancti Iohannis,' with which this MS. concludes, is part of the dying prayer of St. John the Divine as given in the 'Passio S. Iohannis' attributed to Mellitus (Melito).

At whatever date this pseudo-Mellitus may have lived, the prayer probably came ultimately from the Acts by Leucius, which are referred to by him and which may be attributed to the second century. The full text of the prayer is subjoined.[3]

---

[1] It seems impossible to suggest a reason for 'seven patriarchs.' The Irish were always apt to be random in their use of numbers.

[2] The editor is indebted to Mr. Whitley Stokes for the reference to the *Lebar Brecc* and also for the proposed reconstruction of the Hymn.

[3] *Acta Iohannis*, ed. Th. Zahn, Erlangen, 1880, p. 251. J. A. Fabricius, *Codex Apocryphus Novi Testamenti* Hamburgi, 1743, Tom. iii. p. 622. The date of Leucius is discussed by Zahn, p. 195.

Invitatus ad convivium tuum venio gratias agens, quia me dignatus es Domine Jesu Christe ad tuas epulas invitare, sciens quod ex toto corde meo desiderabam te. Vidi faciem tuam et quasi de sepultura suscitatus sum. Odor tuus concupiscentias in me excitavit æternas. Vox tua plena suavitate mellifiua et allocutio tua incomparabilis eloquiis angelorum. Quoties te rogavi ut ad te venirem ; et dixisti, expecta ut populum liberes creditum mihi, et custodisti corpus meum ab omni pollutione, et animam meam semper illuminasti, et non dereliquisti me cum irem in exilium, et redirem, et possuisti ori meo verbum veritatis tuae commemorans me testimonia tuarum virtutum, et

scripsi ea opera, quæ audiri ex ore tuo auribus meis, et vidi oculis meis. Et nunc, Domine, commendo filios tuos, quos tibi ecclesia tua virgo vera mater per aquam et Spiritum Sanctum generavit. Suscipe me cum fratribus meis simul cum quibus veniens invitasti me Aperi mihi pulsanti januam vitæ, principes tenebrarum non occurrant mihi et pes superbiae et manus extranea a te non tangat me. Sed suscipe me secundum verbum tuum, et perduc me ad convivium epularum tuarum, ubi epulantur tecum omnes amici tui. Tu es enim Christus, filius Dei, [qui] cum Patre tuo, et cum Spiritu Sancto vivis et regnas in sæcula sæculorum.

Another and shorter version of this prayer is contained in a ninth century Fleury 'Libellus precum.'[1]

Another prayer of St. John, offered by him before drinking the poisoned chalice, is transcribed from the same source in the Irish Book of Hymns. Deus meus et pater et filius, &c.[2]

The following text from MS. Reg. 2 A. xx. f. 22 r. of the Morning Prayer may be compared with that in the Irish MS. Harl. 7653. commencing 'Mecum esto' at the bottom of f. 2 v.

ORATIO MATUTINA.

(f. 22 r.) Mane cum surrexero intende ad me domine et guberna omnes actus meos et uerba mea et cogitationes meas ut tota die in tua uoluntate transeam.

Dona mihi domine timorem tuum cordis[3] conpunctionem mentis humilitatem conscientiam puram ut terram despiciam cçlum[4] aspiciam peccata odiam iustitiam[5] diligam.

Aufer a me solicitudinem[6] terrenam. gulæ appetitum concupiscentiam fornicationis amorem pecuniae. pestem iracundiae tristitiam saeculi accidiam uanam laetitiam terrenam.

Planta in me uirtutem abstinentium continentiam carnis castitatem humilitatem caritatem non fictam.

Custodi os meum ne loquar uana ne fabuler saecularia ne detraham abstinentibus nemaledicam maledictionem prsentibus.

(f. 22 v.) Sed econtrario benedicam domino et semper laus eius inoremeo. custodi oculos meos neuideant gloriam saeculi concupiscendas eas et nedesiderem rem proximi.

Ut dicam spiritu dauid. oculi mei semper ad dominum et iterum ad te leuaui oculos meos qui habitas incaelo. custodi aures meas ne audiam detractationem nec mendacium nec uerbum otiosum. sed aperiantur cotidie ad audiendum uerbum dei.

Custodi pedes meos necircum eant domus otiosas sed sint inoratione dei. custodi manus meas neporrigantur sepe ad capienda munera. sed potius eleuentur inprecibus domini mundae et purae quo possim dicere cum propheta. eleuatio manum† mearum sacrificium uespertinum.

A rather longer version of the above prayer, with several variations of text, appears in a ninth century Fleury MS. 'Libellus precum.'[6]

---

[1] Edm. Martene, *De antiquis Ecclesiae Ritibus*, Lib. iv. cap. xxxiv. Bassani, 1788, Tom. iii. p. 234.

[2] L.H. p. 268 and Fabricius *ut supra*, p. 618.

[3] Over these first six words a later English hand has written this gloss : 'sele me drith wines eges heortton.'

[4] 'ti' has been written above this word in smaller letters *prima manu*.

[5] A small 'i' has been written between 'l' and 'i' over this word *prima manu*.

[6] This MS. invokes among the martyrs, SS. Monnus, Albanus, Cilianus (Kilian) Columbanus, Columbanus ; among the monks, SS. Columbanus, Furseus, Patricius, Columba, Congallus, Adomnanus, Cheranus (= Kieranus) ; among the virgins, SS. Brigida, Ita, Samsdenna. (Martene, *op. cit.* p. 238.) For the connexion of Celtic MSS. with Fleury at an early date see *Collected Papers of Henry Bradshaw*, Cambridge, 1889, p. 464.

The following is the text from MS. Reg. 2 A. xx. f. 20 r. of the prayer which occurs in Harl. MS. 7653. fol. 4 v. commencing with the same words.

Sp*iritu*m mihi d*omi*ne tuae caritatis infunde, ut amina mea miserationum tuarum [h][l]abundantia semper repleatur et qui es mihi praesidium ipse sis pr*e*mium tuum sit omne q*uo*d uiua*m*.

Presta ut qui sine te esse posum[2] secundum te uiuere ualeam. trah*e* me post te curremus quia dixisti. nemo uenit ad patrem nisi per me

Et nemo uenit ad me nisi pater tracberit eum trahe me ad culmen altum uirtutum.[3]

Considero non sufficere uires proprias nisi a te[4] trahar. trahe me siue per amorem siue per dolorem trahe me per amam et dulcia (f. 20 v.) per aduersa et prospera per angusta et lata per mollia et dura. scio quia neq*ue* uolentis neq*ue* currentis sed miserantis

est d*e*i. trahe me ut uestigia mandatorum tuorum curra*m*.

Ut dixisti uenite post me. trahe me per quod cumque uolueris tantum ut te habea*m* uitae meae unicam atque omnem spem hic et infuturo ut numquam separer ab ingenti ardore amoris tui q*uia*[5] omne q*uo*d desidero tu es.

Neque habeo amplius neq*ue* peto no*n* solum super terram uerum neq*ue* inc*ae*lo excepto hoc ut semp*e*r tecum sim inmisericordia tua tantum gaudebo et gloriabor inte domine.

Nihil terrenum magnopere desidero sed te solum *deu*m integro affectu uiscerum meorum concupisco qui uiuis et regnas per omnia s*e*cula saeculorum amen.

NOTE UPON MS. REG. 2 A. XX.

There is so much similarity, and in certain parts identity, between the contents of this MS. and that of Harl. MS. 7653, and so much reference has been made to it in the notes to the latter MS. that a short account of it, together with a complete catalogue of its contents, may be of interest.

It is a vellum MS. of fifty-two leaves, measuring $9\frac{1}{4}$ inches by $6\frac{1}{2}$ inches, and containing from eighteen to twenty-four lines in a page. It was written in the north of England in the eighth century. The original text exhibits three different handwritings: (1) round, (2) transitional, between round and pointed, (3) pointed. Although No. (3) may be slightly later than (1) and (2), all three handwritings alike may be assigned to the eighth century.

Ff. 2–12 r. are in the (1); ff. 12 v.—38, 41–45 in the (2); and ff. 39, 40, 46–51 in the (3) handwriting.

A good deal of additional matter has been added by an English hand c. A.D. 1000. This additional matter consists of (1) Anglo-Saxon interlinear glosses; (2) Anglo-Saxon headings to the alphabetically arranged series of prayers on f. 29 r.; (3) Latin prayers written on the margins; (4) interlinear Greek words in English characters.

Can we localize this MS. more closely? It is strange that not a single Celtic or Anglo-Saxon saint is invoked or commemorated in any part of it. The early round Northumbrian hand, and the initial letters patched with various colours and surrounded with red dots, very much resemble Irish work, but are found in other Northumbrian MSS. and do no more than testify to the influence which Celtic art had upon a church which was founded by a Celtic Mission in 635, and was only gradually Anglicized after the Synod of Whitby in 664, and which indirectly

---

[1] This letter has been erased.   [2] A later hand has written a long English 's' over this word.

[3] The six words ending 'uirtutum' have been written over again by a later hand on the lower margin.

[4] The original words, which were probably 'ad te,' have been erased and the words 'a te' have been written on the erased space.

[5] The last three letters of this word have been written above the line by a later hand.

through its foundation from Iona, and directly through the nationality and journeys of many of its earlier members, had much communication with Ireland.

The invocation of St. Benedict in the Litany on f. 26 *v.* and the heading and wording of marginal collects on ff. 10 *v.* 13 *v.* connect the MS. with a Benedictine monastery. This does not necessarily mean an original Benedictine foundation ; it may point to some Columban foundation which in the latter part of the seventh or in the eighth century adopted the Benedictine rule.

Two titles of prayers yield further assistance. On fol. 17 *r.* a prayer occurs, entitled, ' oratio sancti hugbaldi abbatis.'

This may be the abbot Hygbald " in provincia Lindissi," mentioned by Bede (*Hist. Eccles.* iv. 3), under the year 669. It is not known of what monastery he was abbot. In Smith and Wace's *Dictionary of Christian Biography* (vol. iii. p. 183) Bardney is suggested, for which there is some, but not conclusive, evidence. Lindsey was a district, south of the Humber, which by conquest and re-conquest oscillated between Northumbria and Mercia, till it remained Mercian after its conquest by Ethelred in 679.

There was another Hugbald, or Hygbald, Bishop of Lindisfarne, A.D. 780–803, but neither the Anglo-Saxon Chronicle which records his accession and death, nor any one of the later Chroniclers who mention him, says anything of his earlier history. If he was an abbot of any monastery before his elevation to the episcopate, that monastery was certainly not Lindisfarne. There is extant a letter of Alcuin to this Hugbald, encouraging him to persevere, in spite of the sack of Lindisfarne by the Danes in 793.[1]

On fol. 40 *r.* there is a poem entitled, ' Versus Cvd. de Sancta Trinitate.'

If this is to be expanded into Cuthberti, we may have preserved to us here an original composition of the great northern saint who was Bishop of Lindisfarne, 685-8. It may, however, be expanded into Cudradi. Cudradus was a presbyter of Lindisfarne, to whom Alcuin addressed a letter in 793 or 794, consoling him after the sack of that monastery by the Danes in 793.[2]

The balance of such evidence as is forthcoming is therefore in favour of connecting the MS. with Lindisfarne.

The curious commemoration of Gallican saints in a marginal collect on f. 13 *v.* has been called attention to in notes, but it does not help us to identify its English home. It rather points to this part of the MS. being a copy of part of a Gallican Service-book.

The Chi-Rho monogram, ℞, is frequently (seventeen times) written on the top margin of this MS. and twice on the left hand margin.

It will be convenient to describe the Scriptural Sections on fol. 2 *r.*–11 *r.* continuously, and then to go back to fol. 3 *v.* 7 *v.* 10 *v.* for a description of the additions on these pages.

Fol.		Fol.	
1	[blank.]	3 *r.*	EUANGELIUM SECUNDUM LUCAN† [i. 5, 6.]
2 *r.*	[SECUNDUM MATTHÆUM i. 1-18 ; xxviii. 16-20.]	3 *v.*	SECUNDUM LUCAM. [xxiv. 48-53.]
2 *v.*	SECUNDUM MARCUM. [i. 1-3 ; xvi. 15-18.]	4 *r.*	EUANGELIUM [SECUNDUM IOHANNEM. i. 1-5.]
3 *r.*	ITEM ALIA. [xvi. 19, 20.]	4 *r.*	IN NATALE SANCTI IOHANNIS BAPTISTA. [i. 6-14.]

[1] Ep. ix. in Migne, *Pat. Lat.* Tom. C. col. 150.

[2] Ep. v. *Ibid.* col. 144.

Fol.

4 *v.* UBI *SEMPER.* [iii. 16, 17.]

5 *r.* xiv. 1–4, part of 5.

5 *r.* SECU*NDUM* IOHANNEM. [xv. 12–16.]

5 *v.* ITEM. [xvi. 33 ; xvii. 1–11 ad te uenio.]

6 *v.* SECU*NDUM* IOHANNEM. [xvii. 11 Pater sancte–13.]

7 *r.* [SECUNDUM MATTHEUM iv. 23, 24.

7 *r.* „ „ viii. 1–17.

8 *v.* „ „ viii. 23–27.

9 *r.* „ „ ix. 1, 2 ; 18–33.

10 *v.* „ „ ix. 36–38 ; x. 1.]

10 *v.* DE MAR*IA* „ [xii. 46–50.]

11 *r.* IN NAT*ALI* SA*NCTI* PETRI

SECU*NDUM* MATH*EUM*† [xvi. 13–19.]

3 *v.* Collects on the margin.

   1. Infunde *domine* benedictionem tua*m* super popu-
lu*m* tuum ut tua resurrectione muniti &c.

   2. Totius mundane uanitatis distructor om*nipotens*
de*us* fac nos &c.

   3. Infunde *domi*ne [in] eclesiam tua*m* caritatem
fraternitatem [tis] et pacis, &c.

7 *v.* Collects on the margin.

   1. Omnipo*tens* semperterne *deus* precibus et meritis
omnium sanc*torum* tuoru*m*, &c.

   2. oratio pro semet ipso.

Omnipo*tens* sempiterne *deus* obsecro te ne me
perire *per*mittas, &c.

10 *v.* Collects on the margin, showing that the MS.
belonged to a Benedictine monastery.

gebiddan fur • • • missa de sanc*te* bene-
dicte.†

   1. Sit *domi*ne beatus benedictus custus† actuum &c.

   2. *precatio* super oblata.

Sacris altaribus *domi*ne ostias superpositas
sanc*tus* benedictus que*sumus* &c.

   3. Existat qu*esumus domi*ne beatissime benedictus
perpetuus interuentor, &c.

11 *v.* ORATIO DO*MI*NICA with Anglo-Saxon glosses ar.d
with 'cotidianum' written over 'supersubstan-
tialem' erased after 'panem nostrum.'

Collect on margin 'Saluator mundi salua nos
om*nes* sancta dei genetrix' &c.

Fol.

12 *r.* SYMBULU*M* APOS*TOLORUM.* with Anglo-Saxon glosses.

Credo inde*um* patrem omnipotentem. et in
ih*esum chri*stu*m* filium eius unicum d*ominum*
nost*rum.* qui natus est de spi*ritu* sanc*to* et
maria uirgine. qui sub pontio pilato crucifixus
est et sepultus. tertia die resurrexit amortuis.
a*s*cendit in caelos. sedit ad dexteram d*e*i patris.
unde uenturus *est* iudicare uiuos ac mortuos.
et inspi*ritum* sanc*tum.* sanc*tam* ecclesiam
catholicam. remisione*m* peccatorum carnis
resurrectionem. amen.[1]

INCIPIT EPISTOLA SALUATORIS DO*MINI*
NOSTRI IH*ESU* CHRI*STI* AD ABAGARUM REGE*M*
QUA*M* DO*MI*NUS MANU SCRIPSIT ET DIXIT.

12 *v.* Beatus es qui me no*n* vidisti etc. with a few Anglo-
Saxon glosses, and three collects on the margin,

   1. Dona *domi*ne uirtutem populum tuum et effice &c.

   2. Remitte *domi*ne iniquitatem plebi tui ostende &c.

   3. Erue *domi*ne animas nostras de manu inferi &c.

13 *r.* Three benedictions, the first two having Anglo-
Saxon glosses, viz.

   1. De*us* omnipotens et *dominus* noster ih*esus* et
spi*ritus* sanc*tus* custodiat &c.

   2. Benedicat me d*ominus* et custodiat me osten-
dat &c.

   3. Sanat te de*us* pater omnipotens qui te creauit &c.

13 *v.* HYMNUS SA*N*CT*Æ* MARI*Æ.* Magnificat with
Anglo-Saxon glosses, and on the margin two
collects which connect the MS. with a Benedictine monastery, viz.

   1. De sanc*te*† benedicti colecta. Intercessione nos
qu[e]sumus *domi*ne beati benedicti abbatis, &c.

   2. Oratio sanc*te* benedicti. Letetur ecl*esia* tua deus
beatorum confessorum tuorum benedicti mar-
cialis[2] taurini[3] atque aquilini[4] confissa[rum]
suffrag[i]is atque eorum pr*e*cibus gloriosis ut
deuota p*er*mane[a]t et secura consistat. p*er*.

14 *r.* CANTICUM ZACHARI*Æ,* with Anglo-Saxon glosses,
and a collect on the lower margin commencing
Oculi nostri ad te *domi*ne semper intendant &c.

14 *v.* CANTICUM TRIUM PUERORUM, with some Anglo-

---

[1] This Creed, with very slight variations of text, also occurs in an eleventh century North Italian liturgical MS.
(Bodl. Liturg. Misc. 345, fol. 56*v.*) Compare the Creed of Chrysologus. (C. A. Heurtley, *Harmonia Symbolica*,
Oxford, 1858, p. 48.)

[2] Martialis, first Bishop of Limoges, in the third century, but a legend grew up about the ninth century, making
him one of the 72 disciples, and ranking him as an apostle, June 30.

[3] Taurinus, first Bishop of Evreux, called in Godwin's list (*De Præsulibus Angliae*, London, 1616. Provinciae
Eboracensis p. 2) a British Bishop of York, which points to a confusion between Ecclesia Ebroicensis and Ecclesia
Eboracensis, Aug. 11.

[4] Aquilinus, Bishop of Evreux, 7th cent. Oct. 19.

Fol.

Saxon glosses, and these two collects on the margins of f. 14 v. Exaudi domine sancte pater omnipotens sempiterne deus mittere dignare sanctum angelum tuum &c.

Domine ihesu christe qui in tronum hierusalem &c., and a collect on the margin of f. 16 r. commencing Domine fons misericordiam† in quae cuncta lauante contagia &c.

16 v. A charm against bleeding, Riuos cruoris toridi contacta uestis obstruit, &c., with these two prayers on the margins.

1. Maiestatem domine suppliciter exoramus ut sicut eclesie tue beatus andreas apostolus &c.

2. Domine ihesu christe adoro te in cruce ascendentem &c.

17 r. ORATIO SANCTI HUGBALDI ABBATIS.
In primis obsecro supplex obnixis precibus &c.

19 v. DEPRECATIO.
Benedictio dei patris cum angelis suis sit

20 r. ORATIO SANCTA.
Spiritum mihi domine tuae caritatis infunde.

22 r. ORATIO MATUTINA.
Mane cum surrexero intende ad me domine

23 r. ORATIO SANCTI AGUSTINI EPISCOPI.
Deus uniuersitatis conditor presta mihi primum &c.

24 v. ORATIO SANCTI AGUSTINI EPISCOPI.
Domine ihesu christi qui de hoc mundo transisti &c.

25 r. ORATIO MATUTINA.
Ambulemus inprosperis huius diei luminis &c.

25 r. ORATIO MILITE† IN TEMPLO.
Pater peccaui in caelum et coram te &c.

26 LAETANIA [see page 89.]

27 r. Ascriptions of praise, viz. :

1. Benedictus dominus et pater domini nostri ihesu christi qui est semper benedicendus &c.

2. Ideo laudandus est a nobis. quia adesta &c.

3. Laudent [eum] caeli quos fecit. terra quam &c.

4. Benedictus es deus pater qui nobis gratis &c.

28 r. HYMNUS ANGELICUS [with a Greek interlinear version in English letters.]
Gloria in excelsis deo &c.

28 r. FIDES CATHOLICA.
Credimus in unum deum patrem omnipotentem et in unum dominum nostrum ihesum christum filium dei et in spiritum sanctum

Fol.

deum. non tres deos sed patrem et filium et spiritum sanctum. unum deum colimus et confitemur.[1]

28 v. A prayer.
Domine deus omnipotens pater qui es omnium rerum creator &c.

29 r. A series of prayers arranged according to the letters of the alphabet. B. is misplaced. The Anglo-Saxon later interlinear headings to each prayer imply that they were composed with reference to events in our Lord's life.
Altus auctor omnium creaturarum deus et æquus &c.

29 v. Cunctis uia es aduitam uolentibus remeare.

29 v. Domine deus meus qui es fons omnis innocentiæ &c.
A slip of vellum is inserted between ff. 29 v. and 30 r. having on the recto a single 'Agnus dei' with its Greek equivalent in English letters underneath it, and on the verso four lines of a prayer omitted at the bottom of f. 30 r.

30 r. Ego seruus tuus ihesu fili magni dei agere &c.

30 v. Beata benedicta incarnataque clementia &c.

31 r. Fidelium omnium aequissimus iudex qui humano &c.

31 v. Gentium sola uitæ exspectatio tu deus &c.

31 v. Humilis excelsi sancta singularisque pietas &c.

32 r. Ihesu domine deus uia uita ac ueritas caelestis &c.

32 r. Karitatis auctor cas[ti]tatis doctor et amator &c.

32 v. Lux lucis inluminans mundum et fons &c.

33 r. Magister bone deus meus deus exercituum &c.

33 v. Nomen tibi est e(m)manuhel noui testamenti &c.

33 v. A poem in eight rude hexameter lines commencing, 'Dextera nos saluos conseruit† in æuum,' some word, such as 'semper,' has been left out in this line. The lines are written in black and red ink alternately.

34 r. O unigenitus dei filius. qui mihi munus &c.

34 v. Princeps pacis patientiæ doctor atque &c.

34 v. Quaesso te preclare clementissime deus ut &c.

35 r. Rex regum et dominus dominantium. tu qui aures &c.

35 v. Sancte saluator sanitas pereuntium medicus saluberrimus mundalium &c.

36 r. Te fortissime magne potens domine qui solus &c.

36 v. Verus largitor uitae perpetuae atque aeternae &c.

37 r. Xpe [i.e. Christe] qui es uita morientium et &c.

---

[1] This creed does not appear to occur elsewhere.

Fol.

37 *v.* Ymnorum solus dignus laudibus d*eu*s &c.

38 *r.* Zelotis sempiterne d*eu*s qui es discretor &c.

38 *r.* Et du d*eu*s iudex iustus qui abhominibus iudi-
catus &c.

38 *v.* On the margin. Or*atio* ad iii*m*.   Tibi subnixis
*christu*m domin*u*m depr*e*cam*u*r ut qui in hac
diei &c.

39 *r.* An elegiac poem of forty lines commencing with
the lines :

Me similem cineri uentoq*ue* umbr*æ*q*ue* me-
m*e*nto

Graminis utq*ue* decor sic mea uita fugit &c.

39 *v.* This collect is on the margin.

Ad uesperum. Gratias agimus d*omi*ne d*eu*s
omn*ipotens* qui nos uiuentes &c.

40 *r.* VERSUS CU*B*[BERTI] DE S*ANC*TA TRINITATE.

Fourteen hexameter lines, forming a metrical creed, commencing—

Mente canam d*omi*no grates l*au*desque re-
pendens &c.

A form of confession. Peccaui d*omi*ne
peccaui coram te et coram angelis &c.

40 *v.* PRECATIO AD S*ANC*TAM MARIAM ET S*ANC*T*U*M
PETRUM ET AD CETEROS APOS*TOLOS.*

Intercede pro me sanc*ta* maria et beatissima
&c.

41 *v.* [Oratio ad Christum.]

Obseruo diuitias bonitatis tu*æ* et longanimi-
tatis &c.

Th*e*se collects are on the margin—

Pacem tuam d*omi*ne de c*æ*lo da nobis et pax
tua &c.

D*eu*s caritas dona p*er* grati*am* sanc*ti* sp*irit*us
tuor*um* &c.

42 *r.* ORA*TIO* MOUCANI [= monachi?]

1. D*eu*m patrem d*eu*m filium d*eu*m depr*e*cor spiri-
*tu*m sanc*tu*m cuius magnitudo &c.

42 *r.* ITEM ALIA.

2. Nunc pænitudinis uerba sedula mihi fatenda sunt
&c.

On the margin 'D*omi*ne ih*es*u *chris*te post
me sis ut me defendas de inpugnatione
diobuli ' &c.

[ITEM ALIA.]

3. Pater peccaui inc*æ*lum et coram te miserere
&c.

43 *r.* [ITEM ALIA.]

4. Fortitudo mea d*omi*ne diligam te sub umbra &c.

Fol.

43 *v.* [ITEM ALIA.]

5. Osanna rex na*z*arene meo exore laudem &c.

6. [ITEM ALIA.]

Erue a fra mea anim*am* mea*m* et demanu
&c.

These collects are on the margin—

Beatorum apostolorum nos d*omi*ne quesumus continua oratione &c.

Auxiliare d*omi*ne querentibus misericordiam
tu*am* &c.

Iniquitates nostras ne respicias omnipotens
d*eu*s set sola tua &c.

44 *r.* 7. [ITEM ALIA.]

Vre renes meos et cor meum ut n*on* intres &c.

44 *v.* 8. [ITEM ALIA.] Erraui in montibus pastor bone
me inumeros tuos impone &c.

9. [ITEM ALIA.] D*omi*ne ih*es*u suscipe sp*iritu*m meum
qu*ia* anima mea turbata est &c.

All these nine prayers, except 7 and 8, end
with this petition 'eloe. sabaoth. ia. adonai.
eli. eli. laba. sabacthani.'

On the margin, D*eu*s qui es omnium sanc-
*to*rum tuorum splendor &c.

45 *r.* ORATIO PENITENTIS.

Gratias ago deo meo quia me miserum pec-
catorem &c.

45 *v.* ORATIO. Obsecro te ih*es*u *christ*us filius d*e*i uiui
p*er* crucem &c. for protection of the various
members of the body.

A charm against the devil.

Eulogumen. patera. caeyo. caeagion. pneuma.
caenym. caeia. caeiseonas. nenonamun.' adiuro
te satanae diabulus aelfae per d*eu*m uiuum ac
uerum et per trementem diem iudicii ut refu-
giatur ab homine illo qui abeat hunc aepist
[olam] scriptum secum innomine d*e*i patris et
filii et sp*iritu*s sanc*ti.*

46 *r.* ORATIO S*ANC*T*Æ* MARI*Æ* MATRIS D*OMI*NI NOS*T*RI.

Auxiliatrix esto mihi sanc*ta* trinitas exaudi
exaudi exaudi me &c.

46 *v.* [ORATIO] Te deprecor pater sanc*te* ut digneris me
saluare &c.

47 *v.* ORATIO S*ANC*TI AUGUSTINI.

D*eu*s iustitiae te deprecor. d*eu*s misericordiae.
d*eu*s inuisibilis &c.

49 *r.* Crux *chris*ti ih*es*u d*omi*ni dei no*s*tri ingeritur
mihi &c.

A charm to stop bleeding.

---

[1] *I.e.* : Εὐλογοῦμεν πατέρα κὰι υἱο᾽ν κὰι ἅγιον πνεῦμα κὰι νῦν κὰι 'αεὶ κὰι εἰς αἰῶνας ἀιώνων. 'αμὴν.

Fol.

Riuos cruoris torridi contacta uestis obstruit,
&c. with variations from the text on f. 16 *v.*

50 *r.* CARMEN SEDULII DE NATALE DOMINI NOSTRI IHESU
CHRISTI. The well-known alphabetical hymn
in twenty-three stanzas, A—Z, with a very few
Anglo-Saxon glosses.

A solis ortus cardine
Adusque terræ limitem
Christum canamus principem
Natum maria uirgine. &c.

51 *r.* Another alphabetical hymn in twenty-three stanzas
A—Z, with title cut away, beginning :

Fol.

Alma fulget in * perpes regn * ciuitas[1]
Hierusalem quae *est nostrum* celsa mater omnium.

At the foot of 51 *r.* are written these words :
In per ennis die sabbati.

52. On this fly-leaf in a twelfth century handwriting are
prayers or charms for sleep, and to stop bleeding, with
references to the 'Septem dormientes, S. Blasius, S.
Cassius.' They include two prayers, beginning :

Domine ihesu christe qui somno deditus in mare &c.
Domine ihesu christe uere deus noster per interces-
sionem &c.

In the above description of this MS. and its contents, use has been made of Sir
E. Maunde Thompson's description of it in the *Catalogue of Ancient Manuscripts in
the British Museum, part ii. Latin.* London, 1884, p. 60, and of Mr. W. de Gray Birch's
description of it on pp. 101–113 of his edition of *An ancient manuscript of the eighth or
ninth century; formerly belonging to St. Mary's Abbey, or Nunnaminster, Winchester,*
Hampshire Record Society, 1889.

---

[1] The first line of this hymn, as given in U. Chevalier's *Repertorium Hymnologicum*, Louvain, 1892, runs thus :
Alma fulget in cœlesti perpes regno civitas.
q.v. for a list of other MSS. in which this rare hymn occurs. It has been printed *in extenso* by E. Duemmler,
Rhythmorum Eccles. Aevi Carolini Specimen, Berolini, 1881. No. ix. p. 14.

INDEX

OF COLLECTS, HYMNS, AND OTHER LITURGICAL FORMS.

The abbreviations made use of are the following :—

ae. = aeternus.
b. = beatus.
d. = deus.
dns. = dominus.
i. = ihesus.
m. = misericors.

o = omnipotens.
p. = pater.
q. = quaesumus.
s. = sanctus.
sem. = sempiternus.
x. = christus.

P

GENERAL INDEX.

[1] The third Anthem after the Hymn of St. Hilary 'Unitas in Trinitate,' &c., quoted from L. H. on p. 38 is also found in the lorica in the Book of Mulling. *Notes on some non-biblical matter in the Book of Mulling*, by H. J. Lawlor. Edinburgh, 1895, pp. 14, 24, 32.

---

[1] In addition to the authorities referred to on p. 61, the Editor is indebted to Rev. B. Zimmerman for the following important reference to Roman ceremonial at an early date, in connection with Easter Day : —

' Matutino irrumpente luce tenebras, surgentes in ecclesia veniunt, et mutua charitate se invicem osculantes dicunt: Deus in adjutorium meum.' Ordo Romanus, i, § 47. Muratori. *Lit. Rom. Vet.*, Venice, 1748, col. 1001.

For further information about the widespread observance of this 'Osculum pacis' before Mattins on Easter Day in Western Breviaries, see paper on *The Breviary of the Humiliati*, by J. Wickham Legg, in the *Transactions of St. Paul's Ecclesiological Society*, vol. ii, part v, p. 281. London, 1890.

ignore

HARRISON AND SONS, PRINTERS IN ORDINARY TO HER MAJESTY, ST. MARTIN'S LANE, LONDON.

13

www.ingramcontent.com/pod-product-compliance
Lightning Source LLC
Chambersburg PA
CBHW030849270326
41928CB00008B/1290